ROUTLEDGE LIBRARY EDITIONS:
HOUSING POLICY AND HOME OWNERSHIP

I0131164

Volume 19

HOUSING AND URBAN RENEWAL

HOUSING AND URBAN RENEWAL
Residential Decay and Revitalization in the Private Sector

ANDREW D. THOMAS

Routledge
Taylor & Francis Group
LONDON AND NEW YORK

First published in 1986 by George Allen & Unwin Ltd

This edition first published in 2021
by Routledge
2 Park Square, Milton Park, Abingdon, Oxon OX14 4RN

and by Routledge
52 Vanderbilt Avenue, New York, NY 10017

Routledge is an imprint of the Taylor & Francis Group, an informa business

British Library Cataloguing in Publication Data
A catalogue record for this book is available from the British Library

ISBN: 978-0-367-64519-9 (Set)
ISBN: 978-1-00-313856-3 (Set) (ebk)
ISBN: 978-0-367-68506-5 (Volume 19) (hbk)
ISBN: 978-0-367-68523-2 (pbk)
ISBN: 978-1-00-313794-8 (Volume 19) (ebk)

Publisher's Note
The publisher has gone to great lengths to ensure the quality of this reprint but
points out that some imperfections in the original copies may be apparent.

Disclaimer
The publisher has made every effort to trace copyright holders and would welcome
correspondence from those they have been unable to trace.

HOUSING AND URBAN RENEWAL

Residential Decay and Revitalization in the Private Sector

ANDREW D. THOMAS

London
GEORGE ALLEN & UNWIN
Boston   Sydney

Allen & Unwin (Publishers) Ltd,
40 Museum Street, London WC1A 1LU, UK

Allen & Unwin (Publishers) Ltd,
Park Lane, Hemel Hempstead, Herts HP2 4TE, UK

Allen & Unwin, Inc.,
8 Winchester Place, Winchester, Mass. 01890, USA

Allen & Unwin (Australia) Ltd,
8 Napier Street, North Sydney, NSW 2060, Australia

First published in 1986

British Library Cataloguing in Publication Data

Thomas, Andrew, 1950–
    Housing and urban renewal: residential decay and revitalization
    in the private sector.—(Urban and regional studies; 12)
1. Public housing—Government policy—Great Britain—History—
20th century   2. Housing rehabilitation—Great Britain—History—
20th century
I. Title   II. Series
363.5'1'0942   HD7288.78.G7
ISBN 0-04-309111-3

Library of Congress Cataloging-in-Publication Data

Thomas, Andrew D. (Andrew David), 1950–
    Housing and urban renewal.
(Urban and regional studies; 12)
Bibliogrpahy: p.
Includes index.
1. Housing—England. 2. Housing—Wales. 3. Urban renewal—England.
4. Urban renewal—Wales. I. Title. II. Series: Urban and regional studies
(George Allen & Unwin); 12
HD7334.A3T49   1984   363.5'0942   85-13532
ISBN 0-04-309111-3 (alk. paper)

Set in 10 on 11 point Goudy by V & M Graphics Ltd, Aylesbury, Bucks
and printed and bound in Great Britain by
Biddles Ltd, Guildford and King's Lynn

Contents

Preface

British housing policy in the 1980s has been dominated by an emphasis on owner-occupation and an adherence to the discipline of the market place. In so much as government is concerned with housing provision and housing quality, the frontiers of intervention are being drawn back. Beyond that which impinges on health and safety, government has argued that choice is the arbitrator of quality, and that owner-occupiers should be free to maintain their homes at a level which suits their income and aspirations. With more elderly and low-income home owners than ever before, many of them living in houses built in the last century, the government has chosen a sensitive moment to consider abandoning all but a residual concern for maintaining the quality of the national housing stock.

It has been assumed by successive governments that they had a role to play in maintaining housing quality. It is perfectly proper that this role should now be questioned, but many of the arguments are difficult to test. The chapters which follow carry assumptions about housing standards, the role of government and the need to intervene in the housing market. With these assumptions goes the view that increased reliance on market approaches would lead to a decline in housing conditions which would result in economic and social costs greater than any short-term savings in public expenditure. This is a matter of opinion, and as such the stance adopted here is not based on a wholly dispassionate, objective analysis of older housing problems. What is presented is more of a synthesis of research experience gathered over a ten-year period. This work began as a thesis at the Oxford School of Architecture, and developed through a series of research contracts at the Centre for Urban and Regional Studies, University of Birmingham.

A substantial amount of research in British universities is carried out under short-term contracts, presenting demands which are often inconsistent with dissemination. In this respect, I was fortunate when, in 1981, Bournville Village Trust provided the opportunity to widen the work of earlier research projects. I am grateful to James Wilson and the trustees for their support, and in particular to Gordon Cherry, who in his role of trustee and Dean of the Faculty of Commerce and Social Science, encouraged me to translate the various strands of work into the present book.

What has emerged is not a work of original academic thought. I have quarried ideas and attempted to interpret current debates. I must therefore acknowledge a wide debt to both academics and practitioners active in the field. Certain work deserves special mention. My description of early rehabilitation and clearance policy draws on the research of Richard

Moore (1980), while more recent policy has been well summarized by Paris and Blackaby (1979) and by the most comprehensive text in the field, Gibson and Langstaff (1982). In terms of the relationship between capital investment and spending on housing exchange, the contribution of Kilroy has been particularly influential. At the Centre for Urban and Regional Studies, colleagues have worked on various related studies over the period of my own research. Pat Niner and Ray Forrest undertook a review of housing action areas, while Valerie Karn, Peter Williams and Jim Kemeny were involved in a programme concerned with the problems of low-income home ownership, leading to work on the reform of housing finance by John Doling, Valerie Karn and Peter Watt.

Apart from the contribution of written sources, it is important to acknowledge the influence of formal and informal comments from contacts will colleagues, students and visitors to the Centre for Urban and Regional Studies. Chris Watson has given generous help throughout my time at the Centre. Material on disrepair in the housing stock draws on work in co-operation with John Doling, and material on capital leakage on work in co-operation with Jim Kemeny. It would not have been possible to carry out the preliminary research without the help of Tony Newson and the Joint Centre library, or without the co-operation of numerous other people: those working for local authorities and housing associations, and local residents interviewed as part of social surveys.

Finally, for their detailed comments on various draft chapters, I would like to thank John Doling, Pat Niner, Ray Forrest and Jim Kemeny. I have tried to understand and act upon their comments, but where errors of fact or interpretation remain they are entirely my responsibility. As always, of course, the conclusions are my own.

The author and publisher would like to thank the following for permission to reproduce copyright material: The Building Societies Association for data from the BSA *Bulletin* in Tables 6.6–6.8; *The Building Societies Gazette* for Table 6.4; the Controller of Her Majesty's Stationery Office for data in Tables 2.12, 2.13, 3.1, 3.2, 3.10, 6.1, 6.2, 6.3, 6.5, 6.9 and 6.10 and Figure 6.3; the Department of the Environment for data in Tables 2.1, 2.3–2.11, 2.13, 3.1, 3.3–3.6, 3.9, 4.1–4.6 and 6.7, Figures 2.1–2.5 and 6.1, and Appendices 1–6; Cambridge University Press for data from the *Journal of Public Policy* in Figure 6.2; Lloyds Bank Review for data in Figure 6.1.

List of Abbreviations

AMA	Association of Metropolitan Authorities
BRE	Building Research Establishment
BSA	Building Societies Association
CDP	Community Development Programme
CHAC	Central Housing Advisory Committee
CSD	Civil Service Department
CSO	Central Statistical Office
CURS	Centre for Urban and Regional Studies
DES	Department of Education and Science
DHSS	Department of Health and Social Services
DOE	Department of the Environment
ECE	Economic Commission for Europe
ESRC	Economic and Social Research Council
FIG	Financial Institutions Group
GDP	Gross domestic product
GIA	General improvement area
GLC	Greater London Council
HAA	Housing action area
HIP	Housing investment programme
HIZ	Housing improvement zone
IAS	Inner Area Study
ICPP	Inner city partnership programme
IEHO	Institution of Environmental Health Officers
IFS	Improvement for sale
MHLG	Ministry of Housing and Local Government
NBA	National Building Agency
NCC	National Consumer Council
NEDO	National Economic Development Office
NFHA	National Federation of Housing Associations
NHS	Neighbourhood Housing Services
NRC	Neighborhood Re-investment Corporation
OPCS	Office of Population Censuses and Surveys
PIBR	Public investment borrowing requirement
PSBR	Public sector borrowing requirement
RTPI	Royal Town Planning Institute
SAUS	School for Advanced Urban Studies
SNAP	Shelter Neighbourhood Action Project
SSRC	Social Science Research Council (now the ESRC)
TUC	Trades Union Congress
UKHT	United Kingdom Housing Trust

1

Introduction

Successive British governments since the mid nineteenth century have been concerned with the condition of privately owned houses. The problem has been tackled by removing the worst substandard property and encouraging the construction of new housing conforming to certain minimum standards. Over time, the emphasis on public-sector involvement has varied. Generally, however, it has been recognized that, if left to itself, the private housing market will fail to provide acceptable conditions for low-income groups; will attempt to maximize profits at the expense of space standards, densities and building quality; and, once housing has been built, will fail to support adequate investment in maintaining the stock. Consequently, legislation has provided for the regulation of quality, for subsidy towards the costs of rehabilitation, and for building by local authorities and housing associations to meet directly the housing needs of poor and disadvantaged groups.

To deal with the condition of existing houses, policies of clearance and improvement have developed along separate but parallel lines. From the late 1960s the emphasis began to swing increasingly towards improvement. But, despite thirty-five years of postwar grant legislation, the clearance activity of the 1950s and 1960s, and successive area-based rehabilitation programmes since 1964, the level of intervention has never matched the scale of the problem. Despite government targets, unsatisfactory housing conditions remain, suggesting that policies have been inevitably inadequate to the task.

As slums have been cleared or improved, new problems have emerged. The benchmark of acceptability has shifted to reflect higher aspirations. Since the Second World War, while progress has been made in the provision of basic amenities, higher levels of disrepair have gradually been recognized as an emerging issue. For the purpose of government policy, poor housing, like poverty, can be held in manageable proportion by the definitions which are adopted. But, while interpretation will vary, the criteria of unfitness in England and Wales have remained largely unchanged for at least fifty years. On this fixed benchmark, the failure of successive policies to prevent further deterioration of the housing stock points to the shortcomings of an attack on what are only the symptoms of a wider market dynamic. If poor housing is a consequence of market forces, then conventional policies of urban renewal can only seek to be ameliorative. Being broadly responsive to wider movements of capital, they will never be able to do better than keep pace with the creation of unsatisfactory housing conditions.

This is a central theme pursued in the following chapters. The aim is to present a contemporary picture of investment trends and policy responses affecting the owner-occupied housing stock. No attempt is made to offer a comprehensive historical account of urban renewal, or to tackle the important and neglected task of cross-tenure analysis. The focus is on owner-occupation, and the policies are specific to England and Wales. But the experience may be relevant to other countries faced with similar trends: a growth in owner-occupation; increasing problems of physical disrepair; and low levels of capital investment in the housing stock.

The Broader Debates

The bulk of material presented in subsequent chapters is concerned with policy as a response to specific issues of housing condition. In no sense is any attempt made to contribute to a more theoretical debate. However, it is useful to draw out the relationship between current theoretical and ideological questions and the more specific policy issues which concern us here.

Of crucial importance is the nature of urban decline and the role of government. Recent structural explanations of urban processes have given primacy to movements of capital. The implication of inevitably uneven development under capitalism asks fundamental questions about the ability of government to intervene in an effective way. This leads to related questions on the role and function of government. If urban renewal policy is ameliorative intervention, in whose interests does government act, and who bears the costs?

Another set of issues concerns processes of consumption and production. The growth of owner-occupation has been achieved through consumption subsidies which have enhanced the value of housing as an investment. Ownership has become an important means of accumulating wealth. But there are at least two major implications. First, this accumulation has not been enjoyed equally by all home owners. There is evidence of social stratification within the tenure, with poorer households finding the costs and responsibility of ownership a burden they are unable or unwilling to carry. Second, the balance of consumption subsidies may act against the interests of capital investment by improving the attractiveness of housing as a form of investment. Both aspects have potential implications for the future condition of the housing stock.

Processes of Decline

Any policy concerned with the condition of older housing must begin with an understanding of the economic and political context. Poor housing is a symptom of economic forces which lead to an unequal distribution of wealth.

Historically, there has always been a close association between housing policy and the problems of older urban areas. The main concern of nineteenth-century housing reform was with public health. There was a clear public benefit from programmes to tackle the worst evils of slum housing. Through continuing programmes of clearance, and a later emphasis on rehabilitation, policies to tackle older housing problems acquired a geographical component which heavily influenced any analysis of the problem. Today, it is not easy to disentangle older housing policy from an assessment of inner-city problems and the difficulties facing older urban areas.

From the early 1970s an analysis of urban problems began to give greater emphasis to the process of structural economic decline. By the early 1980s important potential growth in the national economy appeared to be in high technology, and centred on the M4 motorway between London and Bristol. This new industry was thought unlikely to migrate to the older urban areas farther north. Companies were drawn to the new growth areas by good communications, by links with existing research establishments, by the availability of suitable labour, and by a residential environment attractive to senior executives employed in an international labour market. Left behind in this movement of capital were many of the older urban areas – containing substantial numbers of houses built around the turn of the century to service traditional manufacturing industry. The spatial justification for this housing stock was disappearing, but it remained as a deteriorating asset, providing relatively cheap homes for low-income groups.

On balance, evidence has been pessimistic about the effectiveness of policies to re-establish a resilient inner-area economy. It may be that there is potential for the revitalization of small businesses, though this introduces a potential conflict between demands for increased government intervention and reduced government control. But local economic initiatives appear more marginal if the flight of capital is seen as an irreversible manifestation of market forces. The focus of policy is then to ameliorate the worst social consequences of uneven development. By implication, the prospect of indefinite intervention brings into question the whole basis of policy for older urban areas. Having come to terms with the idea of urban decline, it remains to be seen whether policy can cope with evidence that decline is irreversible.

The Role of Government

Housing decay is a consequence of maintenance patterns, determined by market processes which influence investment performance. Government intervention, whether through clearance or improvement, is then a response to a process of disinvestment which does not affect the causes of obsolescence. The significance and effectiveness of this intervention depends on explanations of the role of government in the urban process, with different theories giving varying weight to the prospects of ameliorative action.

If government is seen as an agent of capital, economic development becomes the irresistible force behind urban change, with individual and collective action being of little effect. In contrast, a consensus view puts forward a mediating role for government. In this perspective, processes of change in urban structure are responsive to the pressures of popular demand. Within this essentially democratic process, groups exercise an influence on urban form through the outcome of pluralistic bargaining. The benefits of urban redevelopment are not then seen to be exclusively directed in the interests of capital, but to enhance general well-being by alleviating problems which have arisen as a result of urban decline (Guterbock, 1980, p. 433).

In terms of government intervention in urban policy, it would seem that the forces controlling the growth and decline of urban areas are conditioned by the needs of capital. Pluralists would see the urban economy as a constraint on policy, while the more sophisticated Marxist perspectives argue that policy is frequently in contradiction with the needs of capital, while bounded by the logic of capital accumulation. Whether we have competing ideocentrisms (London, 1976) or see value in a synthesis of the two contradictory views is a matter of theoretical debate. Guterbock's 'enlightened Marxian' or 'skeptical pluralist' (1980) settles for ineffective amelioration, concluding that political action can alter the course of public policy, but that changes in urban structure tend to benefit the rich rather than the poor, the powerful rather than the weak.

From the theoretical debate, questions are raised about the extent to which government, through intervention, is able to provide adequate housing. In the past, externalities associated with public health and safety were clear objectives of urban renewal. Consequently, there remains a heritage of concern for housing conditions – the traditional policy aim of a decent home for all families at a price they can afford. Through this, government specifies a minimum acceptable level of housing provision, and then pursues targets which imply a global improvement in the quality of housing available for consumption.

The efficiency of intervention through rent control, housing subsidies and improvement grants has been criticized by those who favour direct income transfer as a way of preserving consumer sovereignty and avoiding allocative distortions. However, this attachment to the principle of market choice lacks the direction to pursue politically determined housing objectives (Maclennan, 1982, pp. 160-1). Consumers do not have the opportunity to allocate resources as they feel fit because the market is heavily constrained. In situations of local shortage, the idea of consumer sovereignty is a myth, with any increased income being translated into increased costs of consumption without any improvement in living conditions. Public sector clearance and grants to home owners may be less 'efficient' than income transfer, but they direct spending towards an improved housing stock.

In the mid 1980s, therefore, urban renewal policy reflected a historical acceptance that government had a role in specifying and maintaining housing conditions. This resulted in an untidy, inefficient and sometimes contradictory mishmash of policies, grants and subsidies which are now in need of rethinking and reform. It is an appropriate moment for this to be done. There is no certainty that the present government wishes to perpetuate a concern for housing quality. Both consumption targets and redistributive aims have been abandoned in favour of strident non-intervention, in which the role of government appears to be concerned primarily with improving competition. As one of the main weapons in this regeneration is the reduction of public expenditure, the inefficiencies of direct housing market intervention are a source of continued interest. The future for housing capital investment is questioned in the context of reduced public sector provision, the expansion of subsidies directed at consumption through owner-occupation, and the relegation of investment subsidies such as improvement grants to the role of a welfare benefit.

It is a matter of fact that governments in the past have influenced levels of housing production and consumption. The nature and cost of this involvement has changed over time, but overall it has not proved possible to implement consumption targets without socializing the financial burden. From this emerges a central conflict for urban renewal. There exist expectations about housing quality, housing provision and, within this, the role of local and central government. Present government policy seeks to reduce public expenditure, while looking for opportunities to improve conditions for private profit. Hence the pressure to 'de-commodify' socialized benefits (Forrest and Williams, 1980, p. 6). It is by no means certain that past concerns and expectations can be reconciled with this more competitive ideology.

The role of government in determining and maintaining housing standards is therefore a particularly relevant question during a period when government policy advocates individual solutions rather than collective action. It is central to the current housing debate that government shows no concern to tackle inequalities of income and wealth, or to intervene directly in poor housing conditions. The danger is that 'as soon as the responsibility for housing provision and allocation is shifted to the market place, then inequalities of income and wealth – i.e. market power – manifest themselves in products of widely different quality' (Doling, 1985). Consequently, the specific problems of housing condition discussed in subsequent chapters are simply one component of wider concerns centred on the role of government and the level and effectiveness of intervention in a market economy.

Consumption and Social Stratification

For those concerned with housing policy, perhaps the most depressing feature of postwar years has been the unplanned growth of income support to sustain housing consumption. This has resulted in substantial inequalities between tenures. Owner-occupiers enjoy highly regressive mortgage interest tax relief, while in the rented sector the introduction of Housing Benefit in 1982 began with radically different assumptions about eligibility for subsidy.

The consumption inequalities which exist between tenures also exist within the owner-occupied sector. Housing consumption involves a process of social stratification. Home ownership is a means of wealth accumulation but, as a group, owner-occupiers are not homogeneous. Market situations vary substantially, and owners do not benefit equally. A theoretical debate has surrounded the question whether, despite this heterogeneity, there is a mutuality of interest which is able to structure political alignments. Perhaps of more immediate relevance to policy, however, is that stratification within owner-occupation may have significance in terms of immediate and future material conditions. Where choice is heavily constrained, people may purchase a house they cannot afford, and cannot maintain, and then find that relative movements in house prices have made it more difficult to move up and out to a home in better condition.

The growth of owner-occupation through consumption subsidies is therefore important to urban renewal. As the tenure expands, inequalities of wealth and opportunity seem likely to become more apparent within the sector, leaving the poorest households in the poorest housing stock. Despite arguments that owner-occupation leads to better maintained houses (Yates, 1982, p. 218), the evidence shows there is no correlation between ownership and condition. But the level of owner-occupation is increasing, and with it the proportion of people owning older property.

It is difficult to see how trends in disrepair will be halted without direct government intervention or radical reform of housing subsidies. There is nothing in the proper function of the current housing market which will ensure the improvement and maintenance of lower-priced property. If government were to abandon any concern for quality, assuming perhaps that there would be adjustments through the mechanisms of price, it would place in jeopardy the future security of past improvements in overall housing conditions. Experience suggests that use value and market price would not fall into line, and that in conditions of scarcity households would have to pay high prices for low-quality accommodation.

Consumption and Production

The growth in owner-occupation achieved through favourable housing subsidies has implications which extend beyond issues of consumption. There are consequences for production because of the way limited resources are directed towards the exchange of housing as an investment good.

Ball (1983) has put forward the view that the profit taken in land development and housebuilding is central to the housing problem. Failing to reform the means of production is, in this view, to ignore an element of consumption costs: 'to treat housing solely as a distributional issue is to impose unnecessary costs on households in the name of equity whilst ignoring the creations of the inequalities themselves' (Ball, 1983, p. 373).

However, Ball's emphasis on production is directed largely at the building of new houses rather than investment in the existing stock. It is not entirely clear how rehabilitation fits into the consumption–production debate, but it is recognized that improvement and maintenance work is an important part of total housing investment. It has been noted that 'In presenting a comprehensive analysis of the housing supply process it would be essential to link new housing supply to turnover of and investment and maintenance in secondhand housing' (Maclennan, 1982, p. 103). Thus any study of housing provision and its relationship with wider economic and political forces must concern itself with the performance of housing in use. Whether this is an aspect of production or consumption is less important than a recognition that the way housing is consumed has an impact on levels of investment and, consequently, impinges on the means of production. In this respect, the largely haphazard and expensive framework of tax reliefs, allowances and benefits which facilitate consumption has affected housing investment through distortion of demand.

There are no direct subsidies to housebuilding in the private sector. The market is dependent on the secondary effects of demand management through, for example, interest rates and help for first-time buyers. The nature of subsidy to owner-occupiers therefore operates as a stimulus to consumption rather than directly to production. This has unintended effects on levels of investment which go beyond the production of new housing. Critically, for the quality of existing houses, regular preventive maintenance is not encouraged by either price effects or subsidies. Market values appear highly sensitive to externalities and relatively unresponsive to the quality of individual homes. The level of investment in individual properties is a function of many variables but in so much as the costs of maintenance and repair fail to be reflected in a market price it might be expected that a proportion of this expenditure would be postponed. The aggregate result of this under-investment in capital works would then show as cumulative disrepair. And such a trend would be aggravated by an ageing of the housing stock resulting from low levels of clearance and new building.

Policy Dilemmas

The concentration of poor inner-city housing is an obvious manifestation of the process of uneven decay in the national housing stock. Tenure, age, price and location are factors which influence this concentration. But the spatial component is a consequence of general market processes and is not primarily a causal factor. There will be occasions where specific environmental factors or local planning decisions will have an impact, but generally 'which dwellings and which areas become dilapidated or obsolete does not result from some logical imperative concerned with age or design alone but as a result of the pattern of demand for housing investment and the rate of return on investment and the response of agencies organised around tenure forms, to the pattern of investment opportunity' (Murie, 1981. p. 5). This relationship between market processes and disinvestment provides a perspective which is critical of prevailing policy responses to older housing problems. Government intervention, whether through clearance or improvement policy, is seen as essentially a response to spatial systems of disinvestment. As Murie (1981, p. 6) points out, because spatially based policy intervention ignores causal factors, it can only change the pattern of obsolescence; to influence the rate at which obsolescence occurs, intervention must affect the causes of obsolescence.

In subsequent chapters, the emphasis is on the relationship between disrepair and under-investment resulting from the structure of subsidies, and their impact on the operation of the housing market. Chapter 2 describes the trends affecting the national housing stock and the relatively low levels of capital investment going to maintain existing houses. In Chapter 3 the focus moves to the level of investment decision by individual home owners. The next chapters review policy responses. There is a brief historical introduction as background to the rationale for area-based approaches and the Housing Act 1969. This is followed by an assessment of housing action areas (HAAs) and by a review of more recent initiatives which have sought to simplify and extend area policies, increase the effectiveness of block powers and encourage partnership arrangements.

In presenting this material, the emphasis is not on the failure of urban renewal policy. It should not be forgotten that over 3 million houses have been affected by some form of grant-aided rehabilitation since 1949.

What is criticized is the scale of activity given the rate of decay of the housing stock. The argument developed in concluding chapters is that a more fundamental restructuring of housing finance is required which will alter the nature of investment in the housing stock to achieve continuous maintenance and improvement. If poor housing conditions were truly reflected in lower prices, a trade-off between quality and price would be possible, with expenditure on repair and improvement justified in terms of a return on investment. However, the housing market fails to operate in this manner. The system of housing finance distorts the market so that people cannot benefit from the low historic costs of older property, and are faced with paying a high price for low-quality dwellings. The implication is that if policy is to continue to show an effective concern for people's housing conditions there will be pressure for an extension of help available to owner-occupiers.

To the extent that owner-occupation is already an expensive housing policy, increased support to help with maintenance responsibilities may further distort the housing and personal savings market. The dilemma is therefore to encourage capital investment in repair and maintenance while not increasing the national costs of owner-occupation by inflating the demand for loan capital or exchequer subsidy. This is a specific case of a more general problem surrounding the inequalities and maldistribution of housing subsidies. In the context of older housing the argument is simply that too little capital is being invested in the physical housing stock. At a national level, investment in housing consumption continues to expand, with home ownership representing the most important element in the accumulation of individual wealth (Great Britain, 1977). At the same time, there is a low level of capital investment in the physical stock. The challenge is whether, within the total sum of money spent on housing, a substantial proportion can be directed away from funding the exchange of housing towards capital investment in maintenance and replacement.

At a more individual level, changes in housing finance could alter the performance of housing as a form of investment, influencing individual decisions on the amount of housing being consumed. It is argued that reforms should minimize the opportunities which exist for individual capital gain through the exchange of fixed assets, while maximizing the tendency of prices to reflect physical condition. In the long term, encouraging owners to invest in the maintenance and repair of their homes is seen as the most effective way of reversing existing trends in disrepair.

2

Housing Conditions

The National Housing Stock

Because housing conditions are a function of investment, any description of the national housing stock needs to include both physical deterioration and patterns of spending. There is a physical process of decay which is determined by building materials, construction techniques and environmental conditions. Superimposed on this are economic and social factors which affect rates of decay through the way they influence decisions on maintenance investment.

Left unattended, houses will deteriorate in a cycle from new build, through disrepair and dilapidation, to unfitness and the prospect of clearance. This process of physical deterioration is easily understood in general terms, though it is extremely complex in operation. All houses will deteriorate, but individual elements decay at different rates, with the optimum frequency of replacement varying between elements. Each component of the equation will be subject to modification according to local factors involving the quality of the original design, materials and workmanship, the characteristics of use, and the level of routine maintenance. The way in which a house is built is a variable in its physical performance. Skinner (1981) looked at the way maintenance and condition varied with age, and suggested that future expenditure needs could be predicted on the basis of a more detailed understanding of regional variables and deviations from the average condition due to local design and construction variables.

If dwellings are to have a long life, more attention needs to be paid to the process by which they become obsolete and the methods by which the rate of obsolescence can be slowed down. Subsequent chapters are concerned with the way patterns of physically determined deterioration are modified by social patterns of occupation. In this, the performance of housing as an investment is an important variable. Murie (1983, pp. 223–4) has argued that the underlying determinants of decay are to be found in the investment or exchange values of dwellings, which are in turn determined by the process of economic development, and thus the demand for dwellings in the local housing market. Therefore, by bringing together the physical processes of decay with the economic and social factors influencing the rate of decay, it may be possible to identify thresholds and sequences of events in the physical process of decay and their relationship to, and influence over, decisions about maintenance investment. (Thomas, Karn and Gibson, 1984, p. 52).

It is the role of social research to explain how investment in older housing relates to decisions and processes influencing the operation of the local housing market. The complexity of these processes is enormous, embracing as it does the relationship with new housing construction, land supply, and demand factors influenced by demographic and employment trends, mortgage supply and movements of investment capital. While it is possible to look at global trends in terms of investment cycles and rates of decay, it is important to understand individual investment decisions within the framework of local housing markets. The nature of decisions facing individual home owners will be considered later (Chapter 3). First, this chapter looks at levels of capital investment, beginning with a description of housing conditions and moving on to look at trends in the rate of stock decay in terms of reduced levels of fixed capital formation.

The quality of data available to do this is poor, which leads to apparently contradictory estimates. Bearing these limitations in mind, the material is presented to give a broad indication of existing trends. The picture which emerges is of a substantial stock of poor and substandard housing, which has continued to deteriorate despite the rehabilitation policies pursued during the 1970s.

Levels of investment were criticized as inadequate in the 1960s, and this remained the position twenty years later. Based on research carried out in the mid 1960s, Stone (1970, p. 250) commented on the cumulative impact of under-investment in housing maintenance:

> The maintenance costs for the present stock are about twice as high as the value of the maintenance work currently carried out for housing by the construction industry. This is mainly a reflection of the extent to which dwellings are currently under-maintained, and hence the large cost of arrears of maintenance: eight to nine times current annual expenditure on housing maintenance.

Findings from the 1981 English House Condition Survey (DOE, 1982a) suggested that this under-investment had continued and perhaps worsened during the 1970s as a consequences of economic recession, high unemployment, the relative rise in repair costs, high interest rates and public expenditure cuts. It seemed that conditions were likely to deteriorate still further if the prevailing low levels of investment continued to be channelled towards what was an ageing housing stock. The implications of this were serious because of the way certain groups of people tended to be concentrated in poor housing which they owned but were unable to maintain.

Age Distribution of the Housing Stock

The age distribution of the housing stock reflects rates of clearance and replacement, and is a factor in estimating average repair costs. During the mid 1960s Stone (1970) looked at trends in the average age of the housing stock in Great Britain. He predicted a reduction in the average age of property by the year 2004, based on the then reasonable assumption of demolishing 115,000 houses a year and building 290,000 in the public and private sectors. It is subsequently lower levels of clearance and new building that explain the reversal of Stone's prediction. Though there is a lack of adequate data, it would appear that the average age of the national housing stock was increasing by about six months every year at the beginning of the 1980s.

There is a high level of imprecision about this type of estimate in the absence of detailed information on the age structure of housing in England and Wales. Data for England were provided by the 1981 House Condition Survey (DOE, 1982a), but this offers only a single pre-1919 age band. An alternative estimate is based on a DOE analysis of census data from 1851, approximate rates of new construction before 1919, and assumed ages for losses from the dwelling stock (Table 2.1). Using either estimate, about a third of the stock was built before 1919, representing 5·9 million dwellings. An estimate of the likely age distribution of the housing stock at the end of the century can be obtained by projecting 1982 rates of clearance and new building (Table 2.2). On these figures, there would remain 5·3 million houses (24 per cent of the stock) built before the First World War; and the majority of these would be over a hundred years old. At the same time, because of substantial interwar building, over 9 million houses (43 per cent of the stock) would be at least sixty years old. On these projections, the average age of a house would increase from under fifty to nearly sixty years by the end of the century.

In itself, the age of the housing stock says little about its condition, though Stone showed a correlation at an aggregate level. Using data for

Table 2.1   *Age Distribution of Housing Stock, England and Wales, 1976*

	No. ('ooos)	%	Estimated average age
Pre–1871	1,502	8·3	(120)
1871–1890	1,737	9·5	(96)
1891–1918	2,620	14·4	(72)
1919–1944	4,137	22·7	(45)
1945–1976	8,207	45·1	(16)
	18,203	100·0	(47)

Source: DOE, Housing and Construction Statistics, no. 21, 1977, supplementary table XII.

Table 2.2   Age Distribution of Housing Stock, England and Wales, 2000

	No. ('ooos)	%	Average age
Pre–1871	1,347	6·2	(145)
1871–1890	1,558	7·2	(120)
1891–1918	2,350	10·8	(96)
1919–1944	4,114	18.9	(70)
1945–1976	8,162	37·6	(40)
1977–2000	4,200	19·3	(12)
	21,731	100·0	(59)

1959 on local authority dwellings, he demonstrated a close relationship between the age of a dwelling and the annual cost of repair and maintenance over the first forty years of its life, and felt justified in extrapolating this relationship over a longer period (Stone, 1970, p. 143). An alternative view is that the linear relationship holds to a certain age and then tails off (Skinner, 1981), while different houses built at different times may deteriorate at different rates. However, assuming that a broad relationship does exist between age and condition, an increase in average age implies a growth in average repair and maintenance costs. Following Doling (1983, p. 6) and applying Stone's formula $y = 3·8 + 0·305x$ based on 1982 rates of new building and clearance, would suggest an annual increase in repair and maintenance of about £3 million at 1959 prices; say £18–20 million a year at 1982 prices.

Evidence of Disrepair
From 1967 there was a series of House Condition Surveys for England and Wales, with the results published separately from 1976. The English House Condition Survey provided more comprehensive information, while available tabulations for Wales meant that most results could not be aggregated. Unfortunately, the usefulness of the 1981 English survey was restricted by an extremely limited ability to make comparisons with the results of earlier surveys. The revision of previous results provided insufficient tabulations for comparative purposes, failed to relate to constant prices from earlier studies, and adopted a relatively high figure for its main disrepair comparisons. Whatever the technical merits of the case for re-analysing previous House Condition Survey data, the cautious decision not to make comparisons between repair costs under £7,000 (at 1981 prices) restricted the usefulness of the disrepair time-series. And, while the re-analysis improved the DOE's level of confidence in comparisons between 1971, 1976 and 1981, the effects of surveyor variability and the difference between estimated and real costs remained areas of substantial uncertainty. Consequently, while useful, the House

Condition Survey continued to have considerable limitations in charting changes in the physical state of the housing stock.

Table 2.3 shows that in England an estimated 24 per cent of the stock (4·3 million homes) was unsatisfactory on the measures adopted in the 1981 House Condition Survey. This rather dramatic figure, affecting nearly a quarter of the country's housing stock, was highly sensitive to the definition of disrepair costs. The majority of tabulations in the 1981 survey adopted a figure of £7,000, reducing the total number of unsatisfactory dwellings to just over a tenth of the total stock.

Table 2.3   *Housing Conditions, England, 1981   ('000 dwellings)*

		All unsatisfactory dwellings	
		£7,000 repair threshold	£2,500 repair threshold
Unfit[1] dwellings	1,116		
Fit dwellings lacking amenities[2]	390	2,006 (11·1%)	4,332 (24%)
Fit dwellings with amenities			
requiring repairs over £7,000	500		
requiring repairs £2,500–7,000	2,326		
Satisfactory dwellings		16,060 (88·9%)	13,734 (76%)
All dwellings		18,066	18,066

Source: 1981 EHCS (DOE, 1982a, p. 5).

Notes:

1   A dwelling which on one or more of the following conditions is not reasonably suitable for human habitation: repair; stability; freedom from damp; internal arrangement; natural lighting; ventilation; water supply; drainage and sanitary conveniences; facilities for preparation and cooking of food; disposal of waste water.

2   A dwelling not unfit, but lacking one or more of the five basic amenities: a fixed bath or shower in a bathroom; an inside WC; a wash-hand basin; a sink; hot and cold water to bath, basin and sink.

The issue of definitions lay at the heart of any attempt to describe how conditions had changed over the ten-year period. Analysing indicators of condition separately, Table 2.4 shows that 910,000 dwellings lacked amenities in 1981. Though this problem therefore continued to affect one in twenty homes, the survey suggested a marked improvement from the figure of 1·5 million in 1976. It represented a continuation in the rate of reduction experienced between 1971 and 1976, so that over that period the number of dwellings lacking one or more basic amenities had fallen by about two-thirds. Of this reduction, about a fifth was accounted for by demolition (DOE, 1982a, p. 10).

Turning to unfitness, the 1981 survey provided a figure of 1·12 million

Table 2.4   *Separate Indicators of House Conditions, England 1971–81*
(*'ooo dwellings*)

	Original house condition figures	Revised 1981 house condition figures
Lacking amenities		
1971	2,655	2,815
1976	1,493	1,531
1981	910	910
Unfit		
1971	1,147	1,216
1976	794	1,162
1981	1,116	1,116
Disrepair		
1971	1,636[1]	864[2]
1976	1,997	859
1981	1,049	1,049

Sources: DOE, 1978a, 1982a.
Notes:
1   Repairs costing £500 and over at 1971 prices.
2   Repairs costing £7,000 and over at 1981 prices.

dwellings, unchanged compared with revised figures for 1976. The size of the revision was startling. Table 2.4 shows that the unfitness figure for 1976 was increased by nearly half, while the 1971 figure remained essentially unchanged. The 1981 reclassification affected houses that had been assessed as fit in 1976 and unfit in 1981. The 1976 assessment was reclassified as unfit unless there was evidence that the condition of property had deteriorated over the intervening period. The reason for reclassification was not clear. The 1981 survey simply reported that the number of unfit dwellings was underestimated in 1976 (DOE, 1982a, p. 11). But a revision of nearly 50 per cent could not be described as a minor technical adjustment. Attributing the problem to surveyor variability provided a welcome admission of the subjective nature of unfitness criteria, but it was impossible to judge whether the assessment in 1976 was less reliable than a statistical backward glance by the DOE in 1981.

Revised estimates also affected the original disrepair figures for 1971 and 1976, but comparison was again ruled out, this time by the selection of cut-off values. In 1981 just over 1 million dwellings required repairs in excess of £7,000. This was nearly 20 per cent higher than the revised figure for 1976 (Table 2.4). The revision was not related to an earlier published figure of nearly 2 million, which referred to repairs in excess of £500 (at 1971 prices). In 1981 nearly 4 million dwellings – a fifth of the stock – required repairs costing over £2,500, but no satisfactory comparison could be made with published material from earlier surveys. Table 2.5 summarizes the difficulties at constant prices. From the original 1976 survey, just under 2 million houses had repair costs of over £2,410 (1981 prices); while in 1981 nearly double that number had outstanding repairs of over £2,500. However, the revised figures for 1976 gave no comparable value range. The £7,000 figure was used in 1981 because of the reported unreliability of repair costs under £7,000 in the 1971 and 1976 surveys (DOE, 1982a, p. 37). Again, technical improvements resulted in recalculations, but Matthews (1983) pointed out that the alleged under-estimates in certain cost bands did not seem to justify the high comparative figure.

Table 2.5   *Houses in Disrepair, England, 1971–81   ('ooo dwellings)*

Original house condition figures Repair costs at 1981 prices[1]	1971	1976	Revised 1981 house condition figures Repair costs at 1981 prices	1971[2]	1976[3]	1981[4]
£2,410–4,820	1,000	1,086	£2,500–4,499	—	—	1,930
Over £4,820	636	911	£4,500–6,999	—	—	940
			Over £7,000	864	859	1,049
Total	1,636	1,997				3,919

Sources:
1   Based on 1976 EHCS (DOE, 1978a, p. 10) adjusted to 1981 prices using a factor of 2·06.
2   DOE, 1982a, table 43.
3   DOE, 1982a, table 34.
4   DOE, 1982a, table 17.

More detailed cost information for 1981 was presented by the survey's classification of dwellings according to their need for essential structural repairs. On this new measure, approximately 5 million dwellings needed repairs to at least one essential element. It was this estimate that emphasized the misleading use of £7,000 for comparative disrepair tabulations. Of the 5 million dwellings, about 3 million needed repairs to only one element, and of these half had total repair costs of under £2,500 (DOE, 1982a, table 26).

To summarize the impact of revisions in the 1981 survey, Figure 2.1 compares the stock of unsatisfactory dwellings from the 1976 survey with the position presented in 1981. By an upward revision in the estimate of unsatisfactory property in 1971 and 1976 it was possible to demonstrate a continuing improvement in living conditions, while the £7,000 disrepair figure tended to minimize the impact of stock deterioration. As published, the 1981 survey showed that the number of unfit properties had remained relatively constant over a ten-year period. The number of houses lacking

1976 ENGLISH HOUSE CONDITION SURVEY

1981 ENGLISH HOUSE CONDITION SURVEY

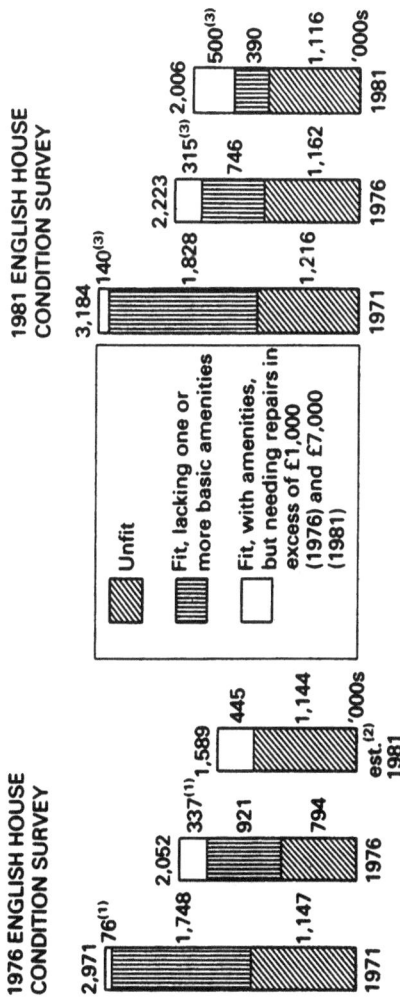

| Unfit |
| Fit, lacking one or more basic amenities |
| Fit, with amenities, but needing repairs in excess of £1,000 (1976) and £7,000 (1981) |

Figure 2.1 *English House Condition Surveys, 1976 and 1981.*

Sources: DOE, 1978a, 1982a; AMA, 1981a.

Notes:

1 Of the 636,000 dwellings in 1971 requiring repairs costing over £1,000 (1971 prices), 12 per cent (76,000) were fit with all amenities (DOE, 1978a, fig. 11). In 1976, 911,000 dwellings required repairs over £1,000 (1971 prices), of which 37 per cent (337,000) were in the category fit with all amenities.

2 The AMA estimated that 1·2 million houses were in serious disrepair and up to 1·144 million unfit (1981a, pp. 2–5). The 1·2 million included unfit dwellings. The 1976 House Condition Survey suggested that 34·1 per cent of unfit dwellings had outstanding repairs of less than £2,000 (at 1976 prices; DOE, 1978a, table 8). The estimate of fit houses in serious disrepair might therefore be in the order of 445,000.

3 Repairs costing over £7,000 at 1981 prices (approximately £1,600 at 1971 prices).

amenities had been reduced since 1971, from 2·8 million to under 1 million, while the number of dwellings requiring repairs costing more than £7,000 had increased by about 200,000.

Within these aggregated figures, the survey highlighted four particular trends. First, there was a deterioration in the condition of dwellings built after 1919. The percentage of all dwellings found to be unfit which had been built in the interwar period increased from about 3 per cent in 1971 to over 10 per cent in 1981 (DOE, 1982a, p. 12). There was also a slight increase in the proportion of significant disrepair contained within the interwar stock. Of dwellings requiring repairs costing over £7,000 in 1971 (at 1981 prices), only 3 per cent were interwar. In 1981 this had doubled to 6 per cent (DOE, 1982a, p. 12). Nevertheless, the incidence of disrepair continued to be closely associated with the age of the property. Over the ten-year period, there was an increase in the number of pre-1919 dwellings requiring expenditure of more than £7,000, despite the loss of dwellings in this age-group due to demolition (DOE, 1982a, p. 13). And of the 3·9 million dwellings requiring repairs costing over £2,500, about 70 per cent were built before 1919, representing over half the pre-1919 stock. Only 5 per cent of the interwar stock required repair expenditure of this scale (DOE, 1982a, table 21).

Second, the number of owner-occupied dwellings which were unfit or in need of substantial repair rose substantially. The 1981 House Condition Survey showed that owner-occupied housing had outstanding repair costs just below the average for the stock as a whole, but accounted for a major share of the total national bill because of the size of the sector (Table 2.6). Within the owner-occupied sector, Table 2.6 also shows that the main problems of disrepair were to be found in the pre-1919 stock, where the average repair cost was approaching twice that for the stock as a whole. A comparison with the 1971 survey shows that the number in need of repair costing more than £7,000 increased by 62 per cent, while those which were assessed as unfit increased by 36 per cent (DOE, 1982a). And bearing in mind the limitations of the data, it would seem that, holding the relative sizes of the tenures constant, owner-occupied houses had deteriorated relative to houses in other tenures (Doling, 1985).

The 1981 House Condition Survey explained these trends as the result of the substantial growth in owner-occupation and the reduction in private renting (DOE, 1982a, p. 4). Between 1971 and 1981 there was an increase of 125,000 unfit dwellings in the owner-occupied sector, while there was a reduction of 250,000 unfit privately rented dwellings. It would be easy to assume that unfit dwellings simply changed tenure, but transfer between tenures was in fact more complex than this. It was known that a change from unfitness to fitness was often associated with tenure change (DOE, 1982a, p. 11), but there was no information about the proportion of dwellings which changed tenure and remained unfit. In the

Table 2.6   *Cost of Outstanding Repairs by Tenure and Age, England*

	Average cost per dwelling (£)	No. of dwellings ('ooos)	% of total dwellings	Total repair cost (£bn)*	% of total repair cost
Tenure					
Owner-occupied	1,883	10,297	57·0	19·4	54·8
Local authority	1,228	5,056	28·0	6·2	17·6
Privately rented	3,559	2,087	12·0	7·4	21·0
Vacant	3,727	626	3·0	2·3	6·6
All dwellings	1,957	18,066	100·0	35·4	100·0
Date of construction (owner-occupied housing)					
Pre-1919	3,777	3,356	32·6	12·7	65·4
1919–1944	1,490	2,477	24·1	3·7	19·0
1945–1981	678	4,464	43·4	3·0	15·6
All owner-occupied	1,883	10,297	100·0	19·4	100·0

Source: Doling, 1985, based on estimates from the 1981 EHCS (DOE, 1982a, table 21).

absence of information from a longitudinal sample there could not be a firm conclusion, but it left the possibility that some of the existing owner-occupied stock moved into unfitness over the period. Similar difficulties complicated comparisons of disrepair. The owner-occupied sector contained 36 per cent of substantial disrepair in 1971 and 51 per cent in 1981, while the private rented sector's share was reduced from 54 per cent to 33 per cent (DOE, 1982a, p. 12). Again, while some of the increase may have been attributable to property transfer, it seemed there had been a deterioration in the repair standards of existing owner-occupied dwellings. Indeed, the former tenure of property could be regarded as insignificant because virtually all pre-1919 property originally began in the privately rented sector. Whatever its original tenure, in 1981, 5 per cent of owner-occupied homes required repairs costing more than £7,000, while over a fifth needed repairs costing at least £2,500.

Third, the 1981 survey pointed to an increase in disrepair and unfitness affecting the South-East of England. While the number of unfit dwellings had been reduced in the North and Rest of England, there was an increase of 100,000 in the South-East (DOE, 1982a, p. 11). In the North there had been a reduction in the number of dwellings in serious disrepair, while the figures for the Rest of England and the South-East increased by 16 per cent and 80 per cent respectively over the ten-year period (DOE, 1982a, p. 12). The survey offered no explanation for this, but commented that the changes tended to even out the distribution of dwellings in poor condition across the country. The extent to which absolute reductions in unfitness and disrepair in the North could be attributed to more vigorous clearance and improvement campaigns remained a point for debate.

Finally, while not noting this in the text, the House Condition Survey showed a reduction in the rate of tackling the worst housing conditions. Published figures showed a fall in the total number of unsatisfactory dwellings from 3·2 million in 1971 to 2 million in 1981. A different picture might have emerged with a lower cut-off point for disrepair, but these figures were not made available. However, on published figures there was a reduction of nearly 1 million unsatisfactory dwellings between 1971 and 1976. Over the next five years progress was much slower, with a reduction of around 200,000 dwellings (DOE, 1982a, p. 13). At that rate it would take nearly fifty years to deal with housing problems identified in 1981.

Projected Growth in Disrepair
The impact of long-term under-investment has little meaning in the absence of information on rates of change. In fact, the 1981 English House Condition Survey did not even provide an estimate of the total cost of necessary work. However, a simple projection suggests that to undertake work to property requiring repairs costing over £2,500 would mean expenditure of around £25 billion,* with a total bill of about £35 billion (Table 2.7). The 1981 survey also failed to make any comparison of changes in the total cost of outstanding works to unfit and substandard property. This was done in 1976, when the cost of outstanding works was much the same as in 1971, despite the reduction in unfit and substandard properties (Table 2.8). Hence the general conclusion that progress in dealing with substandard property between 1971 and 1976 had been entirely outweighed by increased disrepair.

Table 2.7   *Repair Costs by Fitness, England, 1981*

	Unfit		Fit		All	
	No. ('ooos)	Cost (£bn)	No. ('ooos)	Cost (£bn)	No. ('ooos)	Cost (£bn)
Under £1,000	98	0·047	10,918	5·241	11,016	5·288
£1,00–2,499	146	0·256	2,985	5·224	3,131	5·480
£2,500–4,499	195	0·682	1,735	6·072	1,930	6·754
£4,500–6,999	202	1·161	738	4·243	940	5·404
£7,000–9,999	188	1·598	260	2·210	448	3·808
£10,000–13,999	140	1·680	163	1·956	303	3·636
£14,000 and over	147	2·315	151	2·378	298	4·693
All	1,116	7·739	16,950	27·324	18,066	35·063

Source: 1981 EHCS (DOE, 1982a, table 28).

* Throughout the text, billion is used to mean one thousand million.

Table 2.8   *Amenity and Repair Costs, England, 1971–6   (£ million)*

	1971 at current prices	at 1976 prices	1976 at current prices
Cost of installing missing amenities	800	1,880	1,000
Cost of outstanding repairs	3,200	7,520	8,350
Total	4,000	9,400	9.350

Source: 1976 EHCS (DOE, 1978a, p. 11).

Though it is an exercise which cannot be extended on the basis of published data from the 1981 survey, it is possible to make a crude estimate of the rate of physical deterioration over the period 1971–6 based on maintenance expenditure and the change in the costs of outstanding repairs over that period (Doling and Thomas, 1982). That is,

$$d_{1971-6} = r_{1976} - r_{1971} + a_{1971-6}$$

where r = cost of outstanding repair
   a = cost of repairs actually carried out
   d = deterioration over the period.

Estimates of the cost of outstanding repairs can be obtained from the 1971 and 1976 House Condition Surveys. In 1971 the cost was £3,450 million (£8,073 million at 1976 prices). In 1976 separate house condition surveys were carried out in England and Wales. Outstanding repairs in England were estimated at £8,300 million. There was no published estimate for Wales. Assuming a figure proportionate to the size of the stock would give £598 million, and therefore a total figure of £8,898 million.

It is difficult to obtain estimates for actual expenditure on repair and maintenance. Based on published construction output figures for housing repair and maintenance, expenditure over the period 1971–6 was £8,784 million at 1975 prices, £10,541 million at 1976 prices. These figures were for Great Britain. Assuming a 90 per cent figure for England and Wales gives £9,480 million. The statistics included improvement work, but it can be assumed that this formed a constant percentage in any time-period. However, it does seem likely that the statistics under-estimated the value of repair and maintenance work.

If the values of outstanding repair and cost of work actually carried out are applied, an estimate can be obtained for the cost of deterioration over the period:

$$\text{deterioration } d_{1971-6} = 8,898 - 8,073 + 9,480$$
$$1971-6 = £10,305 \text{ million.}$$

Thus, despite incurred expenditure of £9,480 million on housing repair and maintenance over a five-year period, the outstanding repair bill was nearly £900 million more at the end of the period than at the beginning. This estimate must be treated with some caution because of the inadequacies of available data (Doling and Thomas, 1982).

The trend since 1976 depended on whether the rate of deterioration held constant over the period, since the value of construction industry output had been roughly comparable. The AMA (1981a) took the 1971–6 rate of deterioration at 55,000 houses a year and estimated this to increase the repair bill by £1,210 million. This was simply added to the outstanding bill of £17,670 million (at 1980 prices) to give a total of £18,880 million. Lack of comparable data from the 1981 survey made it difficult to assess the projection. It can be seen from Table 2.8 that the outstanding repair bill in 1976 was £8,350 million (for England). Between 1976 and 1981 the output price index for new construction and the retail price index both doubled. At 1981 prices, therefore, outstanding repair costs in 1976 were of the order of £16,800 million. It has also been seen that the 1981 House Condition Survey considered the estimates for 1976 substantially under-estimated repair costs. The report presented revised estimates, but again with no cumulative total. Assuming a similar distribution to that of 1981, Table 2.9 suggests a revised repair bill for 1976 estimated at £31·8 billion. In effect, improvements in survey techniques doubled the previous estimate.

Table 2.9 *Comparison of Repair Costs by Fitness, England (1981 Prices), 1976–81*

| | No. ('000s) | | | | | |
| | 1976 | | | 1981 | | |
	Unfit	Fit	All	Unfit	Fit	All
Under £7,000	698	15,558	16,256	641	16,376	17,017
£7,000–9,999	177	219	396	188	260	448
£10,000–13,999	128	95	223	140	163	303
£14,000 and over	159	81	240	147	151	298
All	1,162	15,953	17,115	1,116	16,950	18,066
	Cost (£bn)					
Under £7,000	0.942	21·003	21·945	2·146	20·780	22·926
£7,000–9,999	1·504	1·862	3·366	1·598	2·210	3·808
£10,000–13,999	1·536	1·140	2·676	1·680	1·956	3·636
£14,000 and over	2·504	1·276	3·780	2·315	2·378	4·693
All	6·486	25·281	31·767	7·739	27·324	35·063

Source: 1981 EHCS (DOE, 1982a, tables, 28 and 37).

At best, therefore, the position is very unclear. The DOE concluded that between 1976 and 1981 the number of dwellings in serious disrepair increased by 22 per cent (DOE, 1982a, p. 12). Inflating the 1976 disrepair figure of £16,800 million (1981 prices) by 22 per cent gives £20,500 million, compared with the 1981 survey figure of £35,000 million. Consequently, either the 1976 survey dramatically under-estimated disrepair, limiting the level of confidence which can be placed in the 1981 survey; or the increase in disrepair between 1976 and 1981 was greater than the 1981 survey reported. All that can be said with any confidence is that on the basis of the DOE's revised figures, the total repair bill increased by 10 per cent over the five-year period to 1981, with the annual rate of deterioration at £660 million.

Housing Investment

There is evidence of growing disrepair in the housing stock, though the data are unreliable in determining the rate of deterioration. Relatively high levels of imprecision concerning trends, and the estimated shortfall in expenditure, form the context within which to consider achieved levels of investment in housing. This is approached from two main perspectives. First, housing output performance is considered in terms of new building, clearance and rehabilitation. Secondly, housing investment is looked at as a component of national resources.

Housing Output
Figure 2.2 shows the trend in new housing starts since 1960. In the public sector total starts fell to 33,000 in 1981, with a slight recovery in 1982 to just over 46,000 (see Appendix 1). This was half the figure achieved in 1973, which was in turn a postwar low. Reflecting this low level of activity, housing associations for the first time accounted for nearly a third of public sector starts in 1982. But associations, though suffering less drastic cuts in relative terms, were down to about half the level achieved in 1976. In the private sector 88,000 starts in 1980 was the lowest since 1953. There was an improved picture over the following two years, reaching 128,000 in 1982. This was largely responsible for the rise in total starts, from a postwar low in 1980, to nearly 175,000 in 1982, with a further increase anticipated in 1983. But even 200,000 a year was well below the average level achieved in the postwar period.

Despite programmes of comprehensive redevelopment affecting most major towns and cities from the mid-1950s, average rates of clearance in England and Wales ran at less than 40,000 a year. It was necessary to go back before the Second World War to find demolitions peaking at 90,000. Figure 2.3 shows trends in clearance activity. In 1979, 27,900 dwellings were demolished, two-fifths of the level achieved in 1971, which was a postwar high (see Appendix 2). From 1979 national statistics

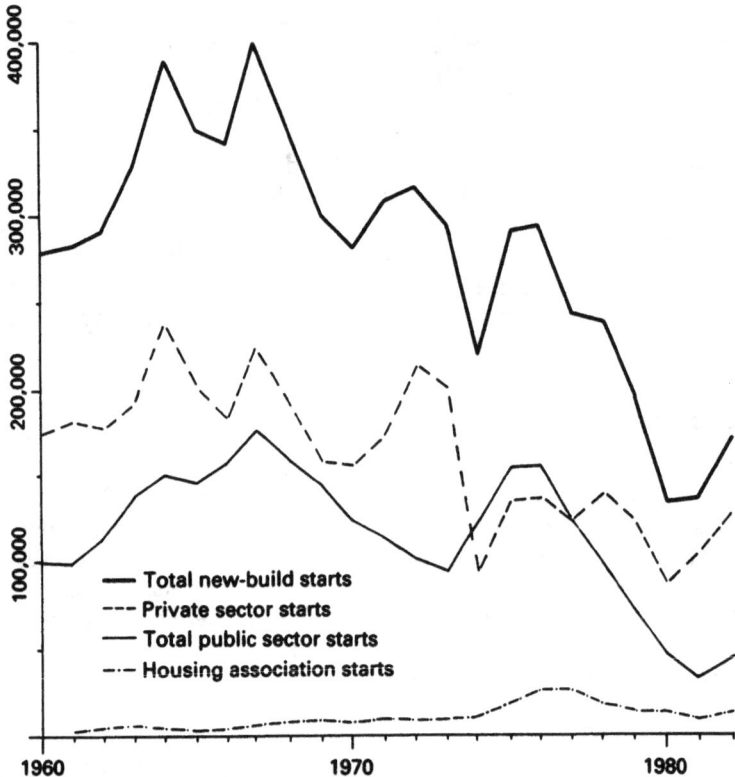

Figure 2.2   *New-build housing starts, England and Wales.*

Source: DOE, *Housing and Construction Statistics* (various).

were published by financial year, but the trend continued downwards. In the 1980/1 financial year, 25,000 dwellings were reported demolished. This level of clearance represented 0·13 per cent of the total stock, an implied assumption that houses lasted over 750 years.

Figure 2.3 also shows the total level of private sector grant activity since 1960. Completions peaked at around 217,000 in 1974 but, in numerical terms, then fell back to levels achieved in the 1960s, a period before rehabilitation was central to older housing policy (see Appendix 3). However, from 1969 grants were primarily for works of improvement and repair. For most of the 1960s more than half of all approvals were for standard grants to provide basic amenities. That change can be seen in Figure 2.4, with a dramatic increase in improvement grant approvals following the Housing Act 1969 (see Appendix 4). The trend in cash terms can be seen in Figure 2.5. Expenditure at the beginning of the 1980s was running at only just above a third of the 1974 level in real terms, but well above expenditure in the 1960s. Spending on improvement grants

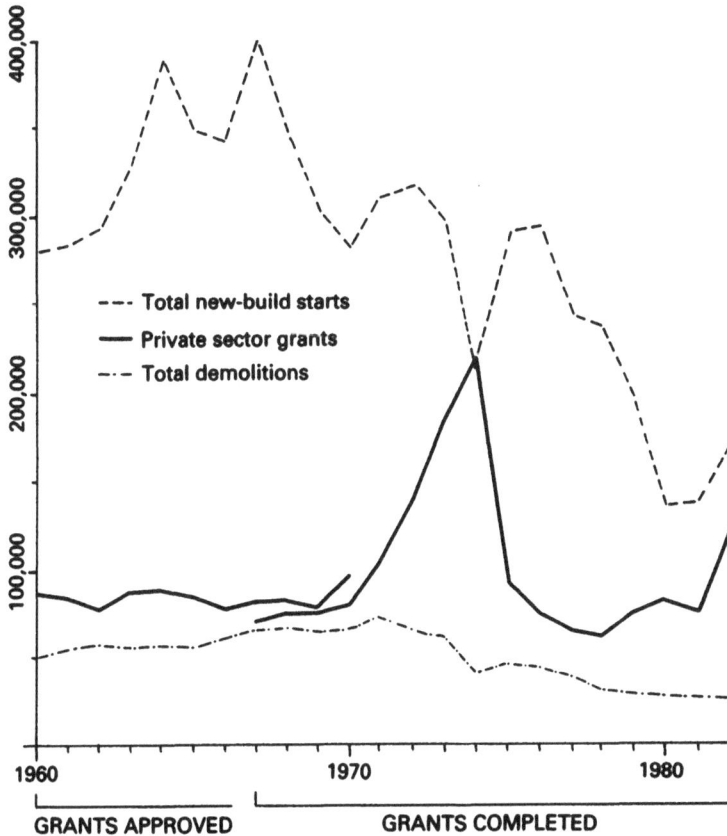

Figure 2.3 *New-build, grants and clearance, England and Wales.*

Source: DOE, *Housing and Construction Statistics* (various).

was the major component; intermediate, special and repair grants together formed only 5 per cent of all expenditure.

In the early 1980s private sector grant completions increased, from 63,500 in 1978 to a provisional 124,000 in 1982. But this figure was only about half the 1974 peak. An important component of the 1982 total was the wider use of repair grants. In 1981 they accounted for 8 per cent of all grants in England, compared with only 1 per cent in the previous year. This trend continued in 1982 when, with the general availability of 90 per cent grants, they accounted for 30 per cent of grants paid to private owners. Higher grant levels also increased the use of intermediate grants, while the number of improvement grants remained largely unchanged (see Appendix 5).

Looking at grant expenditure, payments in 1982 were running at 70 per cent of the 1974 peak (at constant prices). At the same time, the level of grants was running at about 60 per cent of eligible costs, implying that, in

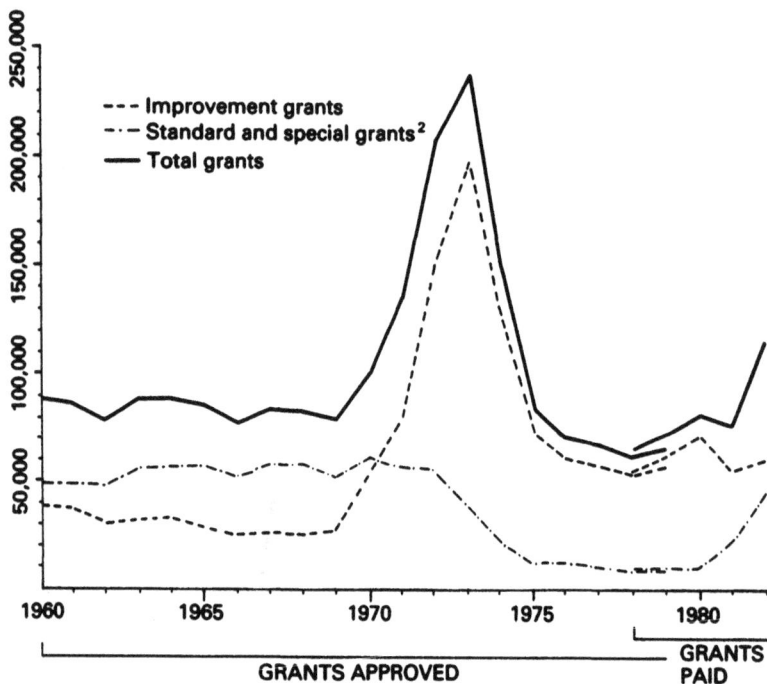

Figure 2.4   Grants approved to private owners, England and Wales.[1]
Source: DOE, Housing and Construction Statistics (various).
Notes:
1   Grants paid from 1978. Including housing associations prior to 1972.
2   Including repair grants after 1974.

real terms, individual properties were receiving higher levels of grant aid in 1982. This may have been a reflection of greater eligible work as a consequence of focusing on the worst housing stock. However, an annual analysis shows that the average grant of just under £1,900 in 1974 (at 1980 prices) was not exceeded during the rest of the 1970s (see Appendix 6). This leads to the conclusion that the sharp rise was due to the higher eligible expense limits and grant percentages introduced in the Housing Act 1980 and by the 1982 Budget. However, these increases did not have a dramatic effect on the real level of grants. Figure 2.6 shows how grant limits should have risen to maintain their 1969 value. Only in London did the 1983 increase restore 1969 purchasing power.

The failure to index-link grant levels was offset, for some people, by higher percentages. In 1969 the maximum grant payable in a general improvement area (GIA) was £1,000 (50 per cent of £2,000 eligible expense limit); equivalent to around £5,850 at 1983 prices. By comparison, the maximum grant in 1983 was £9,180 (90 per cent of £10,200 for a priority dwelling outside London). Even this figure,

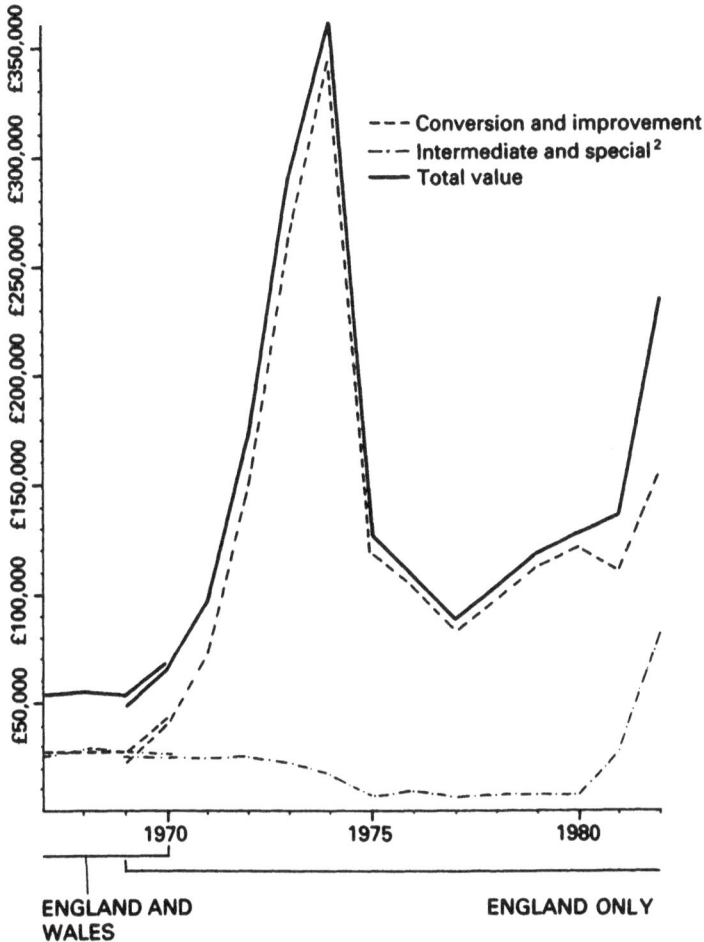

Figure 2.5   *Renovation Grants paid to private owners by value.* [1]
Source: DOE, *Housing and Construction Statistics* (various).
Notes:
1   At constant prices.
2   Including standard grants; and repair grants after 1974.

however, was slightly down in real terms compared with the 90 per cent grant available within HAAs in 1974. Then, the eligible expense limit for an improvement grant was £3,200, with a 90 per cent grant maximum of £2,880 in cases of hardship. To keep pace with inflation, this figure needed to increase to £9,330 in 1983. Therefore, while more people were able to benefit from the availability of 90 per cent grants during the period 1982–4, the purchasing power of these grants had declined slightly in real terms.

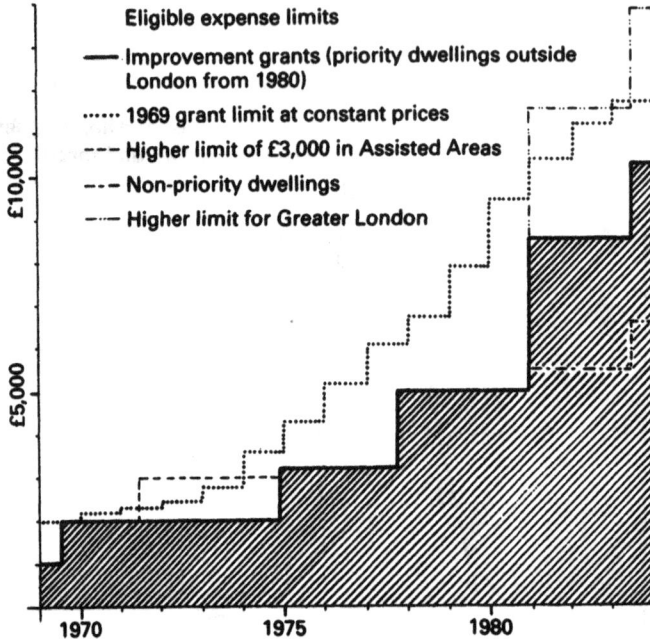

Figure 2.6 *Improvement grant eligible expense limits.*

Summary:
1969: £2,000; 1974: £3,200; 1977: £5,000; 1980: £8,500 for priority dwellings outside London (£5,500 for non-priority); 1983: £10,200 for priority dwellings outside London (£6,600 for non-priority).

Net Stock Gains

The annual net stock gain in England and Wales tended to fall during the early 1970s, but the rise in improvement grants pushed up the total gain of new and improved stock from 2·2 per cent in 1969 to 3·1 per cent in 1973 (Table 2.10). The fall in grant activity in 1975 reduced the percentage gain back to 2·2 per cent. Though new building declined over the late 1970s, grant activity was sufficient to maintain this performance. It was only in 1981 that low rates of new-build completions combined with low grant activity to reduce the overall percentage gain to 1·7 per cent.

To assess the adequacy of performance at this level requires a comparison against both the rate of stock deterioration into unfitness and the increase in household formation. An appendix to the 1977 Housing Policy Review (DOE, 1977a, tech. vol. 1, pp. 159–63) forecast dwellings likely to become unfit. The 1976 House Condition Survey showed 894,000 unfit dwellings in England and Wales. The rate at which properties became unfit was projected at 50,000 a year, on the assumption that the rate would be lower than that thought to have

Table 2.10 Housing Stock: Net Gain, England and Wales, 1969–82

	1969	1970	1971	1972	1973	1974	1975	1976	1977	1978	1979	1980	1981	1982
Completions	306,861	291,793	294,675	272,524	249,713	229,362	261,458	263,426	261,000	241,363	209,457	202,608	170,551	147,062
Demolitions less conversions	57,620	56,650	55,200	45,910	37,920	14,060	30,330	24,635	19,720	15,460	13,310	14,100[1]	14,100	14,100
Stock at end of year ('000s)	15,773	15,980	16,210	16,397	16,573	16,757	16,961	17,174	17,391	17,598	17,777	17,957	18,097	18,220
Net stock gain	249,241	235,143	239,475	226,614	211,793	215,302	231,128	238,791	241,280	225,903	196,147	188,508	156,451	132,962
As % total stock	1·58	1·47	1·48	1·38	1·28	1·28	1·36	1·39	1·39	1·28	1·10	1·05	0·86	0·73
Grant activity	104,588	121,831	163,823	245,290	305,352	298,363	134,452	127,675	120,823	139,012	166,400	191,729	155,392	205,726
Net gain plus improved stock	353,829	356,974	403,298	471,904	517,145	513,665	365,580	366,466	362,103	364,915	362,547	380,237	311,843	338,688
As % total stock	2·2	2·2	2·5	2·9	3·1	3·0	2·2	2·1	2·0	2·0	2·0	2·1	1·7	1·9

Source: DOE, Housing and Construction Statistics. (various).
Note:
1 Estimates since 1980.

Table 2.11   *Projected Levels of Unfitness, 1976–81   ('ooos)*

	1977 Housing Policy Review (England and Wales)	1981 House Condition Survey and actuals (England only)
Unfit 1976	894	1,162
plus becoming unfit 1976–81	250	?
less demolished or closed 1976–81	200	188
less made fit 1976–81	350	?
less made fit in lieu of demolition 1976–81	25	75
Total unfit 1981	570	1,116

Sources: 1977 Housing Policy Review (DOE, 1977a); English House Condition Survey (DOE, 1982a) and *Housing and Construction Statistics 1971–81* (DOE, 1982b).

occurred on the basis of 1971 and 1976 house condition data. Houses made fit were estimated at 70,000 a year. On these figures, the Housing Policy Review suggested that the number of unfit properties would be reduced by over a third to around 570,000 in 1981. In the event, the revised levels of unfitness in the 1981 House Condition Survey (England only) showed that this improvement did not occur (Table 2.11). As demolitions were broadly in line with predictions, it implied that more properties became unfit than were made fit over the period 1976 to 1981. Therefore, if the Housing Policy Review was right to assume 70,000 a year as the number of houses made fit, something approaching 100,000 a year were becoming unfit. Relating this to Table 2.10 offsets the gain in new and improved units by 0·5 per cent a year.

Turning to housing demand in the context of net stock gain, Fleming and Nellis (1982) updated forecasts of supply and demand presented in the Housing Policy Review. This made assumptions about factors which influenced demand: the relationship between household structure and housing opportunities, real income and rates of interest. In the owner-occupied sector, the main factor was the growth of potential first-time buyers as a result of demographic trends. In the public sector, net demand was based on current housing needs and the likely effect of building and modernization programmes. Taking the two sectors together, the housing stock in Great Britain needed to increase by around 300,000 units a year. This would imply a net stock gain of around 1·5 per cent a year for England and Wales. The actual rate was about half this level, confirming the conclusions of the House of Commons Environment Committee that there would be a cumulative shortfall of around 500,000 dwellings by 1985 against the Housing Policy Review projections (House of Commons, 1980, para. 31). In practice this pointed to lengthening public sector waiting lists, strong upward pressures on house prices and private sector rents, an increase in homelessness, sharing and overcrowding, and continued occupation of substandard housing as the stock deteriorated and decisions about replacement and rehabilitation were deferred.

National Allocation of Resources

A decline in housing output is one measure of achieved levels of housing investment. Falling levels of rehabilitation activity have an immediate impact on people's housing standards, while low rates of clearance and new building have a longer-term impact on condition. Indeed, it has been suggested that the rate of new housing provision is a very good barometer, with housing conditions for most people tending to get better during periods when housebuilding is expanding (Ball, 1983, p. 5). The declining level of output during the late 1970s and early 1980s therefore provides a context for understanding the apparent trends in disrepair. An alternative approach is to consider the volume of housing investment within the overall distribution of national resources. Doing this shows how total capital investment has fallen, with increased expenditure on repair failing to offset new housing output.

The 1977 Housing Policy Review showed United Kingdom gross fixed investment in dwellings running at £1,750 million a year (1970 prices) in the period 1973-5. This investment included grant-aided improvement as well as new building, but not purchase of land or second-hand houses. The total level of spending represented a historically high 4·3 per cent of GDP (DOE, 1977a, tech. vol. 1, p. 40, table 1.25). Public expenditure on housing was measured in terms of gross fixed capital formation (including purchase of land and second-hand houses), subsidies by central and local government, and improvement grants. Again, total spending was high, at 4 per cent of GDP in 1975 (£3,694 million at outturn prices; DOE, 1977, tech. vol. 1, p. 41, table 1.26). Between 1976 and 1981 Table 2.12 shows that investment dropped by 45 per cent. Until 1978 about a fifth of all fixed capital formation was in dwellings; but this fell quite dramatically in 1978-80. Over that period total investment declined by 0·4 per cent at constant prices, with housing investment falling by 23 per cent.

Table 2.13 shows construction industry output figures at current and constant prices. These are not comparable with Table 2.12. Gross domestic fixed capital formation (additions to the country's stock of fixed assets) refers to assets in the United Kingdom, which are valued at cost to the purchaser, including fees. And as a measure, it also includes expenditure on improvements to fixed assets, but not repair and maintenance. In practice, this means that all public sector conversion and improvement expenditure is included, but only grant-aided conversion and improvement in the private sector. Output figures, referring to Great Britain, are the amount chargeable by contractors to customers for building work. New construction excludes improvements and extensions,

Table 2.12   Gross Domestic Fixed Capital Formation,[1] United Kingdom, 1970–81

	Investment in dwellings		As % of GDP[2] at factor cost		Total investment[3]		Investment in dwellings as percentage of total investment (1975 prices)
	current prices £m.	1975 prices £m.	current prices %	1975 prices %	current prices £m.	1975 prices £m.	%
1970	1,643	3,926	3·77	4·59	9,470	19,460	20·2
1971	1,898	4,173	3·83	4·76	10,517	19,743	21·1
1972	2,254	4,354	4·07	4·90	11,606	19,823	22·0
1973	2,686	4,152	4·17	4·34	14,238	21,195	19·6
1974	3,187	3,826	4·27	4·03	16,825	20,562	18·6
1975	4,149	4,149	4·40	4·40	20,408	20,408	20·3
1976	4,726	4,265	4·24	4·36	23,556	20,640	20·7
1977	4,695	3,908	3·70	3·94	25,727	20,139	19·4
1978	5,368	4,061	3·67	3·97	29,743	20,845	19·5
1979	5,673	3,615	3·38	3·49	34,469	21,039	17·2
1980	5,984	3,106	3·08	3·06	39,411	20,443	15·2
1981	5,186	2,346	2·46	2·36	39,377	18,774	12·5

Notes and Sources:
1 Expenditure on fixed assets for either replacing or adding to the stock of existing fixed assets, CSO, National Income and Expenditure, 1981 and 1982, table 10.2.
2 CSO, Annual Abstract of Statistics, various years.
3 Including vehicles, ships, aircraft, plant and machinery, other new buildings and works.

which are included under repair and maintenance. What Table 2.13 shows is that new housing output fell over the period, representing 4·2 per cent of GDP in 1970 and 1·7 per cent in 1980. This downward movement during the late 1970s in the proportion of GDP allocated to investment in new dwellings was partly offset by an increase in expenditure on repair and maintenance. This accounted for 32 per cent of total housing investment in 1970 and 52 per cent in 1981. However, this was not sufficient to offset an overall reduction from 5·9 per cent of GDP in 1970 to 3·6 per cent in 1981.

International Comparisons
The 1977 Housing Policy Review showed that a lower proportion of the United Kingdom's GDP was taken by investment in dwellings than the average for other advanced industrial countries, with only Sweden, Norway and the United States being lower (DOE, 1977a, p. 141). Figures for the Economic Commission for Europe (ECE) on domestic fixed capital formation emphasized the United Kingdom's relatively low level of spending. Table 2.14 shows that as a proportion of gross fixed capital

Table 2.13   Investment in New Housing, Repair and Maintenance, Great Britain, 1970–81

	Total new housing output		Current Prices (£ million) Housing repair and maintenance		r & m % total output	Total output	GDP at factor cost	Total output as % GDP
	£m.	% GDP	£m.	% GDP	%	£m.	£m.	% GDP
1970	1,427	3·3	686	1·6	32	2,113	43,574	4·8
1971	1,628	3·3	765	1·5	32	2,393	49,538	4·8
1972	1,915	3·5	946	1·7	33	2,861	55,359	5·2
1973	2,539	3·9	1,279	2·0	34	3,818	64,362	5·9
1974	2,589	3·5	1,504	2·0	37	4,093	74,641	5·5
1975	3,025	3·2	1,658	1·8	35	4,683	94,339	5·0
1976	3,593	3·2	1,788	1·6	33	5,381	111,566	4·8
1977	3,619	2·8	2,110	1·7	37	5,729	127,050	4·5
1978	4,211	2·9	2,622	1·8	38	6,833	146,079	4·7
1979	4,478	2·7	3,242	1·9	42	7,720	167,937	4·6
1980	4,405	2·3	4,114	2·1	48	8,519	194,538	4·4
1981	3,787[P]	1·8	4,130[P]	2·0	52	7,917	210,788	3·8
	1975 Constant Prices (£ million)							
1970	3,556	4·2	1,473	1·7	29	5,029	85,484	5·9
1971	3,682	4·2	1,516	1·7	29	5,198	87,672	5·9
1972	3,701	4·2	1,744	1·9	32	5,445	88,833	6·1
1973	3,762	3·9	1,956	2·1	34	5,718	95,654	6·0
1974	3,056	3·2	1,896	2·0	38	4,952	94,966	5·2
1975	3,025	3·2	1,658	1·8	35	4,683	94,339	5·0
1976	3,285	3·3	1,527	1·6	32	4,812	97,793	4·9
1977	3,048	3·1	1,589	1·6	34	4,637	99,190	4·7
1978	3,164	3·1	1,843	1·8	37	5,007	102,284	4·9
1979	2,791	2·7	1,968	1·9	41	4,759	103,711	4·6
1980	2,245	2·2	2,074	2·1	48	4,319	101,488	4·3
1981	1,737[P]	1·7	1,851[P]	1·9	52	3,588	99,291	3·6

Sources: Housing and Construction Statistics, 1970–81, table 9 (DOE, 1981b, 1982a); CSO, Annual Abstract of Statistics, various years.
Note: [P] denotes a provisional figure.

formation, United Kingdom investment in residential construction fell by 2·7 per cent between 1978 and 1980. A similar pattern was recorded in Denmark and Sweden, with the fall in Canada being more dramatic. In contrast, investment increased in Belgium, France, the Netherlands and Norway. As a proportion both of GDP and of total capital formation, United Kingdom domestic capital formation was lower than for other ECE countries.

Relatively low levels of spending could not in themselves be taken as an

Table 2.14 *Domestic Fixed Capital Formation: International Comparisons*

	Gross fixed capital formation in residential buildings as % GDP				Gross fixed capital formation in residential buildings as % total gross fixed capital formation			
	1970	1978	1979	1980	1970	1978	1979	1980
Belgium	5·6	7·5	6·5	6·4	25·0	35·6	31·6	30·1
Canada	4·1	5·7	5·2	4·7	19·5	25·7	23·4	20·4
Denmark	8·3	7·2	6·9	5·6	33·7	32·2	32·0	29·5
France	6·7	6·6	6·7	6·8	26·6	30·8	31·7	31·4
Germany (FR)	6·6	6·0	6·5	—	25·8	28·3	29·0	—
Italy	6·4	5·0	5·0	—	30·0	27·0	26·8	—
Netherlands	5·3	6·0	5·8	6·2	20·5	27·9	27·0	28·7
Norway	4·9	5·5	5·2	5·1	18·6	17·3	19·0	19·3
Sweden	5·7	4·7	5·0	4·6	25·3	24·7	25·6	23·6
USA	3·6	5·0	—	—	20·8	27·7	—	—
UK	3·2	3·3	2·9	2·7	17·4	18·1	16·6	15·4

Source: Annual Bulletin of Housing and Building Statistics for Europe: ECE (Geneva: United Nations, 1981).
Note: National definitions are not strictly comparable.

indication that capital investment in housing was insufficient. Spending could be related to existing housing conditions. The faster growing economies of other countries may have allowed greater scope for expenditure; but at least on crude indicators of occupancy and amenity provision, the spending was justified because they were relatively poorly housed (DOE, 1977a, p. 141). For similar reasons, the nature of the United Kingdom housing stock was crucial when considering the type and scale of required investment. While there was a continuing demand for housing as a result of new household formation, a trend expected to continue throughout the 1980s and early 1990s (Ermisch, 1981), the age profile of the housing stock suggested that the main share of investment should be in renewal – through rehabilitation or replacement. Indeed it had been argued that, within existing spending patterns, too high a proportion of real resources was being devoted to meet increases in the stock, at the expense of stock renewal (Kilroy, 1981a).

In terms of competition for resources within the total economy, reduced capital spending on housing released resources to be devoted elsewhere. Therefore, while a lower proportion of fixed capital formation had found its way into housing, other parts of the economy could have benefited. Table 2.12 shows a fall in the proportion of resources devoted to domestic capital formation. At the same time, there was all-sector growth in capital investment; while in the public sector there was a decline in new building construction outside housing (CSO, 1981, table 10.2).

Because there had been a decline in housing capital expenditure, one conclusion was that 'Britain's poor industrial performance generally cannot be attributed to the excessive devotion of real resources to housing in recent years' (BSA, 1980, p. 16). However, this relationship between housing and wider economic performance limited the analysis to the use of real resources – new housing construction and improvement work. Housing exchange also had to be financed. The impact of this on the wider economy is a question returned to in Chapter 6.

Disrepair Trends
It has been seen that capital investment in housing fell in absolute and comparative terms in recent years; and though expenditure on repair and maintenance took an increased percentage of lower construction output, there was no growth in real terms. If one accepts revised estimates of disrepair presented in the 1981 English House Condition Survey, the outstanding bill of around £35 billion was an increase of £3·3 billion on 1976, and represented 17 per cent of total GDP. The annual proportion of GDP actually devoted to repair and maintenance was more difficult to estimate. Table 2.13 shows output figures for repair and maintenance in all sectors at £4·1 billion in 1981. The House Condition Survey estimated that during 1981 about £6·1 billion was spent by households on repairs, improvements, maintenance and decoration to the housing stock, of which £160 million came from government grants (DOE, 1983a, p. 14). Including an estimate for the value of households' unpaid labour on do-it-yourself work gave a total expenditure on the owner-occupied stock of £7·3 billion; around 3 per cent of GDP. But it was not known what proportion of this work was devoted to repair rather than conversion, improvement, or extensions. Neither was it known what proportion of do-it-yourself expenditure was directed towards superficial works. However, it was clear that the pattern of expenditure was inconsistent with a professional assessment of the need for investment. The 1981 English House Condition Survey found that expenditure in the owner-occupied sector varied very little with the age of the dwelling, with the result that almost twice as much was spent on postwar dwellings during 1981 than would have been needed to remedy all defects identified by surveyors (DOE, 1983a, p. 14). Clearly, therefore, a substantial proportion of the £7·3 billion spent on the owner-occupied stock had nothing to do with remedial work. In fact, the most common items of expenditure related to work having an immediate impact on comfort and convenience: central heating, replacement bathroom and kitchen fitments, external windows (mainly double glazing), and electrical rewiring (DOE, 1983a, p. 15).

The comparative data presented in the 1981 English House Condition Survey questioned previously held conclusions about national performance in tackling poor housing conditions. But while the re-analysis made it difficult to consider disrepair trends, it confirmed the broad view that external maintenance represented a growing proportion of the bill for outstanding work. Increasingly it was repair, rather than the provision of amenities, which defined the health of the national housing stock. As a response to this problem, the history of policy was one of increasing the proportion of assistance available to home owners, and increasing the repair component. In 1969 all grants were awarded at 50 per cent, irrespective of special area status, and the repair element of an improvement grant could not exceed 50 per cent of the approved cost. The Housing Act 1980 increased the repair element to 70 per cent, and during the period 1982–4 a substantial proportion of all grants were awarded at 90 per cent. Birmingham, in its envelope approach (see Chapter 5), provided the logical conclusion to this trend with a scheme which was essentially a 100 per cent repair grant to secure the external fabric of the property.

The disadvantage of grants is that they represent a major but infrequent injection of capital without being able to influence the future pattern of maintenance activity. They are a firefighting measure which fail to tackle the reasons why owners in aggregate continue to invest in property repair at a level which is insufficient to prevent its deterioration. As the average age of the housing stock increases, due to low levels of new building and clearance, it was to be expected that the need for maintenance expenditure will increase. While there is not a linear relationship between age and repair expenditure, there is a tendency for the annual costs of repair to increase with age. To the extent that this theoretical relationship holds true, a deterioration in the national housing stock can be attributed to increasing costs rather than reductions in expenditure. But the overall level of investment seems inadequate to prevent further deterioration.

3

The Process of Disrepair

Investment and Disinvestment

Chapter 2 described the relatively low and inadequate levels of national investment in an ageing housing stock. The cumulative impact was expressed as a rate of deterioration in cash terms. To understand further the processes of disrepair it is necessary to abandon the macro analysis and consider investment decisions at an individual level.

It is easy to see that condition and likely future maintenance costs may be factors influencing the original decision to purchase a house. But once acquired, other considerations will operate. People's strategies for coping with maintenance problems will be related to factors like income, housing condition, and their perception of the need for investment. There may also be patterns of investment behaviour relating to movement intentions, with people deciding that selling would provide a better return than carrying out expensive repairs. Alternatively, they might anticipate moving, with this determining the nature and level of investment in terms of a potential sale price.

In the absence of any clear price incentive, it seems likely that owners will under-invest in capital works and that this will show as cumulative disrepair. Such a trend would be aggravated by an ageing of the housing stock resulting from low levels of clearance and new building. However, these are broad generalizations which do not explain why some houses remain well maintained while others deteriorate to the point where they no longer provide satisfactory housing.

Some areas of housing will always be of higher status than others because of the heterogeneous nature of the stock and the unequal distribution of purchase power. Even in the absence of absolute scarcity, symbolic value would induce what Hirsch described as social scarcity. Absolute improvements in living standards will increase the effective demand for environments that are socially or physically scarce, placing excess pressure on these environments, which either leads to their deterioration or to their protection through the exclusion mechanism of price (Hirsch, 1977, p. 41).

In this process, it is apparent that physical factors are relatively unimportant. It is true that certain characteristics of construction tend to hasten obsolescence; for example, the non-traditional building systems of the postwar period. But there is much that has survived from earlier periods which gives a different meaning to the view that building standards have changed over the years. Following the logic of constructional obsolescence would leave little Georgian or Victorian property. Most were built without adequate foundations or a damp-proof course.

Similarly, design is not generally a critical variable. It is the case that form can have an impact on social obsolescence. Suitability for purpose has, to varying degrees, influenced the useful life of deck access and tower blocks; while poor orientation, sound insulation and lack of open space are factors which may encourage people to move from inner city terraces to suburban areas. But older property can be remarkably adaptable. At some point inconvenience, lack of privacy and inadequate car parking becomes a town house with character and a desirable central location.

In looking at why some houses receive adequate maintenance while others are allowed to deteriorate, traditional economic explanations have been couched in terms of a balance between levels of investment and the flow of benefits received (see, for example, Richardson, 1971). Whether or not to carry out repairs, and the level of repair to be undertaken, is balanced against likely financial returns: 'if the discounted present value of the costs exceed the present value of the future revenue then it would be rational for the individual property owner to allow the property to deteriorate' (Jackson, 1980, p. 226). Future revenue is assessed both in terms of the increased flow of services enjoyed through improvements, and by increased benefits occurring in relation to neighbourhood effects. Both economic and policy debates have focused on these externalities in a search for a theory which predicts urban decay and regeneration. The tendency has been to concentrate on individual decisions in the context of perceptions about broader investment trends. Consequently, much emphasis has been given to the disincentives implied by a valuation gap between improved and unimproved property; the valuation gap being the shortfall between the selling price of an improved house and its pre-improved valuation plus the costs of improvement. Where grants fail to make good the shortfall, there is an assumed disincentive to carry out the work.

The existence of a valuation gap has been used to explain the problems facing individual owners. One study of the implementation of a housing action area in the West Midlands identified valuation gap constraints affecting both new and continuing owner-occupiers. For many first-time buyers the finance of house purchase was extremely marginal. People who exchanged property did not need a maximum mortgage of either valuation or income and could afford to carry out any required or necessary repairs out of capital. The first-time buyer, however, was often looking for the highest possible mortgage, found problems with retentions, and was not able to borrow for additional improvements because of valuation. But this buyer, the least able to carry out repair work, might well be buying the property most in need of attention. Capital sums were required for deposit, fees, furnishings and fittings. The proportion of income devoted to mortgage repayments could be high, even though the house was in an HAA. If money had to be borrowed for the deposit or related expenses, the commitment was even more onerous. In these circumstances, residents in the study area were effectively unable to meet their share of improvement costs. At that time, for a house costing £4,500 with £7,000 of improvement costs, a 75 per cent grant on prevailing eligible expense limits left the owner with a potential mortgage of £7,750; unobtainable because it was higher than the improved property valuation (Thomas, 1979, p. 238).

For established owners, valuation problems were not such a severe constraint on borrowing due to lower initial purchase prices. But a survey of the area showed that of the seventy owner-occupiers who had not inquired about a grant, nearly a quarter gave as a reason that they could not afford to finance their share of the costs. Of those that had inquired about grants but had not made an application, 18 per cent said the grant was too small. But even if they could afford it, rehabilitation was not an attractive proposition in objective terms. Where a family had purchased in the 1960s for £2,000 they could sell unimproved for around £4,500, showing a capital growth of £2,500. If they invested £3,000 of their own money in improvements and sold for £6,000, their capital growth would be reduced to £1,000. Owners planning to remain in their homes might be prepared to invest money without wishing to add to their property's value, and in time, the general increase in house prices might justify the financial investment. But in the immediate future, and in the absence of any dramatic rise in local house prices, it was concluded to be economically advantageous to invest in a modern property elsewhere rather than improve an old house in the HAA (Thomas, 1979, p. 150).

Thus, for both first-time and established owner-occupiers alike, straightforward economics often argued against rehabilitation. The existence of a valuation gap meant that it was impossible to recoup all the invested capital. Where a valuation gap continued to exist, having taken into account improvement costs net of subsidy, investment was potentially deterred unless the owner was more concerned with the benefits improvement would bring than with value added to the property; or if improved property carried a price premium reflecting the inconvenience of the improvement process; or if neighbourhood price effects would cancel the valuation gap as the whole area was improved (Harrison, 1977).

The existence of a valuation gap helps to explain investment behaviour. It has also been linked with the prisoner's dilemma to suggest that the pursuit of individual self-interest leads to a position where no owner invests, and therefore, where everyone loses. In this formulation, the consequences of pursuing uncoordinated self-interest would be similar to those described by Paris (1977), where the only improved house on the street might prove the most difficult to sell. Investment returns to individuals would be reasonable where all maintained their homes: but because of the narrow divergence between improved and unimproved prices, individuals would be better off not maintaining their property while others did. In this fundamental market contradiction, it is the dislocation between condition and value which is at the root of the valuation gap. The difference between the cost of work and the resulting investment value not only discourages capital spending but means that it is usually cheaper to buy a better house than carry out major repairs, because the cost of work exceeds its investment value by more than the transaction costs of moving.

Expenditure by Home Owners

At root, there would appear to be three broad and interdependent influences on levels of maintenance expenditure: the characteristics of the building; the income of the household; and their housing aspirations (Sigsworth and Wilkinson, 1971). The relationship between stock condition and rates of obsolescence then become factors in a process of access and consumption within the housing market. The consequence of this pattern of consumption is that resources will be allocated in a way which handicaps certain groups, resulting in a familiar concentration of poor people living in poor housing conditions unable to maintain their homes.

Looking at spending by individual home owners, there is evidence of at least short-term reductions in levels of maintenance expenditure which have paralleled trends in increased disrepair. Findings from the Family Expenditure Survey suggested that average spending on repair and maintenance by home owners had declined throughout the 1970s relative to rehabilitation costs and incomes. Table 3.1 shows that weekly repair and maintenance expenditure did not keep pace with indices of earnings and costs. The general economic climate might provide an explanation, it seeming reasonable to postpone long-term maintenance for immediate capital savings during a recession. If owner-occupiers did this, it would reflect similar decisions in the public sector to lengthen maintenance cycles. A closer look at consumer spending, however, gives little support to explanations linked to economic performance, though time-series data are too brief to confirm any firm trends. During the 1970s, consumer spending on repair, maintenance and improvement remained fairly steady in real terms and as a proportion of total consumer spending. Real disposable income rose over the period, with maintenance expenditure failing to reflect the increase (Table 3.2). The figures are global and insensitive to the nature of work being carried out. It is possible that other underlying trends had an influence. Perhaps those enjoying greater

Table 3.1 *Owner-Occupiers' Expenditure on Repair and Maintenance*

	Households' average weekly expenditure[1] £	Index of weekly expenditure	Repair and maintenance materials cost index[2]	Housing repair and maintenance index[3]	Average earnings index[4]
1970	0·95	100	100	100	100
1971	1·11	117	106	108	112
1972	1·06	112	112	116	126
1973	1·34	141	127	147	143
1974	1·81	191	163	179	168
1975	1·81	191	196	222	212
1976	2·42	255	235	261	245
1977	2·30	242	276	296	269
1978	2·48	261	304	327	304
1979	3·43	361	355	405	352
1980	3·75	395	425	490	424
1981	3·96	417	467		479
1982			502ᵖ		524

Sources:
1 Family Expenditure Survey (London: HMSO, 1982).
2 DOE, *Housing and Construction Statistics*, various years.
3 From Doling, 1983, table 1, based on DOE supplementary memorandum to House of Commons Environment Committee (Private Rented Housing Sector). The index includes VAT.
4 Department of Employment.
  Note: ᵖ denotes a provisional figure.

disposable income did not see repair as a problem, or maintenance expenditure as a priority. People may have recognized the need for repairs, while choosing to spend in some other way. For low-income owners, the element of choice was likely to be more severely constrained, introducing a real conflict of priorities.

The individual implications of an unwillingness or inability to pay for repair and maintenance underlie aggregate levels of under-investment in the national housing stock. For one household living in Birmingham and faced with repair costs, the price of owner-occupation was the family holiday. In a second case, the wife went back to work specifically to pay the costs of rewiring. A third household regretted the purchase of their pre-1919 house because they were never likely to see a return on their maintenance expenditure (Karn, Kemeny and Williams, 1982). In another part of the city, an elderly couple living in an interwar semi-detached house needed a £4,000 interest-only loan so that they could replace their rotten windows (Carvel, 1983). These experiences, though random, are indicative of the individual problems experienced by people

Table 3.2 *Consumer Expenditure on Maintenance, Repairs and Improvements, United Kingdom 1975 constant prices £ millions*

	Expenditure on maintenance repair and improvements (A)	Total consumer expenditure (B)	Real disposable income (C)	A as % of B (D)	A as % of C (E)
1970	1,692	57,814	63,709	2·9	2·7
1971	1,827	59,724	64,643	3·1	2·8
1972	1,874	63,270	70,783	3·0	2·6
1973	1,991	66,332	75,086	3·0	2·7
1974	1,815	65,113	75,023	2·8	2·4
1975	1,845	64,749	73,768	2·9	2·5
1976	1,720	64,815	73,304	2·6	2·3
1977	1,732	64,583	71,763	2·7	2·4
1978	1,870	68,222	77,696	2·7	2·4
1979	2,132	71,409	82,134	3·0	2·6
1980	1,936	71,454	84,501	2·7	2·3

Source: CSO, *National Income and Expenditure*, table 4.7 (London: HMSO, 1981).

living in homes they could not afford to maintain.

The high repair costs imposed on low-income families was pointed out by Coates and Silburn (1970) arising out of their work in Nottingham. Not only were the poor living in homes which required more maintenance, but, if repairs were done, they had to be done in a relatively expensive way. It was an example of how rich you had to be to be poor. Because a poor family could not afford expensive fundamental repairs, maintenance was either neglected or undertaken in a piecemeal fashion, which in the long term was neither efficient nor cheap. It could also shift the burden of costs from one element of the family budget to another. Ignoring repairs to ill fitting windows could lead to higher heating bills, as might the fight to combat damp. Higher initial expenditure, an option denied by lack of cash and credit, would have meant lower future outgoings: 'To be poor is to pay more, and to pay more often' (Coates and Silburn, 1970, p. 95).

Income and Housing Conditions

The correlation between income and housing conditions was confirmed by findings in both the 1976 and 1981 English House Condition Surveys. The social survey in 1981 showed that households living in the poorer stock had lower average incomes than those in satisfactory dwellings, and that those in dwellings found to be unfit or lacking amenities had the lowest average incomes of all (DOE, 1983a, p. 10). Households living in unsatisfactory houses were more likely to be elderly, to consist of just one or two people, and to have been resident at their current address for a long period (Table 3.3). Housing conditions of households whose heads were born outside the United Kingdom also tended to be worse than those of the indigenous population (DOE, 1979a, p. 6). Reflecting the relationship between the age of a house and its condition, terrace houses were more likely to lack amenities, be unfit and have higher outstanding repairs (Table 3.4). At the same time there was a broad relationship between house form and income. Of those living in a terrace house, 51 per cent had a weekly gross income of £80 or less in 1980. This was true of 41 per cent of those who lived in semi-detached houses and 31 per cent of detached houses. Of those with a gross income of more than £160 a week, 41 per cent lived in detached, 32 per cent in semi-detached, and only 16 per cent in terraced houses (OPCS, 1982, table 3.18).

Table 3.5 shows that the elderly were more likely to be living in poor housing conditions. It was found that a third of unfit property in serious disrepair was occupied by an elderly household, though this group accounted for only a quarter of the population. The elderly were also found to be over-represented in pre-1919 houses which, as has been seen, were more likely to lack amenities, to be unfit or in disrepair. The concentrations of elderly people might explain the relationship between length of residence and condition. Of people living in satisfactory dwellings, 51 per cent had been there for less than ten years, and 25 per cent for more than twenty years. When property was assessed as fit but in serious disrepair, 34 per cent had lived there for less than ten years and 42 per cent for more than twenty years (DOE, 1983a, table 11).

These figures covered all households and were not analysed by tenure. It may therefore be possible to explain correlations in terms of the concentrations of particular groups in the private rented sector. It is indeed the case that the private rented sector contained high proportions of these low-income groups but, in numerical terms, owner-occupation was more significant. For example, a third of private rented tenants were elderly households (DOE, 1978b, table 4), but 49 per cent of elderly households were owner-occupiers, with only 15 per cent living in the privately rented sector (DOE, 1978b, table 3).

Rather better information by tenure and household characteristics was available from the 1979 Greater London House Condition Survey. Analysis of this shows that repair costs were above average for elderly owner-occupiers (GLC, 1982, p. 7); and that Asian owners were more likely to have repair costs in excess of £1,000 (GLC, 1982, p. 83). An analysis of owner-occupiers by socio-economic group showed that, in London as a whole, 60 per cent of unskilled manual workers had repair costs over £1,000, compared with 42 per cent of non-manual workers and 36 per cent of professional and managerial workers. Length of residence was not significant for owner-occupiers, though it was marked in the privately rented sector (GLC, 1982, pp. 115–18 and p. 143).

Survey and research evidence of a correlation between low income and

Table 3.3 *Household Characteristics and Dwelling Condition, 1976–81*

	1976			1981			
Characteristics of households	*Sound dwellings*	*Dwellings in need of rehab.*	*Dwellings lacking amenities*	*Satisfactory dwellings*	*Fit but in medium disrepair*	*Lacking amenities*	*Unfit and in serious disrepair*
	%	%	%	%	%	%	%
Single person aged under 60	4·6	8	7	5	7	8	10
Single person aged over 60	10·8	19	26	14	14	28	27
Family with children	34·0	25	21	28	26	19	18
Head retired	19·4	29	34	22	25	45	38
Head looking for work	9·8	14	16	4	5	3	6
Head working full-time	67·8	53	46	62	56	34	38
Long-term resident[1]	23·4	45	51	25	35	45	59
Median income[2]	£64	£54	£50	£5,566	£3,937	£2,238	£2,224

Source: DOE, 1979a, figure 2.1; DOE, 1983a, tables 3, 5, 6, 8 and 9.
Notes:

1 1976: Lived at address for 17 years or more.
   1981: Lived at address for 20 years or more.
2 1976: Median weekly wage of full-time workers.
   1981: Median annual household income.

Table 3.4   *Condition by Type of Dwelling, 1981*

	Terrace houses %	Semi-detached %	Detached %	Purpose-built flats %	All types %
Lacking one or more basic amenity	9·0	3·0	2·4	2·7	5·0
Unfit	11·9	2·5	4·4	1·9	6·2
Repair costs over £2,500	31·2	17·8	20·6	4·0	21·7

Source: DOE, 1982a, part 1, tables 7, 14 and 22.

Table 3.5   *Age of Head of Household by Housing Conditions, 1981*

	Proportion of total households %	Satisfactory dwellings %	Unsatisfactory dwellings with amenities but medium disrepair %	unfit and serious disrepair %
Under 25	4·3	4	5	7
25–59	60·3	61	59	50
60–65	9·7	12	10	9
66 and over	25·7	23	26	34
All	100·0	100	100	100

Source: DOE, 1982a, table 5, and Census 1981.

poor housing is clear and unremarkable. No one should be surprised that an inadequate income will only purchase an inadequate house. Many families with low incomes have been forced into owner-occupation by lack of choice. As a form of tenure it offers the future advantage of enforced saving, but for low-income groups this saving may not be one they wish to make (Doling, 1983, p. 12). Reflecting the high costs of being poor, they will have to pay more for the money they borrow to purchase or improve their homes. Karn (1979) demonstrated how dependent parts of the Birmingham inner-city area were on fringe banks and informal sources of loans. National statistics give support to these findings. Owners with a mortgage living in a pre-1919 house were more likely to have a loan from a local authority or bank; and 5 per cent borrowed from 'other organisations or individuals' compared with 2 per cent overall (OPCS, 1982, table 3.34). This higher level of lending from 'other' sources was also a feature of people having gross weekly incomes of under £100 (OPCS, 1982, table 3.32). In the circumstances of high costs and poor quality, the rational and perhaps inevitable response for low-income owners might be to neglect repairs.

Owners' Perceptions of Maintenance Problems
It would be inaccurate to attribute disrepair solely to under-investment by low-income groups. Their problems are symptomatic of a more general problem. Poorer households tend to inherit the consequences of a longer process of decay related to more general patterns of consumption within the housing market. Neither does the existence of substandard property prove that people have consciously decided to under-invest, because this would assume a common or agreed standard. There is evidence to confirm the subjective nature of standards, with home owners not sharing the values of housing professionals. It is the case that people living in poor conditions are more dissatisfied than average with their homes, but survey evidence also suggests that some people are quite satisfied with poor housing and show a lack of awareness concerning housing defects. Clearly such attitudes and perceptions could determine whether people carry out improvement work. For example, a survey in London of grant take-up in housing action areas suggested that people's view of the condition of their property was a more important factor in lack of take-up than the administrative and technical problems associated with rehabilitation (GLC, 1980, p. 9).

The 1981 House Condition Survey showed that 9 per cent of those in satisfactory dwellings were dissatisfied with the state of repair of the house, compared with 29 per cent in dwellings which were assessed as unfit and in serious disrepair (DOE, 1983a, table 12). Owner-occupiers were less likely to be dissatisfied whatever their housing conditions. Looking at property assessed to be unfit and in serious disrepair, the proportion of owner-occupiers who were dissatisfied was 15 per cent, compared with 26 per cent of private tenants and 57 per cent of local authority tenants (DOE, 1983a, table 14). It is important, however, to distinguish between satisfaction and views about the existence of defects. The 1981 House Condition Survey concluded that a low proportion of people in the unsatisfactory stock considered their dwelling to be in bad condition, with owner-occupiers, and to a lesser extent the elderly, being especially prone to give a favourable assessment (DOE, 1983a, p. 9). However, the 1981 survey asked attitude questions in a different way from the 1976 survey, when a distinction was made between satisfaction and views concerning the need for maintenance. This showed that of the houses assessed to be in need of essential repair the need was recognized by 88 per cent of households (DOE, 1979a, p. 38). Owner-occupiers were less likely to acknowledge a problem; and, if they did, were less likely to describe it as urgent (Table 3.6). The reluctance of owners to criticize their accommodation is perhaps a more significant factor than the distinction between professional and non-professional opinion.

Table 3.6 *Houses Needing Essential Repair by Occupants' Assessment, 1976*

	View as to whether repair needed			Total
	Not needed	Needed		
		big and urgent	not big and urgent	
	%	%	%	
Owner-occupied	27	21	52	100
All renters	18	40	42	100
All needing essential repairs	22	32	46	100

Source: DOE, 1979a, table D3.3.

Rodwell (1981) looked in more detail at the importance of state of repair as a factor influencing an occupant's satisfaction with his home. Presenting data from the 1976 House Condition Survey and the 1978 National Dwelling and Household Survey, levels of satisfaction appeared to be influenced by characteristics like the number of bedrooms, cost of repairs and use of amenities. This in itself was insufficient evidence that any of the characteristics actually caused the degree of dissatisfaction recorded. However, looking more specifically at dissatisfied occupiers, private tenants were particularly likely to mention state of repair, while owners were more concerned about the number and size of rooms (Rodwell, 1981, p. 17). And again, some sections of the population appeared tolerant of poor housing conditions. Of those people living in unfit housing, 81 per cent of owner-occupiers and 57 per cent of tenants said they were satisfied with their houses.

There are difficulties in assessing the implications of these findings. It would be wrong, for example, to conclude that people 'chose' to live in unfit houses; but they might be unwilling to express dissatisfaction with circumstances attributable to their own actions. Tangential support for this is provided by a separate Building Research Establishment (BRE) survey investigating the views of households. This showed that respondents from higher-quality homes were significantly more likely to identify selected items as basic necessities than were respondents from lower-quality accommodation (Britten, 1977, p. 15). However, the sample contained few households living in unfit or substandard housing, so it was difficult to obtain a realistic statement of their priorities. Britten concluded (1977, p. 26) with the possible explanation that:

> each respondent has his own 'received standard', his own idea of what is required of a home for someone in his circumstances. This received standard varies slowly over time with changes in expectations and abilities, but it is not possible to state exactly how it is determined for a particular individual. Any changes that are made to the respondent's accommodation, either by improving it (within the limits set by

finance, tenure, personal skill or structural configuration) or by moving to a different house, will generally bring the house closer to his own received standard. But at each stage in the process, the level which has been attained will now be regarded as the basic quality, below which he would no longer be prepared to live. This 'achieved standard' differs from the target 'received standard' in being composed largely of basic necessities, rather than including a number of desirable items. Therefore any apparent variations in opinion with tenure, social class, house type, etc., merely reflect the differing base levels which have been achieved by (or may indeed be possible for) the differing groups.

By its nature, Britten's work was concerned with the house itself, and not with external factors, which survey evidence suggests are more likely to influence levels of satisfaction. The 1976 House Condition Survey asked people what they liked and disliked about their homes. The most frequent replies contained no comments about the house itself, only about the neighbourhood or area. Rodwell used these responses in an attempt to predict levels of satisfaction. The four most significant factors were, in order of declining importance, satisfaction with the neighbourhood, tenure, density of occupation (people per room), and cost of necessary repairs. But, even in combination, these factors gave a poor prediction, with only a 30 per cent level of confidence (Rodwell, 1981).

Rodwell also considered the ability of occupiers to recognize the need for repair. From the 1976 House Condition Survey he noted that:

> occupants in general did not list as many faults as the surveyors. The fact that some of the faults identified by occupiers were not noted by the surveyors could mean (a) that the faults were missed in the relatively quick inspection of the property, or (b) that they were seen but not rated as important. One can certainly see how a fault with a high nuisance value can take on considerable importance to an occupier although structurally it may be unimportant. It does seem though, that the elderly and those who have been in residence for a long period do accept many shortcomings in their homes even if they are aware of them.

Further evidence of differing perceptions or priorities came from a detailed survey of residents in six housing action areas throughout England. The survey discovered 192 owner-occupiers living in property which had not received attention during the action period. Of these, 34 per cent were living in houses assessed as unsatifactory by the local authority. However, the survey suggested that not all owners of property assessed to be in need of improvement thought the work was necessary. Altogether, only 58 per cent of owners lacking or sharing one or more amenity said that their property needed attention (Niner and Forrest, 1982, p. 77).

Though there is uncertainty about the importance people attach to housind conditions, it is perhaps not surprising that they severely underestimate the cost of major repair work. In the 1976 House Condition Survey, where the surveyor estimated repair costs at over £1,000, the median value of household estimates was £280 (DOE, 1979a, table D3.4). This does not prove that people are underestimating the extent of disrepair; they may have had insufficient information on which to base a costing. Looking at dwellings in need of rehabilitation, people's view about the need for this work was influenced by their age and income, but only marginally by their period of residence. In all cases, a substantial proportion of people expressed satisfaction with state of repair, even where they acknowledged that repair was necessary (DOE, 1979a, Table D3.7).

It is difficult to summarize the picture which emerges from this survey information. There is a suggestion of differences between professional and resident assessment of investment requirements, but also some evidence that the need for repair is recognized by at least a majority of owners. There seems reason to suppose that this is broadly the case, with the divergence occurring in assessments of the scale, urgency, priority and cost of the work. But there is a need to look elsewhere for an assessment of repair as a problem. The House Condition Surveys show whether people recognize, for example, the need for roof repairs; but not whether they are worried about the problem or where it comes in their scale of priorities. It is here that it is necessary to draw on the more anecdotal evidence of repair programmes, supplemented by survey work in Birmingham.

Housing Maintenance Problems

The difficulties of home maintenance facing owner-occupiers have been remarkably slow to emerge as a problem. While tenants have long complained about the failure of landlords to carry out repairs, the relative lack of comment in the owner-occupied sector might have been taken as an indication that problems did not exist. However, evidence of cumulative under-investment was always capable of predicting the eventual emergence of such problems. Grant policy was clearly having a marginal impact on conditions. In 1982, for example, only one owner-occupied property in a hundred was affected by grant payment of any kind. Of the remaining ninety-nine, just under half were built after the Second World War and might therefore have escaped the need for major works. The others would be increasingly in need of attention, requiring either relatively expensive building work, which those on low incomes would find difficult to afford, or quite ambitious do-it-yourself activity, which would be beyond the capacity of many owners. Amongst these, obvious problems were faced by the elderly.

The increasing number of elderly owner-occupiers, many of whom found it difficult to do their own major repairs, was noted by Donnison (1979) when Chairman of the Supplementary Benefits Commission. Tinker and White (1979) pointed to the lack of systematic research into the repair problems facing elderly owners, but drew on the experience of national charities, who had expressed anxiety at the scale of the problem. Age Concern conducted a survey in the early 1970s which suggested that the elderly had considerable problems maintaining their property (Britton, 1974). Conscious of these difficulties, Anchor Housing Trust established a small-scale experiment to help elderly owners to repair and improve their homes. The report of this initiative (Anchor Housing Trust, 1980) was influential in its advocacy of 'staying put' as a policy option (Wheeler, 1982) and in focusing attention on both the problem and means of providing comprehensive support and guidance. The larger-scale programme launched in the wake of the initial experiment helped to reveal the varied and complex nature of the housing problems facing elderly home owners (Wheeler, 1983).

The Anchor Project was only one of a variety of initiatives. Other countries with an ageing population of home owners responded in different ways. In Scandinavia the preference appeared to be for programmes of income support (Struyk and Soldo, 1980, p. 12), while in the United States, there were direct aid experiments to provide repair services. These government-funded programmes, like 'Handy Andy' and 'Mr Fix-it', were part of what was acknowledged to be the need for a coherent housing maintenance programme. A Senate Committee argued that home repair services were justified as being not only cost-effective but also compatible with the preference of many older home owners to age in peace in a familiar environment (US Congress, 1977).

In practice, the early American repair aid programmes were said to have achieved a very thin coverage, and usually provided once-only assistance (Struyk and Soldo, 1980, p. 297). However, possible developments were demonstrated by projects in Pittsburgh and Baltimore. In Pittsburgh, a housing maintenance service was launched in 1975. Following the repair or improvement of properties it was seen to be important to maintain them, but this was made more difficult by the low income of residents. Therefore a scheme was devised whereby for an annual payment (then $96) a subscribing owner would receive an annual maintenance evaluation of the house, normal exterior and interior preventive maintenance, one emergency call, materials supplied at cost and access to a tool library (Ahlbrandt and Brophy, 1975, p. 139).

In a similar project, in Baltimore, the service fee entitled the household to an annual inspection, when any minor repairs that might be required were carried out, and a small number of emergency calls each year. This experiment provided the model for a British pilot project in Ferndale,

South Wales, established by Shelter and Help the Aged as a low-cost repair service for elderly households. The project was again prompted by a concern that the elderly were living in homes they did not wish to leave, but that as they grew older they were increasingly unable to carry out the maintenance which would make their continued independence possible. Demand for the repair service left those involved in no doubt of the need for help in the area. Due to economic decline and consequent differential migration, about 54 per cent of households in the project area were elderly people on modest pensions, with more than half being women living on their own (Morton, 1982, p. 8). With 80 per cent of all households in Ferndale being owner-occupiers, the responsibility for maintaining the largely nineteenth-century terrace housing stock fell on people with modest retirement incomes and little ability to carry out the work themselves. Their failure to cope was evidenced by visible dilapidation and the not uncommon abandonment of upper floors in the face of high rainfall and deteriorating roofs. Those involved in the Ferndale project sensed that many of the elderly were overcome by the scale and complexity of their maintenance worries, and that the feeling of helplessness had given way to resignation.

Another pilot project showed that the difficulties of home maintenance were not a problem restricted to the elderly. Cardiff's South Riverside project emphasized the more general problems facing low-income home owners. Though nearly threequarters of owner-occupiers in the area owned their homes outright, they often faced high repair and maintenance costs on very low incomes. With 85 per cent of household heads earning less than £75, take-up of improvement grants had been extremely low (Leather, 1982). An evaluation of the project (Leather and Murie, 1983) showed that over half the sampled owners had spent less than £500 on repairs over the past five years. This proportion would probably have been higher if it had not been for the incidence of flood damage covered by insurance. Though low income had restricted people's ability to carry out work, they remained conscious of the disrepair problem. Nearly threequarters of respondents felt there was a need to carry out at least one item of major repair from a checklist of elements covering fabric and amenities, and half identified three or more elements.

A number of points emerged from an analysis of project take-up. As an indicator of concern, 43 per cent felt that their homes were in a worse condition than when they moved in. For 59 per cent of service users, repair expenditure over the last five years amounted to less than £100, and 51 per cent had not made any use of paid labour. As virtually half of all users were retired and a further 16 per cent permanently sick or disabled the scope for do-it-yourself activity appeared limited. The evaluation also found extraordinarily high levels of satisfaction with the repair service provided. Users were almost exclusively on low incomes and valued the 100 per cent labour cost subsidy. But it seemed they valued the quality and reliability of the service as much as its cheapness. A number seemed to have experienced problems with private sector repair firms, and in this sense the more general difficulties reported by the Office of Fair Trading (1983) were felt more severely by those unable to attract the established, reputable firms. Consequently, in South Riverside, many users of the service would not apparently consider the use of private firms, and this, as much as fears of upheaval and financial constraints, had caused them to tolerate poor housing conditions over a long period of time. The experience of difficulties with building firms in Cardiff, while consistent with other case study evidence (see, for example, Niner and Forrest, 1982) was not confirmed by the English House Condition Survey, which suggested that the overall level of satisfaction with contractors was very high (DOE, 1983a, p. 17). It is not clear why these differences existed, though local variations might be expected.

Faced with evidence from Cardiff and Ferndale, it might be concluded that household characteristics like age could provide reliable predictors of likely investment behaviour. This is not the case. A survey of HAAs carried out for the DOE (Niner and Forrest, 1982) looked at grant-aided and non-grant-aided improvement activity. A re-analysis of this data (Table 3.7) shows that there was a significant variation in activity between different areas. In South Tyneside, with its concentration of small households, childless couples did a disproportionate amount of grant-aided work; while small families were more likely to do work without grant aid, though there was very little in total. In Sandwell, with a more even distribution of household types, it was the large households who were disproportionately represented in grant take-up. Again, there was very little non-grant-aided work of any kind. In Burnley, the distribution of work was closer to the population as a whole, though, as in South Tyneside, small families were slightly more likely to have taken up grants. Only in Southwark was non-grant-aided work significant. Just 29 per cent of owner-occupiers had experience of grant-aided improvement, compared with 75 per cent in Sandwell, 79 per cent in Burnley and 82 per cent in South Tyneside.

Looking at age of head of household, the bulk of work in South Tyneside was carried out by young people, reflecting the area's generally young age profile. People in the 35–44 age band undertook disproportionately high levels of both grant-aided and non-grant-aided work. In Sandwell, with a more even age profile, middle-aged households were responsible for over 60 per cent of work. It was the younger age group in Southwark that was carrying out a disproportionate amount of grant and non-grant work. In all four areas, the elderly were less likely to be carrying out work, but there were variations. The elderly were over-represented amongst the small number of non-grant-aided improvers in Sandwell, while in Burnley the over-55 age group carried out over 40 per cent of grant-aided work. This finding alone should caution against any

Table 3.7 Property in HAA Survey Affected by Improvement and Repair

	South Tyneside			Sandwell			Burnley			Southwark		
	All %	grant %	non-grant %	All %	grant %	non-grant %	All %	grant %	non-grant %	all %	grant %	non-grant %
Household type												
Single person	24	23	(14)	16	7	(24)	29	29	(16)	23	24	18
Childless couple	28	36	(21)	14	7	(15)	26	23	(39)	25	27	28
Unrelated sharers	—	—	—	1	2	—	—	—	—	3	5	7
All adult	5	6	(7)	14	16	(30)	8	2	(8)	17	13	18
Single parent	4	—	(7)	12	—	—	5	5	(6)	2	2	—
Small family	31	28	(43)	12	7	(9)	24	33	(23)	20	20	15
Large family	6	6	—	19	34	—	7	7	(8)	7	7	14
Extended family	1	—	(7)	13	27	(22)	—	—	—	2	2	—
Family with unrelated sharers	1	—	—	—	—	—	—	—	—	—	—	—
Weighted base	383	172	20	264	62	19	158	80	16	416	57	76
Age head of household												
Under 34	54	48	(35)	27	4	(9)	22	26	(8)	29	37	46
35–44	20	29	(36)	17	20	—	14	17	(21)	18	21	16
45–54	13	11	(21)	21	34	(30)	12	14	(8)	15	17	11
55–64	9	9	—	17	30	(31)	21	19	(33)	7	5	11
65 and over	4	2	—	14	9	(30)	30	23	(23)	30	20	2
Weighted base	383	172	20	264	62	19	158	80	16	416	57	76

Source: Unpublished tabulations from survey of HAAs by the Centre for Urban and Regional Studies, University of Birmingham.

Notes: Action was classified by house: it cannot be certain that work was done by the household living there at the time of the survey.

Parentheses indicate a weighted base of less than 50.

conclusion that elderly households were invariably uninterested in undertaking improvement work.

Inner-City Home Purchase

The problems facing home owners were also apparent in a physical and social survey of thirty-two households living in a Birmingham HAA. All houses were pre-1919, two-storey mid- or end-terrace properties which had been purchased freehold. The house condition survey showed varying states of repair. Some needed major structural work, usually to the roof. Others required relatively minor maintenance. There was, however, no correlation between an owner's worries about repairs and the assessed condition of the houses. Some owners expressed concern about the future maintenance problems of properties which were in better condition than other houses where the owner either failed to recognize problems or felt that they were unimportant.

Overall, a third of the sample felt that carrying out repairs to their home was a problem. In four of these eleven cases this was serious enough for them to express regrets about having bought that particular house. In each case, money was identified as the central problem. But only one of these houses had been assessed by the condition survey as of below average quality. In this single case the immediate housing outgoings did not look unduly high. The purchase price was only £3,000, with an outstanding loan of £1,000 from relatives. However, the household was faced with borrowing a further £1,500 to meet its share of grant work, with the prospect of two informal loans having to be paid off as quickly as possible on a household income of about £75 a week. The other three owners who regretted their purchase faced a more familiar problem. Each had purchased with the help of a building society mortgage for about £6,000, with the building society requiring repairs as a condition of the mortgage. In each case the required works were small, between £300 and £500, and no retention had been imposed. But all three families had experienced difficulty in financing the required work on their incomes of about £80 a week.

Of the other seven families who expressed concern about repair problems, but had no reservations about buying their homes, all were aware that repairs needed to be carried out involving expenses they would find difficult to cover. There was, however, no straightforward relationship between income, housing costs and financial difficulties. Four families had mortgage payments accounting for under 10 per cent of disposable income. The housing costs of the other three accounted for about a quarter of their budgets – one because an informal loan was being paid off as quickly as possible, the others because they had borrowed as much as possible for mortgage and deposit on relatively low incomes.

In all eleven cases, owners recognized the need for repairs but found that for financial reasons these would be difficult to carry out. However, this was not related to the purchase price of the house, the need for repair, or relative housing costs. Table 3.8 summarizes housing costs by repair category. Bearing in mind the small sample, neither house price nor income seemed to offer an explanation for repair being viewed as a problem. As might be expected, there was some relationship between state of repair and the likelihood of it being seen as a problem, but a quarter of the people who expressed no concern about repairs were living in houses assessed as being in poor condition. In an attempt to explain repair problems, housing conditions were analysed by household characteristics. Place of birth, age, family type and income level were all of no use in predicting individual attitudes and perceptions.

Table 3.8   *Attitude to Repairs by Condition and Purchase Price, 1980*

	Assessed condition[1]	Number	Average purchase price £	Average housing costs[2] %
Repairs a problem	poor condition	4	5,000	30
	fair condition	6	6,260	13
	good condition	1	6,000	28
Repairs not a problem	poor condition	5	4,860	24
	fair condition	10	6,375	16
	good condition	6	5,525	25

Notes:
1   Condition refers to state of repair, assessed at survey prices: good, less than £1,000; fair, £1,000–£3,000; poor, more than £3,000.
2   Mortgage repayments as a proportion of average weekly take-home income.

Though the sample size is very small, and therefore not reliable, it would appear that people living in the cheaper properties, in the worst state of repair, were paying a relatively high proportion of their income for housing, irrespective of their expressed concern for dealing with repair problems. There seemed to be several reasons for these relatively high housing costs: first, mortgages of 90 per cent or above on low weekly incomes; second, quite small informal loans which Asian families were trying to pay back quickly; third, and again, quite small loans (less than 50 per cent of purchase price) from high street banks being paid back over short periods. In none of these cases were rates of interest unusually high, and there was no evidence that longer-term loans could not have been obtained. To an extent, at least, relatively high housing costs were being traded off against early outright ownership.

Irrespective of perceived problems, most people in the sample said that they had undertaken repairs to their home since purchase, or intended to do so once it could be afforded. The most commonly mentioned items were replastering, roofing, guttering, window frames and rewiring. Over half the sample had actually carried out repairs. This generally left work still to be done, and most owners indicated their intention to carry out further work when savings permitted. However, compared with average costs of outstanding repairs, expenditure by owners was very low. The assessed cost averaged nearly £7,000 per house, compared with the national average for property in HAAs of £5,870 (DOE, 1982a, table 25). By comparison, owners' expenditure was in the order of a few hundred pounds, averaging £340 from the date of purchase of the property. This was often do-it-yourself expenditure, so the savings in labour had to be offset against the character of work carried out.

Turning to wider survey evidence, work at the Centre for Urban and Regional Studies on inner-city home ownership surveyed recent buyers in parts of Birmingham. This showed that only 7 per cent of households used Housing Act grants to pay for repair and improvement work. The bulk of expenditure was financed through savings, and over half the longer-established buyers had postponed carrying out items of major repair, mostly for financial reasons (Karn, Kemeny and Williams, 1982, p. 104). For this group, repairs were singled out as the most serious problem with their housing; and half of them thought repairs would become an increasing problem as time passed. A third of all households thought that if they ran into financial difficulties in the future they would have to neglect repair work:

> The pessimism of households concerning their ability to cope with repairs crops up again and again in interviews with buyers ... Thus, repairs and maintenance was stated to be the major disadvantage of having bought rather than rented, having bought an old rather than a new house and of having bought that particular house. (Karn, Kemeny and Williams, 1982, p. 105)

These concerns reflected the need for substantial investment from owners with relatively low incomes. In these circumstances, investment decisions were constrained by lack of choice. People recognized the need for repair and maintenance, but lacked the income to pay for the work.

Investment Decisions
Income is one of several variables influencing investment decisions. It has been seen that some households do not see disrepair as a problem, or under-estimate the cost or urgency of the work. Others, particularly the elderly, are unwilling to face the disruption of improvement work. Where household income is sufficient to meet the cost of necessary works, a valuation gap can dissuade otherwise willing investors. In these

circumstances it is hardly surprising that work carried out tends to be done by those on higher incomes, is often cosmetic, and avoids property in the poorest condition.

Table 3.9 shows that, though they were less likely to live in houses needing rehabilitation, those on higher incomes were more likely to have carried out major works. And, as might be expected, general expenditure on repairs and maintenance rose with income (Table 3.10). However, even when it was required, expenditure might not be on works of a fundamental nature. Even on properties in need of rehabilitation, between a third and a half of owners' expenditure involved decoration and cosmetic repairs or improvements rather than essential work (DOE, 1979a, p. 13). It would also seem that the physical condition of a property had little influence on levels of expenditure. Owner-occupiers living in property in need of rehabilitation were less likely to carry out work and to carry out work of over £500 (1976 prices) than were owner-occupiers in general (DOE, 1979a, table D4.5). Perhaps it was to be expected that the property most in need of repair and maintenance expenditure would actually receive lower levels of investment, given the correlation between income and housing conditions and between income and maintenance expenditure.

Table 3.9 *Rate of Rehabilitation, Pre-1919 Houses, 1976*

Income of head of household	Households in category %	Households who carried out major works %	Households in dwellings needing rehabilitation %	Rehabilitation rate %
Under £1,560	29	3·1	45·9	7
£1,560–£3,900	46	4·9	36·6	13
More than £3,900	25	8·9	22·2	40
All	100	5·5	33·5	16

Source: DOE, 1979a, table D4.9.
Note: Rehabilitation rate = % households carrying out major works in past 12 months,
                              % households in dwellings needing rehabilitation

Investment and the Housing Market

Individual investment decisions have to be seen in the wider context of a planning, institutional and market framework. Planning blight, building society lending practices, tenure patterns and relative shifts in locational preference provide the background against which individuals determine levels of investment against other calls on disposable income, movement intentions, aspirations and their interpretation of likely financial returns. This chapter has been concerned with investment decisions affecting the

Table 3.10   *Owner-Occupiers Average Weekly Expenditure on Repair,*
Maintenance and Decoration by Income

	Under £80 £	£80– £179 £	£180 and over £	All £
Outright owners				
1980	2·19	3·37	3·56	2·99
1981	2·13	2·29	6·09	3·40
Owners with mortgage				
1980	(1·19)	3·03	5·28	4·23
1981	—	2·42	5·21	4·33

Source: CSO, *Family Expenditure Survey 1980 and 1981* (London: HMSO, 1982).

existing homes of owner-occupiers. These decisions have been treated in isolation from the original process of acquisition. However, they are clearly related and, conceptually, subsequent maintenance investment patterns cannot be divorced from the factors which determined the initial purchase. It is at the point of purchase, for example, that the poorer owner-occupiers find themselves living in houses which require relatively high levels of maintenance investment. The prior question is, therefore, how people come to own houses in need of major repair and improvement. It is possible to see people making choices about the solution to their housing needs as operating as individuals in a 'free' housing market which is harmonious and self-regulating. But presumably people do not actively aspire to housing in disrepair. Rather, their choices must be seen as heavily constrained. People may wish to live in a particular area, which perhaps determines the quality of house available to them. Or their housing needs – perhaps for a four-bedroom house – conflict with price, requiring a compromise on quality.

As a means of consuming housing, owner-occupation is an increasingly important factor in the distribution of wealth, but owners are not a homogeneous group enjoying uniform benefits. There is a relationship between price and quality, and, with income groups having different abilities to consume housing, the wealthier owners are able to command the better properties. Low-income owner-occupiers move into and within a cheaper, poorer quality housing stock. There is nothing particularly remarkable about a pattern of housing consumption which leads to poorer people occupying the poorer houses: 'If housing is produced and consumed predominantly according to market criteria, a hierachy of housing conditions inevitably develops, determined by differential access to power and resources' (Forrest and Williams, 1980, p. 11).

The effective demand for low-cost housing can be seen to reflect institutional structures and decisions rather than individual expressions of demand and preference (Murie and Forrest, 1980b, p. 91). But for lower income groups, perhaps forced into purchase by the lack of tenure options, cheaper property has expensive consequences. Mortgaging difficulties may lead to a short-term, high interest loan from a fringe bank. The potential long-term benefits of ownership – such as lower mortgage repayments as income increases – may be eroded by higher maintenance costs. And the price performance of certain sectors of the market suggest that low-income owners may become trapped in poorer quality housing with little opportunity to trade up. This will lead to a residualized stock, accommodating high concentrations of the elderly and poor, with these owners being relatively disadvantaged in terms of access to better housing, health care, education and the accumulation of wealth. Even owner-occupiers on very low incomes tend to benefit from wealth accumulation compared with non-owners. For those who rent there is clearly no opportunity for accumulation through housing. However, it is not the case that all owners enjoy advantages over non-owners in the consumption sphere: 'as the commodification of housing progresses and more people on lower incomes buy the cheaper, older dwellings, more dwellings may become liabilities rather than assets' (Forrest and Williams, 1980, p. 15).

The concept of a stratified housing market should not introduce too rigid a notion of housing ladders and associated ideas of filtering. As a process, the concept of a housing ladder may apply to young owners with a growing income. But there are problems when this is applied as a description of the housing stock. While housing in a particular location or price range may attract mobile owner-occupiers – with possible implications in terms of a relationship between maintenance investment and rate of turnover – this does not mean that individual houses hold a rigid market location. The homes of long-term elderly owner-occupiers, for example, may be subsequently purchased and improved by middle-income families. Consequently, houses cannot be identified simply by condition and then placed in a particular market location. There are problems, therefore, in any analysis which approaches investment decisions from a housing stock perspective. It is apparent that market processes result in low-income owner-occupiers living in the poorer housing stock, and that relatively high housing costs and low disposable income influence their ability to undertake repair and maintenance. But it is more difficult to conceptualize the relationship between household situation and housing quality because neither element has a set location within the housing market. Even low-income owner-occupiers experience some variation in their ability to consume housing, while what they own is not defined within a static sub-market. The distinction, however, between general market processes and the action of individual owners may be a useful way of simplifying the picture. Through such an approach it is possible to separately identify a set of factors influencing national patterns of investment in the housing stock, while analysing the motivations and perceptions of people acting within this market framework. The theoretical problem lies at the level of interaction – the extent to which the housing market is the sum of individual actions. National disrepair trends can be seen in terms of under-investment encouraged by the process of accumulation – a view considered in more detail in Chapter 6. The accumulation and transfer of wealth through housing processes is important for individuals both in terms of inheritance and exchange. The operation of subsidies makes housing an attractive form of accumulation, and could be partly responsible for low levels of capital investment. In this sense, disrepair in the older housing stock can be seen as a consequence of the process of accumulation. But the impact of low investment is particularly dramatic in certain sectors of the market. And people living in the worst housing – which has received the lowest levels of investment – are the least likely to benefit from the accumulation process. Relative house prices make it difficult to trade up or take out capital on exchange.

Outside these market constraints, however, the indivual actions of owners will be influenced by a variety of factors. Income level will condition opportunity, while age may influence inclination. People's views of disrepair problems will vary, while the extent of investment may be influenced by their expectation of returns. In effect, investment decisions can be seen to be influenced by pragmatic or rational responses (the return on investment), by awareness of the problem (the extent to which the need for repair is recognized) and by ability to tackle the problem.

This is the context within which, in the following chapters, the nature of policy response is considered. Britain has an ageing and deteriorating stock. Levels of investment are apparently inadequate to arrest or reverse this decline. Individual capital investment decisions are discouraged by processes of accumulation, while the poorest sections of the community benefit least from increasing exchange values and live in the property most in need of repair.

4

Redevelopment and Renewal

Historical Background

Since the mid nineteenth century, the history of urban renewal has been one of the parallel development of clearance and rehabilitation policies. A number of themes introduced themselves at an early stage, and these formed a recurrent feature of policy debate over subsequent years. The problems associated with clearance activity were quick to emerge, as were the pragmatic attractions of rehabilitation. Nineteenth-century public health legislation began with powers to improve insanitary conditions because more direct intervention was seen as an unwarranted attack on property ownership. A century later, the shift towards improvement in the late 1960s can be partly attributed to the impact of clearance activity on owner-occupiers.

The history of urban renewal is also one of conflict between a desire to improve housing standards and a recognition of the imposed costs, both in terms of national resources and their effect on people living in the worst housing stock. Because of the relationship between income and housing conditions, policies focusing on the worst houses have an impact on the lowest and most vulnerable income groups. Even in the early programmes of closure, it was recognized that intervention had displacement effects (Treble, 1971; Wohl, 1971). But, while nineteenth-century slum clearance legislation contained provisions for rebuilding, it was not until 1930 that reference was made to the rehousing of displaced residents.

The Early Legislation
The early response to poor housing conditions was based very firmly on a concern for public health. A succession of reports and inquiries drew attention to the conditions in which the poor were housed, beginning with the Chadwick Report (Poor Law Commissioners, 1842). There also followed a long sequence of Acts designed to improve housing standards, usually by conferring powers on local authorities.

The first powers of demolition were contained in the 1868 Torrens Act. But this legislation also included powers of compulsory improvement, with clearance seen as a back-up procedure following a failure to comply. For this reason, Moore (1980, p. 20) has characterized the 1868

Act as the true beginning of improvement legislation, with the main thrust of slum clearance powers coming in the 1875-9 Cross Acts. These Acts permitted local authorities to formulate schemes for both the clearance and the rebuilding of slum areas, and as such were the forerunners of modern comprehensive redevelopment legislation.

The criticisms levelled at slum clearance during the 1880s and 1890s were very similar to those voiced nearly one hundred years later - those of planning blight, social displacement and high costs. The nineteenth-century response was somewhat similar to that of the 1969 Housing Act. Criticism by the 1885 Royal Commission on the Housing of the Working Classes led to the 1890 Housing of the Working Classes Act - the first area-based rehabilitation legislation, with provision for gradual renewal and environmental improvements (Moore, 1980, p. 25).

National action on slum clearance, with central government taking a really positive lead, did not come until the 1930s. The early legislation on slum clearance placed the initiative with local authorities. This discretion generally resulted in sporadic action, with successive amendments to the Cross Acts attempting to encourage a more concerted approach.

It was the Greenwood Housing Act of 1930 which entirely reformed the nineteenth-century legislation and provided the framework for current procedures. The Greenwood Act enabled local authorities to deal with slums by declaring clearance areas, with compulsory purchase and clearance order procedures. It also introduced specific subsidies for the rehousing of families displaced by this clearance. Local discretion to ignore clearance was limited by requiring urban authorities with populations exceeding 20,000 to prepare five-year programmes to deal with housing conditions in their areas. Programmes submitted at the end of 1930 provided for the demolition of 96,000 houses (English, Madigan and Norman, 1976, p. 21).

The aim of the slum clearance drive of the 1930s was to abolish slums in a five-year programme. What followed was a massive effort. By its own high ambitions, the policy was a failure, but more houses were cleared than ever before, and the demolition of 90,000 properties in 1939 was a figure that has not since been equalled.

The Immediate Postwar Period

The Second World War halted clearance programmes and resulted in widespread neglect and deterioration. It was not until the mid 1950s that slum clearance was resumed. Housing policy in the late 1940s and early 1950s was largely concerned with replacing the stock of dwellings destroyed during the war. In this context, central government's extension of house improvement subsidies from 1949 onwards seems, at least in part, to have been prompted by the realization that substandard houses would have to be utilized in the short term to make good overall shortages. In the longer term, policy and economic circumstances were notable for their extension of owner-occupation as the primary form of housing tenure. But the substance of debate – the scale of slum clearance, the role of public sector housing, and intervention in the privately rented market – was very similar to that of the prewar years (McKay and Cox, 1979, p. 129).

The first national legislation to provide for improvement grants had been the Housing (Rural Workers) Act 1926. The maximum grant was two-thirds of the cost of works, up to a limit of £100, with half the grant provided by the exchequer. The Act, introduced by Neville Chamberlain and drawing on his Birmingham experience, originally included provisions for reconditioning and municipalization in urban areas. These provisions did not make the statute book, but some of the larger urban authorities continued with substantial improvement programmes. In the late 1920s, the rate of reconditioning was variously estimated at between 300,000 and 500,000 houses a year.

The Housing Act 1949 extended the 1926 Act to provide improvement grants in urban as well as rural areas. Grants were intended particularly for the installation of basic amenities, though they could also be used for conversion. Discretionary improvement grants for all owners therefore become part of national housing policy. The justification used then, and for many years to follow, was that grants were not to subsidize work which should have been carried out by owners, but to provide basic facilities in houses which had been built without amenities (Cullingworth, 1966, p. 207).

The Act's improvement provisions were not a startling success. Between 1949 and 1953, a total of only 6,000 discretionary grants were awarded. The explanation for this low level of take-up was probably rooted in the government's own policy, which preferred to emphasize new building and discouraged temporary works of repair or patching. There was a continued reluctance to subsidize private landlords, while the Act's strict conditions were designed to ensure high standards.

In 1953 a major reorientation of official housing policy was announced. With a background of growing postwar affluence, and a housebuilding programme running at 300,000 a year, it was proposed to direct more attention to maintaining and improving the stock, and to the resumption of slum clearance. The 1953 White paper and its consequent legislation – the Housing Rents and Repairs Act 1954 – was perhaps most significant for its emphasis on the increased role of the private housebuilding industry. But the White Paper also recommended an increase in improvement activity, proposing powers for the purchase and patching of dilapidated property prior to demolition (MHLG, 1953).

According to the 1953 White Paper, the main reason for the 1949 Act's lack of success was the inadequate publicity given to improvement schemes during the years of labour and material shortage which followed its introduction. In order to stimulate improvement, the Housing Act

1954 relaxed the 1949 Act grant conditions. As a result, and assisted by a determined publicity campaign, improvement take-up increased to over 30,000 a year, the total of grants approved between 1954 and 1959 being about 154,000. Most of these grants seem to have been for the installation of baths and hot-water systems, while about 90 per cent went to owner-occupiers (Cullingworth, 1966, p. 43).

As with previous legislation, grants awarded for improvement under the 1954 Act were at the discretion of local authorities. It was not until the House Purchase and Housing Act 1959 that a mandatory grant was introduced. In a continuing effort to encourage a higher rate of improvement, the Act further relaxed discretionary grant conditions and introduced a 'standard grant' which could be claimed by owners of eligible property, as of right, towards the cost of installing five basic amenities: a fixed bath or shower, a wash-hand basin, a water closet, a ventilated food store, and hot and cold water supply to the bath or shower and basin.

The introduction of standard grants, together with extended publicity, brought a fourfold increase in improvements – about 131,000 in 1960, of which 64 per cent were standard grants (Spencer, 1970). It seems that relatively few private landlords took advantage of the grants, even after the Housing Act 1961 allowed rents to increase by a maximum 12.5 per cent of the owners contribution (Cullingworth, 1966, p. 50). In the five-year period to 1964, 600,000 grants were approved, over twice the number between 1949 and 1959, but only a fifth went to landlords (Gibson and Langstaff, 1982, p. 55).

The peak level of grant take-up achieved in 1960 was not sustained. By 1968 approvals had fallen to a level of 114,000, with 60 per cent being for standard grants. Over the period from 1960 to 1968, discretionary grant approvals remained at about the same number, whereas standard grant approvals fell from 83,000 in 1960 to 68,000 in 1968. This decrease was the result of two main factors. First, fewer dwellings were eligible for standard grants as property was improved and slums cleared. Second, the maximum grant level, fixed at £155 in 1959, remained unchanged until 1969, while costs were rising. In 1960 the average grant for private owners was £91; by 1968 it was £135. It is therefore probable that owners were having to contribute more than half the cost of improvement, while associated repair work had to be carried out without grant assistance.

Background to the 1969 Act

Between 1949 and the mid-1960s, various pieces of legislation were introduced to improve houses, but levels of improvement activity remained relatively low. The main emphasis of government policy was on new building. Even after the introduction of standard grants in 1959, and the improvement areas of the Housing Act 1964, rehabilitation remained essentially a marginal policy. Indeed, much of the housing demolished in the 1950s was undoubtedly substandard and had to be cleared. But older housing, whether fit or unfit, was regarded as having a strictly limited life. The 1960s altered the picture, bringing together a variety of factors which recognized improvement as an essential part of a long-term housing strategy. Comprehensive redevelopment came under increased attack at a technical and social level; fresh evidence became available on the number of substandard houses; and this awareness of the scale of the problem coincided with a deterioration in national economic performance.

Academic evidence on the social dislocation created by clearance programmes reflected similar concerns expressed a century earlier. The social costs of redevelopment, and in particular the disruption of community, was highlighted in a series of sociological studies, notably by Young and Willmott (1957) and Jennings (1962). While the process of comprehensive redevelopment faced increasing criticism, actual progress in clearing slum properties also came under sharp attack. The 1955 local authority returns showed just under 850,000 unfit houses, setting a target clearance rate of 75,000 a year. This was never achieved, though the rate increased from 24,000 in 1955 to about 60,000 in the early 1960s. However, Cullingworth argued that local authority returns were a gross under estimate of the problem. He maintained that demolition should be at the rate of 200,000 a year to deal with identified slums and reverse the trend in deterioration. As this level of activity was unsustainable, there was a need for a parallel programme of rehabilitation (Cullingworth, 1960, p. 53).

Cullingworth's support for rehabilitation policy was based on the view that the necessary level of clearance was economically unsustainable. This sparked off fresh academic debate on the economics of improvement in an attempt to ascertain the relative costs of redevelopment and rehabilitation (Needleman 1965 and 1969; Sigsworth and Wilkinson, 1967 and 1970). But the scale of substandard housing, which formed a background to the debate on the economies of renovation, was only one of a number of contributions to the climate of change. Two official reports stressed the need for a more effective grant system (MHLG, 1965; CHAC, 1966), while the Deeplish study (MHLG, 1966) was the first systematic attempt to inquire into attitudes about home improvement since the introduction of improvement grants in 1949.

The 1968 White Paper

The Housing Act 1969 was formulated amidst mounting political and professional pressure against comprehensive clearance programmes in the context of quite severe national economic constraints. With the balance of payments crisis of November 1967 heralding the formal abandonment of targets established in the National Plan, the constraint on public sector expenditure was the most important single reason why policy shifted towards improvement.

While economic expediency may now be accepted as the prime motive, it is hardly surprising that the government presented its change of direction in a different light. It chose to publish the results of the 1967 House Condition Survey as part of the 1968 White Paper 'Old Houses into New Homes' (MHLG, 1968). For the first time there was an independent estimate of the scale of the problems of older housing. The results were not reassuring. Returns made by local authorities in 1965 gave a national total of just under 800,000 unfit houses (MHLG, 1966, p. 56). The 1967 estimate of 1·8 million unfit dwellings in England and Wales more than doubled the earlier figure. The White Paper suggested that more unfit houses ought to be cleared and that obstacles to rapid clearance procedures should be identified and removed (MHLG, 1968, p. 9).

Following the recommendations of the 1968 White Paper, the Housing Act 1969 introduced the concept of general improvement areas (GIAs). In essence, GIAs were intended to achieve the comprehensive improvement of houses by a concentration of improvement grant effort on an area basis, and the enhancement of external amenities through a series of environmental works. The 1969 Act introduced consultation into GIA declaration procedures, provided grants for environmental works and abandoned powers of compulsory improvement, preferring to rely on voluntary activity. Local authorities retained powers of compulsory purchase, and could acquire for improvement or conversion. But the emphasis was on participation and the voluntary take-up of grants.

Though the 1969 Act is mainly associated with GIAs, these were essentially an operational concept rather than a legislative innovation. There was nothing new about the area-based approach; the 1964 Act had been a recent expression of an idea rooted in the nineteenth century. Within a GIA, individual owners did not receive any direct financial advantage from its status. The level of grants available was no higher than elsewhere. The main advantage of declaration was argued to be the removal of uncertainty. The approval of grant achieved a standard of improvement consistent with a notional future life of thirty years. In some cases this made it easier for existing residents and potential purchasers to obtain loan finance. Residents could also benefit from environmental works where local authorities chose to avail themselves of the exchequer subsidy. While not generous, central government finance for this purpose was new, though an emphasis on the quality of the environment was not. Octavia Hill landscaped derelict land in Marylebone in 1865 (Moore, 1980, p. 17). Bevan made suggestions for the visual improvement of long streets when introducing the 1949 Housing Bill (House of Commons, 1949). And in 1954, under a Conservative administration, the policy document 'New Houses for Old' advocated planting, street closures and the tidying up of derelict open space (MHLG, 1954).

While its provisions were not particularly innovative, the 1969 Act was notable in two main respects. First, improvement strategies were elevated to the same level of importance as slum clearance. It was not suggested that rehabilitation should replace clearance. Rather, it was hoped that GIAs would be declared in essentially 'sound' areas, where a statement assuring the houses of a long-term future, together with environmental works, would be sufficient to encourage investment and restore market confidence. Second, the Act recognized that improvement should not be considered as a purely housing issue, and that for it to be fully effective attention should be paid not only to the condition of dwellings but also to their physical and social environment.

The 1969 Act in Practice

Although the Housing Act 1969 was placed on the statute book by a Labour government, it was largely implemented by the Conservative administration which took office in 1970. They actively encouraged the improvement programme, achieving a peak level of activity in the mid-1970s which was not subsequently equalled. However, GIAs were not responsible for this increased activity. The main reason was the Housing Act 1971, which, in an attempt to stimulate the construction industry, gave an increased level of grant aid to the intermediate and development areas for an initial period of two years, later extended until August 1974. Grants to private owners were increased in these areas to 75 per cent of the approved cost of work, while the contribution by the exchequer towards these grants increased from 75 per cent to 90 per cent of the annual loan charges.

This measure was very effective in increasing the level of grant-aided improvement. Council property was a particular beneficiary. In the years 1969–73, 31 per cent of all grant approvals were for local authority dwellings (DOE, 1977a, tech. vol. 3, p. 118). The measure also demonstrated a relationship between the level of subsidy and the take-up of grant. Table 4.1 shows improvement grant activity for Great Britain

Table 4.1 *Improvement Grants in Development and Intermediate Areas, Great Britain, 1971–4*

	1971	1972	1973	1974
Total grants: Great Britain	232,511	368,068	453,496	300,482
Annual % increase (decrease)		+58	+23	−34
Grants in development and intermediate areas	59,400	234,071	329,075	210,092
Annual % increase (decrease)		+294	+41	−36
Grants in development and intermediate areas as % total grants	26	64	73	70

Source: DOE, *Housing and Construction Statistics*, no. 12, table 30 (London: HMSO, 1974).

during the period the Act was effective. It can be seen that the increase in grant approvals between 1971 and 1973 was more than accounted for by the increase in approvals in development and intermediate areas. By 1973 grants in these special areas accounted for nearly three-quarters of all approvals in Great Britain.

In the context of grant activity over the period 1969–73, improvement work in GIAs represented a relatively small component of increased take-up. Under the 1969 Act, 273 local authorities in England and Wales declared 904 GIAs containing 273,000 dwellings (House of Commons, 1975). By the end of 1974 just over one in four dwellings had received grant approval (Table 4.2), with work completed on 14 per cent. Of most importance, in terms of the national picture, completions within GIAs never reached 16,000 a year, and at their 1973 high represented only 5 per cent of all grant work in England and Wales.

Table 4.2   *General Improvement Areas, England and Wales, 1970–4*

	1970	1971	1972	1973	1974
Dwellings in declared areas	33,982	58,046	89,122	63,185	30,152
Cumulative total	33,982	92,028	181,150	244,335	274,487
Grants approved in GIAs	2,571	5,453	18,239	32,621	15,799
Cumulative total	2,571	8,024	26,263	58,884	74,683
Grants approved in England and Wales	156,557	197,481	319,169	360,954	231,918
Grants approved in GIAs as % of total approvals	1·6	2·8	5·7	9·0	6·8
Work completed in GIAs	1,119	2,300	7,271	15,143	12,960
Cumulative total	1,119	3,419	10,690	25,833	38,793
Work completed in England and Wales[1]	121,831	108,823	245,290	305,352	298,363
Work completed in GIAs as % of total work	0·9	2·1	3·0	5·0	4·3
Total work completed in GIAs as % of total dwellings in declared areas	3·3	3·7	5·9	10·6	14·1

Source: DOE, *Housing and Construction Statistics*, no. 15, table 31 (London: HMSO, 1975).
Note:
1   Private grants paid; local authority and housing grants approved.

In evaluating the contribution of GIAs, it is important to separate performance within declared areas from the more general contribution of GIAs to improving the national housing stock. In broad terms the conclusion must be that, within a wide range of achievement, GIAs were individually quite successful, but contributed very little to an overall improvement in housing conditions. By 1974, only 14 per cent of properties within GIAs had been improved. But further work was in the pipeline, and not all houses were a target for improvement activity. Two years later, 43 per cent of target stock had been treated, permitting the conclusion that:

> area based improvement has shown a considerable measure of success within the spirit and intention of the Act, many GIAs have undoubtedly become better places to live in even if results are not always dramatic as far as the take-up of grants is concerned. (Williamson and Wrigley, 1978, p. 76)

Turning to the wider impact of GIAs, the unavoidable conclusion must be that they had little impact on the total stock of substandard property. In 1971 the National House Condition Survey estimated that there were 3·84 million substandard houses in England and Wales. By comparison, GIAs contained a total of less than 300,000 dwellings. Because GIAs contained a relatively small proportion of the national target stock, Roberts (1976, p. 154) was justified in concluding that estimates of grant activity within declared areas revealed a very marginal contribution to national house improvement progress.

The background to the Housing Act 1974 was therefore one of considerable dissatisfaction with GIA performance, albeit in the context of limited empirical evidence. The House of Commons Expenditure Committee commented on the slow progress of GIA declarations and on the equally disappointing rate of house improvement within them (House of Commons, 1973, paras 58-9). A White Paper in the same years emphasized the extent to which official enthusiasm for GIAs had cooled; they had 'so far failed to raise the standards of our older residential districts to the extent that the government considers both desirable and possible' (DOE, 1973b). This official dissatisfaction with the performance of the 1969 Act was reinforced by a body of detailed criticism relating to inadequate eligible expense limits and grant percentages, to the absence of effective compulsory powers, and to the over-emphasis on voluntary action at the expense of those in greatest need. The social consequences of grant legislation – who benefits – was increasingly emphasized by debates in the early 1970s. It was widely recognized that grants were going mainly to improve interwar council houses and the owner-occupied stock, while least activity occurred where it was most needed, in the privately rented sector. Not only were grants going to the relatively better housed, rather than being focused on the worst stock; but they were going to help the more affluent groups.

To summarize the position in the early 1970s, the 1969 Act had been introduced as a reaction to increased doubts about the effectiveness, social consequences and financial costs of comprehensive redevelopment. There was a significant increase in the level of grant take-up after 1969, but this was chiefly as a result of the special levels of grant available in development and intermediate areas. The central concept of the 1969 Act, that of area improvement, failed to make a major contribution towards upgrading the worst private sector stock, while there was widespread criticism that grants were going to properties least in need of improvement. At the same time, the implementation of grant policy, particularly in GIAs, had social implications which figured prominently in discussion on the effectiveness of the strategy. Much of the background to the 1974 legislation was concerned with proposals to limit abuses of the grant system and to guard against unintentioned secondary effects.

Background to the 1974 Act

The Housing Act 1974 and the introduction of HAAs was a response to criticisms levelled at the operation of improvement grant legislation in general and GIA performance in particular. In this sense, HAAs were a development of the GIA concept in a way which attempted to direct special funds to the worst areas for the benefit of local residents. Consequently, the 1974 Act involved an adjustment in rehabilitation strategies rather than any major redirection of policy. From the range of criticism levelled at the 1969 Act it is possible to identify three main objectives behind the introduction of the 1974 legislation. First, a recognition that slum clearance had become so unpopular that improvement policy had to be promoted as an alternative to demolition. Second, and linked to this, an attempt to direct resources towards dwellings and people most in need of help as part of an emphasis on the small area approach. Finally, a desire to produce a more discriminating grant system which both aided people in stress areas and prevented the kind of speculative abuses which in some cases had led to gentrification.

Opposition to Slum Clearance
The introduction of the Housing Act 1969 was influenced by the increasing unpopularity and cost of clearance. Programmes were seen to affect a growing proportion of both property which was not unfit and houses which were owner-occupied. The inclusion of more fit property may have reflected the lack of spatial concentration of unfit properties. The first National House Condition Survey in 1967 showed that about 700,000 of the 1·8 million unfit dwellings were widely scattered and would have to be dealt with individually rather than within clearance areas (MHLG, 1968, para 4). What happened was rather different. Between 1969 and 1974, the overall decline in demolition activity occurred outside clearance areas. Though the series is not strictly comparable, Table 4.3 shows that the proportion of houses demolished in clearance areas increased throughout the 1960s and early 1970s, accounting for over 90 per cent of all demolitions in 1974. So activity continued to be

concentrated within clearance areas, but there is no evidence of any dramatic increase in the proportion of fit houses being demolished. Again, bearing in mind the problems of comparability between statistical series, Table 4.4 suggests a slight rise in the proportion of fit property in clearance areas towards the end of the 1960s, before tailing off again.

Table 4.3 *Clearance Area Demolitions, England and Wales, 1960–79.*

Year	In or adjoining clearance areas no.	Demolished Not in clearance areas no.	Total no.	Clearance area as proportion of total %
1960	33,620	22,941	56,561	59
1961	37,941	24,028	61,969	61
1962	38,707	23,724	62,431	62
1963	40,529	20,916	61,445	66
1964	41,153	20,062	61,215	67
1965	42,588	18,078	60,666	70
1966	48,076	18,706	66,782	72
1967	51,517	19,635	71,152	72
1968	53,875	17,711	71,586	75
1969	53,399	15,834	69,233	77
1970	52,538	15,266	67,804	77
1969	55,543	11,700	67,243	83
1970	54,710	11,682	66,392	82
1971	59,455	10,950	70,405	84
1972	55,956	9,831	65,787	85
1973	54,674	8,247	62,921	87
1974	37,871	3,406	41,277	92
1975	41,772	4,910	46,682	89
1976	38,581	5,351	43,932	88
1977	34,134	4,414	38,545	89
1978	26,670	4,614	31,284	85
1979	23,747	4,171	27,918	85

Source: 1960–70: *Housing and Construction Statistics*, various quarterly returns; 1969–79: DOE, *Housing and Construction Statistics* (London: HMSO), various years.

The second assertion was that, as clearance continued, it moved increasingly into better-quality areas with higher proportions of owner-occupied houses. There is little reliable information to confirm this, but it is the case that during the 1950s large numbers of people began to purchase old houses which had previously been rented privately (Cullingworth, 1966, p. 48), and these may well have been in areas which were later affected by clearance action. Certainly, by the late 1960s, owner-occupied houses made up at least a quarter of property in clearance areas. A survey carried out at that time showed that 28 per cent of property in the sample clearance areas were owner-occupied (English, Madigan and Norman, 1976, p. 155) – comparable with the 1967 and 1971 House Condition Surveys which showed that 27 per cent of property in potential clearance areas was owner-occupied (MHLG, 1968, table 3; DOE, 1973b, table 4).

Table 4.4   *Houses Demolished within Clearance Areas, 1960–78*

Year	Unfit no.	Included by reason of bad arrangement no.	Others no.	Total no.	Not unfit as proportion of total %
1960	31,334	419	1,867	33,620	7
1961	34,668	439	2,834	37,941	9
1962	35,328	376	3,003	38,707	9
1963	37,216	530	2,783	40,529	8
1964	37,629	537	2,987	41,153	9
1965	38,964	570	3,054	42,588	9
1966	42,847	922	4,307	48,076	11
1967	46,913	543	4,061	51,517	9
1968	47,637	955	5,283	53,875	12
1969	46,746	1,163	5,490	53,399	12
1970	47,259	689	4,590	52,538	10
1971	49,676		6,510	56,186	12
1972	47,964		5,478	53,442	10
1973	46,841		5,898	52,739	11
1974	34,073		3,798	37,871	10
1975	38,500		4,751	43,251	11
1976	36,893		3,673	40,566	9
1977	—		—	32,895	—
1978	—		—	25,882	—

Source: DOE *Housing and Construction Statistics* (London: HMSO), various years.

Though the weight of argument may have exceeded the evidence, it is clear that government acknowledged the shortcomings of clearance programmes and the strength of feeling which had built up against them. Indeed, a circular accompanying the 1974 Act indicated acceptance of an increasing level of opposition to large-scale slum clearance (DOE, 1975a, para. 4). It may also be that delays inherent in redevelopment programmes became even greater between 1969 and 1974, though for reasons unconnected with the 1969 legislation. Inflationary pressures during the early 1970s, fuelled by the expansionary Barber budgets, were one reason for a decline in public sector housing construction. With yardstick revisions lagging behind rapidly increasing costs, it became difficult to obtain competitive tenders from a construction industry enjoying the lucrative benefits of a commercial property boom. This added further delay to the building programmes of local authorities and did not improve the overall performance of comprehensive redevelopment.

It was in this context that improvement policy was put forward as an alternative to redevelopment, in contrast to the parallel programme advocated in 1969. However, it was not the first time that improvement had been seen as an alternative strategy. There were similarities between events from the mid-1960s and those of the late 1920s. In both periods, rehabilitation policies were first introduced as a temporary measure pending clearance. And in both periods, as economic problems continued, rehabilitation was advocated by government as a direct alternative (Moore, 1980, p. 113).

Targeting Stress Areas
The second criticism of the 1969 Act focused on the problem of directing resources towards areas of concentrated stress. Following the 1969 legislation there was a growing concern that grants in general were not being directed at the worst housing stock, and that GIAs failed to balance this tendency. This was undoubtedly the case in many local authorities. It was broadly in line with circular advice, which tended to discourage the declaration of GIAs in stress areas. As a general rule it was indicated that the worst areas of housing should be avoided, though it was conceded that in certain areas of multiple deprivation there might be a social reason for declaration (MHLG, 1969, paras 12 and 37).

Given that GIAs tended to avoid the worst areas of housing, it became increasingly obvious that there were a large number of houses which did not fall into either clearance areas or GIAs. Criticism of the 1969 Act suggested that policy was insufficiently focused on this middle range of houses, and that they would gradually deteriorate over a number of years until they were clearance material. Responding to this, the 1973 White Paper proposed to redirect priorities to 'those areas where the worst housing problems were increasingly concentrated' (DOE, 1973b, para. 17). It was therefore the intention of the 1974 Act to concentrate rehabilitation resources in areas of poor physical and environmental conditions and on works of essential repair.

In attempting to achieve this concentration of resources within areas of housing stress, the 1974 Act was operating within a wider policy climate which emphasized the spatial nature of social deprivation. HAAs were just one of a series of area-based policies aimed at directing resources towards people in need. It was a period during which policy was particularly concerned with locally based solutions to social problems. The analysis was one of disadvantaged groups rather than structural economic decline, and the prescriptions involved locally based solutions rather than fundamental social and economic reform. Lawless (1981) identified two major assumptions. The first was that improved local government management techniques would help to identify and assist people living in areas of deprivation. This idea could be found in the Maud Report's concern to encourage a corporate approach to policy analysis and service delivery (MHLG, 1965b), in the Seebohm Committee's proposals for reorganizing the personal social services (1969), and as a theme sustained through later experiments in area management (Harrop *et al.*, 1978) and comprehensive community programmes (Spencer, 1980; Wicks, 1983).

The second assumption related to a whole series of arguments on the concept of social and individual pathologies apparent in the operation of cultures of poverty. In the 1960s, considerable emphasis was given to the failings of the poor themselves – a phenomenon which became known as blaming the victim (Ryan, 1971). The thesis, transferred from the United States, was that in certain areas people were brought up in circumstances which encouraged transmitted deprivation.

A variant of the culture of poverty theory (Lewis, 1965) was propounded by Keith Joseph (then Secretary of State for Health and Social Security). He proposed that there was a cycle of deprivation which was transmitted from one generation to another in certain families (Holman, 1977). Consequently, the policy response ought to be directed towards the functioning of the family and local community rather than the broader economic and social structure.

Though questioned by the findings of subsequent research (Rutter and Madge, 1976), the cycle of deprivation hypothesis formed the background against which three experimental programmes were launched in the late 1960s. Each gave new impetus to the idea that social problems could be tackled by focusing special resources on a small area basis. Education priority areas were action-research projects established by the DES and SSRC as a response to the Plowden Report (1967). The other two programmes, Urban Aid and the Community Development Project, were both administered by the Home Office and aimed at a wider set of policy goals.

The urban programme initiative, while not exclusively a race relations policy, was deliberately announced as a direct challenge to racialism (Wilson, 1971, p. 525) and as a response to the government's own political difficulties in the face of arguments for immigration control (Edwards and Batley, 1978, p. 32). The first urban programme circular (Home Office, 1968) indicated that expenditure priorities were for education, housing, health and welfare in areas of special social need. The target areas were characterized as having a poor physical environment, substantial immigrant populations, a high proportion of children in care, and above average levels of unemployment. The funding for Urban Aid was not additional money but a sum already available in the rate support grant which was taken out of the general allocation and put into the special grant category. Local authorities could ápply for funds from this special grant for specific projects, which could be funded for up to five years with a 75 per cent government contribution.

The Community Development Project (CDP) was a series of local programmes to initiate and monitor practical ways of meeting the needs of people living in areas of high social deprivation. By 1972, twelve CDPs had been established in areas suffering from high unemployment and declining industry. Demuth (1977, p. 6) set out their aims to:

> encourage local self-help and initiative in poor areas on the grounds that improvements could be made through the greáter motivation and involvement of the people living there. To this end CDPs were established in small areas of severe deprivation with local authority teams employed to identify needs; promote the greater co-ordination and accessibility of services at the field level; foster community involvement and increase contacts between the people and local services.

The urban programme had only a very limited practical impact, and was judged a failure within its own terms of reference. Indeed, some writers effectively dismissed ten years of urban programme experiments as an economy measure. The problems were to be tackled by redirecting existing resources, but very little was actually spent because all the effort went into actually identifying areas of deprivation, or trying to find out what would be the best thing to do if they could be identified (Evans, 1980). Because they lay outside mainstream spending programmes, the urban experiments achieved a relatively high political impact at small cost. The entire range of urban policies could be seen as an example of incrementalism in expenditure. As most of central government's budget is committed in advance, all manoeuvre on policy takes place at the margins. Consequently, the urban programmes were marginal both in terms of the primary policy concerns of government departments and because they could neither rival nor threaten the integrity of existing and established expenditure programmes (Higgins *et al.*, 1983, pp. 174–5). But to dismiss the CDP experience on these grounds is to ignore their important contribution. They gathered useful information on economic and social decline, fulfilled an educative function by illustrating the potential and limitations of different forms of social action, and helped to change the climate of opinion as a contribution to policy change (Higgins *et al.*, 1983, pp. 45–6).

Abuses of the Grant System
The third and final area of criticism surrounding the 1969 Act related to

the grant system and its failure to discriminate. In this sense, the argument was that GIAs had succeeded in targeting poor areas of housing, but to the disadvantage of poorer residents. There was rising concern about the use of grant aid in parts of London and for weekend or second homes. Disquiet about the activities of speculators was particularly acute in certain inner London boroughs. Hamnett (1973) demonstrated the high proportion of improvement grants going to landlords in inner London, with particular concentrations in Camden, Westminster, Kensington and Chelsea, and Hammersmith. He concluded that the stock of privately rented property in London was being diminished as a result of the operation of improvement grants. More detailed evidence on the displacement of tenants was provided by McCarthy (1975), who found that for various reasons the improvement process tended not to benefit original residents. Of sampled grant applications, two-thirds had been preceded by outward movement of at least one household, and almost three-quarters of all households had moved away. The bulk of this outward movement was not so much a part of a process of property vacation followed by improvement, but rather property vacation, sale and then improvement. This tended to confirm the correlation between increases in professional and managerial groups and increases in owner-occupation at the expense of privately rented accommodation.

During the 1972/3 Session, the House of Commons Expenditure Committee inquired into the operation of the 1969 Housing Act. Evidence received by the committee placed considerable emphasis on the Act's social effects (House of Commons, 1973, para 14). The 1974 Act responded with an explicit recognition of the social implications of area-based policies. Earlier provisions on the repayment of grant were reintroduced and extended through stipulations on the future use of property, and a limited attempt was made to protect the interests of existing tenants. In procedural terms there was an emphasis on flexibility in the application of standards and encouragement for the involvement of housing associations to provide an alternative to the private landlord. But, both philosophically and practically, the 1974 legislation found it difficult to reconcile social concerns with the problems of physical improvement.

The 1974 Act

Under the provisions of the Housing Act 1974, local authorities had at their disposal the choice of three types of statutory area declaration. The 1969 Act GIAs remained in a modified form, together with the introduction of priority neighbourhoods and housing action areas. Inevitably there was a certain lack of conceptual distinction between the three. GIAs were intended to consist of fundamentally sound houses in areas offering scope for environmental improvement, and containing stable communities largely free from housing stress. Powers remained essentially unchanged from 1969, except that grant assistance to owners was increased from 50 per cent to 60 per cent. A new repair grant was introduced which was available only to owners in GIAs and HAAs. Grants for environmental works remained unchanged at their 1972 level of £200 a dwelling. Because of reliance on voluntary action, high concentrations of privately rented accommodation were thought unsuitable for GIA action (DOE, 1975a, para. 18).

Priority neighbourhoods were designed to prevent housing conditions from deteriorating in areas immediately outside HAAs and GIAs, to restore public confidence in the future of the area, and to pave the way for later, more intensive action once resources became available. Grants were only at the standard level of 50 per cent, which was an immediate disincentive given the prospect of future higher grants on declaration of an HAA. The main powers were the extension of notification procedures established within HAAs and designed to protect the interests of private tenants, and the availability of Section 43 compulsory purchase powers, also introduced to further the goals of HAA declaration.

Housing action areas were intended to achieve the rapid improvement of housing conditions in areas where bad physical and social conditions interacted (DOE, 1975b, para. 1). This reflected the central concern of the 1974 Act, which was to concentrate resources on a 'worst first' basis. To this end, in declaring HAAs, local authorities were to present evidence of severe physical and social conditions. It was this combination of physical and social factors which was used to define housing stress; poor physical conditions on their own were not considered sufficient to justify an HAA declaration (DOE, 1975b, para. 13). The normal life of an HAA was set at five years, extendable with DOE approval for a further two years; GIAs, by comparison, continued to have an indefinite life. The time limit on HAAs was designed to encourage rapid progress towards three legislative goals. Two were concerned directly with housing – improving physical conditions and aiming for the effective use and management of accommodation. The third was social, more difficult to define, and potentially in conflict with the first two, relating as it did to the 'well-being' of residents. Improvement of housing conditions was intended to benefit existing residents, with local authorities having an explicit responsibility to consider the social function of the area and to maintain this function wherever possible.

In pursuit of these objectives, certain additional powers became available in HAAs. Perhaps the most significant, reflecting the experience of the 1971 Act, was that grant levels were increased to encourage a high rate of voluntary take-up. They were paid at 75 per cent of allowable cost, with the local authority having discretion to increase this up to 90 per cent in cases of hardship. Apart from revised grant levels, there was also a new grant for repairs. Available only in GIAs and HAAs, its introduction attracted remarkably little political attention. It further undermined the well established justification for grant aid, which distinguished between original provision and the continuing maintenance responsibilities of owners. The new repair grant was intended to help owners to carry out basic repairs which they would not otherwise be able to finance. Improvement and special grants continued to be available, together with an intermediate grant – replacing the former standard grant – providing assistance with costs of repair associated with the provision of basic amenities. Local authorities were also eligible for exchequer subsidy at 50 per cent, up to an eligible expense limit of £50 a dwelling, for modest environmental works to land in private ownership.

Under the 1974 Act, conditions were imposed on the future occupation of all dwellings improved with renovation grants. Outside HAAs, owner-occupiers could be required to repay grants if they sold their homes within five years of carrying out the work, while landlords had to continue to let their property for the same period. Within HAAs the specified time was seven years. Two further discretionary conditions were mandatory in HAAs. First, following grant-aided renovation, rented property had to be let on the basis of a tenancy rather than any other form of occupancy. And, second, grants could not be given to an owner-occupier within twelve months of a tenant leaving the same dwelling. The penalty for default on these conditions was normally repayment of the grant.

A consistent criticism of the 1969 Act was its failure to tackle the lack of investment in privately rented property. Policies of compulsory improvement or purchase were not encouraged, but neither was it accepted that private rents should be allowed to increase substantially following improvement. The ineffective compromise was to allow conversion to a fair rent where a dwelling was improved to a given standard. Various groups argued that to tackle the problems of stress areas local authorities needed to intervene on a major scale to acquire the property of absentee landlords, that this needed to be done rapidly rather than following protracted attempts at voluntary improvement, and that it needed to be set in the context of security of tenure for furnished tenants (see, for example, Holmes, 1973, pp. 19–22). In recognition of the inadequacy of voluntary policies to deal with housing problems in stress areas, the Labour government's HAA strategy initially encompassed a commitment to municipalization linked with a new emphasis on housing associations to bring the rented sector into social ownership. To this end, local authorities were given a new power of compulsory purchase to acquire dwellings in pursuit of HAA objectives. Also, authorities could initiate proceedings for the compulsory improvement of tenanted dwellings – proceedings which outside HAAs and GIAs could only be started by the tenant. Finally, a requirement was placed on landlords to notify the local authority when a tenancy had expired, or when a notice to quit had been given, or when a formerly tenanted dwelling was being sold. The intention was to assist the council in identifying cases where existing residents were being disadvantaged or where the sale of property was prejudicial to the goals of the HAA. Though this notification procedure was designed to curtail speculation, there was no statutory duty placed on the local authority to take action and prevent eviction or sale. A proposal included in the 1973 White Paper (DOE, 1973b, para. 27c) but omitted from the Conservatives' Bill and subsequent legislation was that councils should have the right of first refusal on all property for sale in an HAA.

Progress in HAAs

The 1974 Act involved an unusually detailed programme of monitoring. The need to give careful attention to the implementation of policy had been recommended by the House of Commons Expenditure Committee, albeit in the context of scepticism concerning the adequacy of HAA procedures to achieve an effective and rapid improvement of rented accommodation (House of Commons, 1973, para. 56). Powers consistent with this recommendation were included in the legislation and resulted in three levels of monitoring being set out by the DOE (1975b). In addition to documentation submitted at declaration, quarterly statistical returns on GIAs were extended to cover progress in HAAs; a series of in-depth case studies were initiated; and annual progress reports were requested for each HAA covering improvement activity, population turnover, acquisition, notifications and compulsory action. Subsequently, monitoring procedures were simplified with a more standardized form of annual progress report replacing the quarterly returns (DOE, 1977b). The in-depth case studies were originally of six and later seven HAAs. They were commissioned and carried out in different ways and did not provide comparative data, but reports were published on four of the areas (Lomas, 1978; NBA, 1979; Thomas, 1979; Bradley, 1980). The final stage of this monitoring involved updating of progress in six of the areas together with an examination of residents' attitudes to their homes, the environment, and to the improvement process itself (Niner and Forrest, 1982).

HAA Declarations
From the beginning, the rate of HAA declaration was comparatively slow. In the first six months, only 30 were declared in England and Wales, with 73 in the full year. Just over 22,000 dwellings were included in these declarations, compared with 156,000 dwellings within GIAs declared during the first year the 1969 Act was in operation. Though authorities like Birmingham and later Liverpool moved forward with substantial programmes of HAA declaration, for the majority a more cautious approach was the rule. As with GIAs, the tendency was to begin with an experimental declaration as a preliminary step before looking at a more ambitious programme. But another factor was also at work. In the early

years at least, HAA declarations were concentrated within the major conurbations (Kirby, 1977). There was a widespread belief amongst many of the more rural authorities that HAAs were designed mainly with the problems of the larger urban areas in mind. Others felt that they could not identify within their authority the combination of HAA stress criteria which justified declaration. Indeed, some authorities set themselves outside the legislation because the declaration of an HAA appeared to admit to a combination of housing and social problems which they did not wish to acknowledge (Thomas, 1979, pp. 220-2). In this respect, authorities were being unduly restrictive in their interpretation of circular guidance. Factors characteristic of inner urban area stress, like multiple occupation, overcrowding and tenanted property, were mentioned. But so too was the concentration of households likely to have special housing problems – elderly people, large households, single-parent families, the unemployed and those on low incomes. Circular advice made it clear that not all the suggested social indicators would be relevant in every area, and recommended local authorities to bear in mind the extent to which physical and social factors combined and interacted to create unsatisfactory housing conditions (DOE, 1975b, para. 13).

Improvement Activity
An assessment of improvement activity within HAAs is dependent on the date of declaration and the proportion of property considered to be a target for renovation. Overall, the 1981 House Condition Survey showed that, since 1976, 19 per cent of dwellings within HAAs had been subject to improvement activity (DOE, 1983a, p. 24). A slightly higher figure was obtained if action was considered in terms of target dwellings – that is, excluding houses identified for clearance or already considered to be in adequate condition. These overall percentages, however, concealed wide variations at a regional level and indeed between individual HAAs. Overall progress seemed to have been most rapid in the Northern region, where approaching 60 per cent of target dwellings had been improved by early 1980, compared with less than a fifth in the East Midlands. At the individual level, some HAAs experienced total improvement, while there were others where virtually nothing had happened (Jones, 1980). There also appeared to be a correlation with public sector intervention. In general terms, progress seemed to have been most dramatic where implementation included compulsory action and public sector acquisition. Reliance on voluntary grant take-up alone tended to lead to lower levels of improvement.

One of the problems with area policies was the temptation to assess achievements at too early a stage. Certainly, initial progress within HAAs was not very encouraging (Wintour and Van Dyke, 1977; DOE, 1979b), and slower than the DOE originally anticipated. Some of the reasons for this early lack of progress were identified by local studies. In Leicester, for example, the time taken to process grant applications was seen as a serious problem. Staff shortages, high costs and drop-out rates combined to produce a situation where, over the period 1978-9, houses were being included within the area improvement programme at a much faster rate than completions (Lomas and Howes, 1979).

Where assessment concentrated on HAAs reaching their maturity, there was more encouraging evidence of improvement activity. A survey of 67 HAAs by Jones (1980) showed that in the HAAs declared early the average level of improvement was about 30 per cent, but that this figure increased to 70 per cent if account was taken of those in the process of being improved, or included within local authority or housing association renovation programmes. This impression was confirmed by the DOE's own monitoring programme, which had always stressed that progress was related to the length of time an area had been an HAA (DOE, 1979b, p. 30). The DOE's analysis of the earliest declared HAAs showed that initial activity was usually modest, and that improvement action generally peaked in years three and four, with housing association improvement and compulsory action being particularly slow to gain momentum. For HAAs which had been in existence for at least four years in April 1980, the average rate of progress was approaching 60 per cent of target dwellings, with even higher rates amongst the earliest HAAs. Detailed studies of six HAAs in existence for at least five years confirmed this relatively substantial progress. Overall, about 70 per cent of all occupied dwellings had been affected by some kind of work, with slightly over half this action being by local authorities and housing associations (Niner and Forrest, 1982, p. 19).

Voluntary Grant Take-Up
While the Housing Act 1974 contained new powers of intervention through compulsion and control, and encouraged partnership with housing associations, the main emphasis of policy, particularly in the owner-occupied sector, continued to be on voluntary improvement. Grants were a central element in attacking problems of poor owner-occupied housing, and in practice this meant that voluntary grant take-up was the single most important means of achieving progress within HAAs. Nearly half of all improvement activity was carried out by private owners, largely using improvement grants, though this percentage masked considerable regional variations.

Grant take-up by owner-occupiers was not achieved without difficulty. A range of factors influenced non-take-up, and amongst these it would be wrong to over-emphasize financial constraints. Differing aspirations, different priorities and an unwillingness or inability to face a complex and disruptive process were all factors which were in operation to varying degrees, as was a continuing lack of confidence in an area's future. After years of uncertainty and blight in what might have been a former clearance area, residents were not always convinced of the local authority's long-term commitment to improvement policies (Paris and Blackaby, 1979, p. 29). Future clearance remained a possibility if HAA policies 'failed', while genuine ambivalence accompanied an authority's encouragement of voluntary grant take-up in areas where doubt surrounded the relative value and quality of rehabilitated houses. In such circumstances, the caution of many residents was not surprising.

While low levels of grant activity could not be wholly explained by the inadequacy of the economic incentive, the nature of the financial package on offer attracted widespread comment. Because of the concentrations of physical and social stress within HAAs, some of the poorest owner-occupiers were being asked to improve some of the worst property, with an inevitable impact on the rate of grant take-up. Relatively low incomes, coupled with expensive credit, meant that owners had a very limited ability to finance their share of improvements. And, with eligible expense limits falling behind the rate of inflation, their share of the costs was often prohibitively expensive. The original grant limits were fixed in December 1974 at £3,200 for an improvement grant, and remained at that level until August 1977. During that period, building prices increased dramatically, with rehabilitation costs in Birmingham ranging from £4,500 to £6,000 by the end of 1976 (DOE, 1979b, p. 14). This meant that an owner-occupier receiving a 75 per cent grant was being asked to contribute £3,600. Paris (1977, p. 11) reported that between June 1974 and June 1976 the costs of grant work increased by 50 per cent. If an owner was receiving a full 75 per cent grant in 1974, by 1976 his share had increased by 200 per cent. In Sandwell, the picture was similar. Average costs increased by about 75 per cent over three years, to £7,500 by March 1978, so that even with higher eligible expense limits the grant was covering only just over half the cost, leaving the applicant to find around £3,500 (Thomas, 1979, p. 94). Over the same three-year period, new house building costs increased by half, suggesting that the costs of improvement work had increased faster than building work generally.

Though grant limits were periodically revised from 1977 onwards, there was always a tendency for the cost of works to exceed the expenditure limits. In the context of low incomes and high housing costs, grant limits and lending policies inevitably featured as primary factors influencing levels of improvement activity. However, the 1974 Act also introduced more stringent grant conditions: the rateable value limit, certificates of future occupation, and the exclusion of certain categories of property and certain types of work. Though these restrictions were introduced mainly to control the speculative use of grants, they had various unforeseen consequences. For example, owner-occupiers were not eligible for a grant on a property which had been tenanted during the previous twelve months. This was intended to discourage landlords from selling unimproved property with vacant possession. But one of the results was delay for sitting tenants who wished to purchase and improve their homes.

In certain areas of the country, rateable value limits were a constraint on grant activity. In the years immediately following the 1974 Act, owner-occupied property was not eligible for an improvement grant if it had a rateable value of over £175 (£300 in Greater London). The effect of this was to prevent a proportion of substandard houses in certain inner-city areas from receiving grant assistance. The notion of a rateable value limit was introduced into the legislation as a means of targeting grants. In the absence of an income test, it was seen as a measure of the condition of property, and of an owner's ability to pay for the work. But as a way of directing grant assistance towards the property most in need it proved to be an ineffective device. First, it was not a satisfactory indicator of property condition because there was substantial local and regional variation in the rateable value of essentially similar property. Second, as a measure of people's ability to pay, there was a low correlation between rateable value and income. There was no reliable relationship between rateable value and income generally. Benson (1978, p. 84) compared standardized rateable values with relative incomes, showing that the variation in average income was much less than the variation in standardized rateable value, and concluded that there was no clear relationship between household income and rateable values, either within authority areas or between them. The earlier Layfield Committee had formed a similar conclusion. They conceded a broad correspondence between average incomes and average rateable values, but then found that there was likely to be wide variation in the incomes of individual households living in similar houses even in the same area (DOE, 1976b, pp. 155–8).

Direct Intervention
Success in promoting voluntary grant take-up inevitably varied according to local circumstances but, overall, tended to be limited when dealing with tenanted stock. Renovation grants were available to landlords, who in turn were affected by many of the same financial and legislative constraints as owner-occupiers. There did, however, seem to be very little incentive for landlords to improve their property. The general picture was one of a low level of grant take-up despite the continued concentration of substandard property in the rented sector. Within HAAs, where landlords were subject to increased pressure to improve, about 30 per cent of completed grants were in the rented sector, though they accounted for 43 per cent of all property (DOE, 1979b). This figure masked wide regional variations, with grants to landlords accounting for more than half of total payments in the Northern region, compared with 11 per cent in the North-West.

The limited attraction of grants to private landlords was not unpredicted. Evidence submitted to the House of Commons Expenditure Committee in 1973 had made it quite clear that it was more profitable for a landlord to sell a property than to let at a fair rent, and that there was a very restricted role for the private landlord in voluntary improvement (House of Commons, 1973). In these circumstances, local authorities had two main powers of intervention within HAAs – compulsory improvement and acquisition. Local authorities could serve a notice requiring a landlord to improve the property, or serve a compulsory purchase notice and either to do the work themselves or transfer the property to a housing association. However, both procedures proved very slow. In fact, they were broadly similar to the powers available under the 1964 Act and these were generally abandoned as unworkable.

Partly for this reason, compulsory improvement using 1974 Act powers accounted for a very small proportion of activity within HAAs as a whole. The powers were initiated in about 44 per cent of HAAs. However, over half the provisional notices were not followed up by a full notice, perhaps because local authorities were attempting to prompt action and had no intention of proceeding further. Where a full notice was served, just over a quarter had resulted in completed work by 1980. It was not clear what happened to the remainder, though it may have been that the problem was solved by transferring ownership to the local authority or a housing association. On balance, however, the whole procedure was regarded as cumbersome and time-consuming.

This was recognized in the 1977 Housing Policy Review, which recommended a separate study with the aim of making compulsory improvement more simple and effective (DOE, 1977a, para. 10.32). In the absence of this reform, authorities seem to have been dissuaded from action both by the length of procedures and by concern over capital costs. These could be incurred in the event of owners responding with a purchase notice on the local authority, or where the authority had to do the work in default because the owner failed to comply with the improvement notice. Despite these fears, however, there were examples to demonstrate that determined application of compulsory powers could achieve results, and that the required work was generally undertaken by owners once the authority had demonstrated its ability to pursue default work. Notably, two London authorities showed that compulsory improvement could be used effectively. Between them, the GLC and Royal Borough of Kensington and Chelsea served half the national total of improvement notices during the early years of HAA implementation (DOE, 1979b, p. 18). As with repair notices, the serving of provisional improvement notices sometimes resulted in sale or voluntary improvement, possibly with grant aid. Experience in Kensington and Chelsea suggested that, given sufficient commitment at member and officer level, the whole process from provisional notice to completion could average under two years, and as such the approach provided a useful means of improving tenanted property (NBA, 1979).

The Role of Housing Associations
Rather than improve and manage property themselves, local authorities had the option of transferring the role of intervention to housing associations. The Housing Act 1974 provided for a new system of subsidy – housing association grant – which was payable to associations registered with the Housing Corporation. The new grant was available on both new build and rehabilitation schemes and was designed to cover the deficit between fair rent income and expenditure on allowable management and maintenance costs and capital loan repayment. The result was a rapid growth in housing association activity, with a doubling of their stock in ten years, mostly in the form of new build or rehabilitated houses or flats let to tenants at fair rents. Renovations increased from about 4,000 units in England during 1974 to nearly 19,000 in 1977. This was the peak year, and activity fell back to under 14,000 in 1981 – but still accounted for 10 per cent of all publicly funded rehabilitation, and one in five of all renovations in the public sector.

The new housing association grant and a larger Housing Corporation budget made it possible to involve housing associations in an expanded programme of rehabilitation in stress areas. Circular advice encouraged local authorities to involve housing associations in HAA implementation (DOE, 1975b, para. 26). Though their role varied enormously, housing associations made an important contribution to national levels of improvement activity within HAAs, owning about 10 per cent of houses within declared areas, but by 1981 accounting for nearly 30 per cent of all improvement activity.

This contribution was not achieved without difficulty. Early Housing Corporation procedures involved a high level of scheme scrutiny. To acquire and improve property, associations had to submit schemes on three separate occasions to the Housing Corporation: at acquisition; for rehabilitation proposals; and finally at tender stage. A small study of improvement pipelines in one West Midlands housing association showed that, on average, an individual scheme took about 21 months from registration to completion, and during this time spent about four months at the Housing Corporation in the process of checking and approval (Thomas, 1979, pp. 112–18).

Widespread criticism of the Housing Corporation's appraisal procedures led to the development of streamline procedures and later to scheme work audit (Housing Corporation, 1981). But other administrative problems remained. The district valuer was always involved in acquisition, and this presented difficulties for housing associations trying to acquire property in a rising market. In such circumstances, not only did some valuations fail to reflect current prices, but the procedure made it difficult to compete against other potential purchasers. When a sample of housing associations were interviewed in 1981, over half complained about the low level of valuations made by district valuers in relation to current market prices, which was thought to be a particular problem in areas where the housing market was more competitive (Brown *et al.*, 1984, pp. 34–5).

Two other factors influenced the ability of housing associations to acquire and improve property within HAAs. First, there were problems associated with purchase by agreement. Housing associations purchased property in the same way as a transfer between individuals, but with the Housing Corporation involved in the role of mortgagee. However, the whole process was made more complex by the number of agencies involved. In the West Midlands study, the period between an initial offer and completion averaged 36 weeks, but occasionally extended to well over a year (Thomas, 1979, p. 127). At any time during this period the vendor could withdraw, leaving the housing association with an administrative cost and a gap in their development programme.

Second, and inevitably, housing associations experienced difficulties carrying out work within cost yardsticks. The system which operated between 1974 and 1982 combined acquisition and rehabilitation costs within limits which varied between local authority areas. Where acquisition costs were high, this increased the pressure on renovation budgets, and encouraged conversion schemes with the maximum number of units, irrespective of property characteristics or local housing need. If, despite this, schemes were over cost limits, further delays would occur as savings were negotiated with the lowest tenderer. As cost limits were adjusted only periodically, inflation eroded values, pushing an increasing proportion of schemes over the limit in any one period. This forced savings to reduce capital costs, which in turn threatened to present housing associations with longer-term maintenance problems.

A separate difficulty was the practice of annual budgeting, with no ability to carry forward underspend into the next financial year. Given the delays involved in acquisition of individual properties on the open market, it proved very difficult for associations to plan expenditure programmes. They were not helped by a series of spending moratoria imposed by the Housing Corporation, which itself was also handicapped by an annual budget. Given the problems of operating a capital programme in such circumstances, there were calls at various times for some form of three-year cash allocation on a rolling programme, reviewed annually. Similar comments were made about local authority housing investment programmes, and it would seem that a good deal of sympathy existed for these proposals within the DOE. However, the Treasury continued to hold to a rigid system of cash control which did not admit to the practical difficulties of building and improving houses.

The Implementation of HAAs

Despite the emphasis of HAA policy on the voluntary take-up of grants by the private sector, responsibility for implementation rested squarely with local authorities, which raised questions about the adequacy of the powers and resources available to them. Given the central role of local authorities, two important factors set the context within which other constraints were to operate. The first was a product of the general economic climate – the problem of resource constraints. The second, and more fundamental, was the co-ordination and management role of the local authority. Given the emphasis on grant take-up, authorities were being asked to encourage the improvement of property through the voluntary actions of owner-occupiers and landlords, supplemented by the negotiated purchases of housing associations. The problems of simultaneously sustaining and co-ordinating an agreed policy involving a range of different owners inevitably led to questions about the ability of local authorities to manage improvement programmes in a way which was responsive to local needs.

Resource Constraints
Uncertainty surrounded the availability of finance almost as soon as the 1974 Act came into effect. Accompanying government circulars were closer to financial regulators than guidance notes on housing policy. Circular 13/75 (DOE, 1975a) introduced renewal strategies with a brief statement on the prevailing economic climate, leaving one contemporary commentator with the impression that gradual renewal was not so much a panacea as an absolute necessity (Fleetwood, 1975). The objective was to reduce rates of obsolescence until additional resources could be found to tackle the problem on a more comprehensive basis. Indeed, the Welsh Office equivalent of Circular 13/75 was more explicit, urging that 'maximum use should be made of the existing housing stock, bad as it is, in order to buy time to enable the new house-building programme to catch up with demand' (Welsh Office, 1975).

In March 1975 there was a cut in allocations for the rehabilitation of local authority owned stock. This was greeted with widespread and vehement protest, leading to a reassessment and reallocation, mostly at the expense of local authority mortgages. But it set the climate of doubt and financial restraint which was to be the theme of HAA policy in future years. After 1976, capital expenditure within HAAs was brought under increasingly tight control by cash limits which also restricted the ability of housing associations to contribute to renovation programmes. Healey's Budgets of 1975 and 1976 were already looking for reductions in the public sector borrowing requirement before the International Monetary Fund intervened with further reductions for the 1977/8 financial year. Local authority housing investment fell by a quarter between 1975/6 and

1977/8. New council housebuilding was affected, but so too were policies central to effective intervention in area-based renewal – municipalization, local authority mortgage lending and renovation grants, the value of which fell rapidly behind the rate of inflation. The introduction of housing investment programmes (HIPs) in 1977/8 gave some theoretical flexibility within capital budgets but local authorities, mindful of non-subsidized expenditure, continued to be cautious about the rate at which they declared HAAs.

Though capital restrictions on public sector acquisition, improvement and mortgage finance were increasingly important factors in the rate of declaration and progress of HAAs, restrictions on local authority manpower budgets were perhaps more significant in their immediate impact. The resource-intensive nature of HAA policy had always been recognized. The demands on staff were identified at an early stage (Haringey, 1975) and acknowledged in circular advice (DOE, 1975a, para. 10). It was appreciated that staff costs had to be incurred in advance of capital programmes, and that extra costs were imposed by attempting to achieve this spending in the poorer housing areas.

There was a clear implication, therefore, that the type of intervention appropriate to HAA policy was staff-intensive and that there was a relationship between progress and the availability of staff resources. There appear to have been two main explanations why these were not forthcoming. First, some authorities found themselves under-established in certain departments following local government reorganization. Second, this situation was then aggravated by central government controls over the growth of local government manpower. A circular in late 1974 had instructed authorities not to employ additional staff (DOE, 1974b). While there were substantial variations between authorities, the overall trend was of manpower reduction, with successive rate support grant settlements having the effect of cutting total employment within local authorities through the postponement of recruitment and the voluntary retirement of staff (DOE, 1978c, para. 19). The specific advice on HAAs was that extra staff should only be devoted to the work if compensating savings could be made in other services (DOE, 1975a, para. 10). This was done in a number of authorities, where renewal teams were established through internal secondment. But staff transfer meant a reallocation of resources and therefore a reappraisal of priorities.

Local Authorities as Managers
The HAA concept envisaged a relatively sophisticated approach to physical and social problems in which housing renewal was used as the base from which to move towards an overall improvement in living conditions. These related physical and social objectives presented a considerable challenge to local authorities. They were required to devise and implement programmes sensitive to the needs of a particular area,

involving resident participation, corporate planning and the co-ordination of external agencies. This had to be done in the period immediately following a major reorganization of local government and with very little direct experience on which to draw.

As a broad generalization, local authorities did appear to grasp the message that HAAs required new organizational responses. Following the Bains Report (1972), the climate was relatively receptive to corporate ideas, and various authorities reacted through some form of special management structure. In Newcastle, for example, older housing policy was part of the area management priority areas, with grants processed through area teams to a central revitalization team. This was part of, but largely independent from, the housing department, and provided a comprehensive, co-ordinated grant service for all applicants, covering plan preparation, grant administration and proof of title. Both in Newcastle and in South Tyneside (Bradley, 1980), improvement grants were seen as a product which could be packaged and a complete service offered to applicants. Birmingham adopted a different procedure on grant administration, but devolved the renewal programme to area-based project teams which were ultimately to enjoy a considerable degree of autonomy. Other local authorities adopted similar area team approaches. In their own way, these were quite radical, and the forerunners of the more comprehensive decentralization exercises which were to follow.

Whatever the organizational structure adopted, few if any local authorities immediately grasped the complexity of urban renewal as a management task. In the early days of Birmingham's renewal strategy, for example, one research project saw corporate management as being more concerned with the production and management of a policy than with changes to the environment, more a public commitment than a clearly defined programme of action informed by available resources (Paris and Blackaby, 1979, p. 159). The main management problem was not the devising of policies or services, many of which were straightforward, but the co-ordination of service delivery. An area sometimes required services it was not receiving, or a greater share of resources which were already being allocated. For example, substantial improvements could be achieved in an area without incurring expenditure under the financial heading of HAA or GIA environmental works. Better street cleaning, improved street lighting and footpath repair were needs commonly mentioned by residents (Niner *et al.*, 1975, p. 64). In a similar way, rapid and sensitive rehousing of tenants within an HAA could have a significant but unspectacular impact on programme implementation, and this priority and flexibility in rehousing arrangements could be achieved in a variety of ways. Consequently, an important management task within an HAA was one of improving the response and delivery of a range of existing services. This was not a problem unique to HAAs:

Many local authorities are not as effective as they might be in meeting the overall needs and problems which exist in particular localities; many services and facilities are provided on the basis of assumptions of uniform needs or according to professional or national standards; there are no mechanisms for achieving a corporate approach to planning for the area to ensure the right balance of services is provided; and opportunities for the public to make known their views on the problems of a particular area are inadequate. (Inner City Working Group, 1977, para 3.29)

As was shown by other experiments, an enhanced responsiveness to local needs proved to be difficult to achieve. In area management, for example, this was partly because its structure failed to challenge fundamentally the existing basis of decision-making and, conversely, because it generated political opposition simply by its threat both to the existing principles of organization and to established interest groups (Harrop *et al.*, 1978, p. 200). This meant that area management was not notably successful in changing the broad pattern of resource allocation at local authority level, though some schemes secured improvements in the services provided to individual communities, suggesting an ability to increase responsiveness to area needs in terms of service delivery (Harrop *et al.*, 1978, p. 180). This could also apply within HAAs, and would be consistent with the broader social aims of declaration. It was never certain, however, that HAAs were appropriate vehicles for such a wide-ranging approach. With good management relying on clearly defined objectives, there was much to be said for concentrating on the development and implementation of a strategy for older housing as part of an attack on social deprivation, rather than converting the strategy into a vehicle for improved service delivery.

Social Change
Central to the HAA concept was a concern for the well-being of existing residents. Programmes were to achieve physical improvement in a way which did not disadvantage people already living in the area. Broad generalizations about the social characteristics of HAAs were virtually worthless, the differences between areas far exceeding their points of comparison. But concern for the well-being of existing residents brought into focus the issue of mobility and posed the question of who benefited from HAA policy. It then became important to recognize that HAAs were often declared in areas of high mobility. In part, this was a heritage of the clearance programmes, which tended to avoid areas of multiple occupation because of their substantial rehousing implications. Consequently, housing markets adjacent to redevelopment areas were often characterized more by change and heterogeneity than by stability and homogeneity (Paris and Blackaby, 1979, p. 20). It was these areas which were commonly the focus of HAA policy.

Having recognized that HAAs were often areas of high mobility, the question of who benefited from HAA status needed to be reformulated. The assumption was not that post-declaration migration implied failure. Rather, the concern was that households wishing to stay in the area should not be displaced because of HAA activity (DOE, 1979b, p. 37). In practice, this was a difficult question to pursue. Various monitoring studies could answer questions about changing household characteristics within HAAs, and of residents' attitudes to the process. But data sources in England made it difficult to trace people moving from an HAA. Conclusions on social change therefore tended to be inferred from the results of comparative surveys within an HAA. This approach lacked information on the reasons for moving out, the choices involved, whether people would have preferred to stay, and whether they were forced out by HAA activity. To complicate the issue further, there were unanswered questions of impact on potential users. The level of activity within an HAA meant that housing conditions improved for those households living in the area, but, in terms of tenure transfer, at a cost to some of the functions previously performed by the area. In the context of fixed resources, improved quality and access for some groups must have been achieved at the expense of others. In line with the intentions of the legislation, it might have been possible to safeguard the welfare of existing residents, but it would be more difficult to plan for the needs of households who were potential users of the area.

These issues were highlighted by the impact of housing association activity within HAAs. Because associations were concentrated in a small area over a long period of time, they inevitably influenced the tenure pattern and housing function of the area. Their acquisition and improvement activity did not increase total housing opportunities. It almost invariably occurred in the context of reduced private-sector rented accommodation. Whether it reduced levels of owner-occupation depended on the original tenure balance and the extent of transfer from private renting to owner-occupation. A particular loss was access to furnished accommodation (Thomas, 1979, p. 133). What was gained in return was better quality, self-contained fair-rent flats. But, particularly for tenants in multi-occupied property, the acquisition policies of both housing associations and local authorities in pursuit of area improvement had an impact on local housing markets. Without alternative provision of easy-access furnished accommodation suitable for relatively transient tenants, the displacement effects of HAA policy on at least one section of the population threatened to be similar to those associated with clearance programmes.

The Overall Contribution
In terms of who benefited, it began to look academic whether improvement within HAAs was enjoyed by new or existing residents. As a

result of declining levels of improvement activity large numbers had not benefited at all.

Individual HAAs were successful. In terms of physical improvement, the available evidence shows that living conditions within HAAs improved as a result of declaration. Grant take-up was stimulated, while public sector improvement, particularly by housing associations, and the use of compulsory powers made an important contribution to progress and were dependent on declaration. A whole range of local factors conditioned the speed and extent of progress: existing physical and tenure characteristics, income levels relative to the costs of work, and the commitment of the local authority through grant promotion, compulsory powers and housing association activity. On balance, however, the highest levels of improvement were achieved where policy involved direct local authority and housing association activity to back up grant take-up by owner-occupiers.

In national terms it was not the rate of progress within individual HAAs that caused concern, but its interaction with the number of areas declared. While levels of improvement activity might be considered reasonable, the small number of declarations meant that, overall, too few houses were being renovated. If 30 per cent of houses had been improved in HAAs by 1980, this represented an estimated total of around 56,000 properties, or approximately 9,300 improved homes a year over the six years the policy had been in operation. Even allowing for initially low levels of activity, this hardly represented a major contribution to the attack on the condition of older housing. In Birmingham alone, one estimate showed that 93,000 dwellings needed repair or improvement (Birmingham City Council, 1981).

Overall levels of progress were of even greater concern when viewed against the generally lower levels of grant take-up achieved in the second half of the 1970s. Since 1974, spatial analysis of grant take-up tended to focus on HAA policy, ignoring the broader implications. As grant take-up fell dramatically after 1974 (Appendix 3), any success in achieving voluntary improvement within declared areas was reflected in a fall in activity elsewhere. In 1974, grants in GIAs represented 4 per cent of total grant activity. In 1979, work in HAAs and GIAs accounted for 11 per cent of all grants, but total activity was down by nearly half (Table 4.5). This trend did not necessarily mean that the worst areas had benefited compared with other areas within a local authority; there could have been a more dramatic redistribution of grants at a national level. However, from the limited local evidence available it would appear that the redistribution had indeed been at an intra-authority level, with HAAs and GIAs gaining a larger share of a smaller cake.

By the middle of 1982, just over 500 HAAs had been declared in England, with the rate of declaration slowing down from an average of just under a hundred a year over the first few years to about fifty a year in

Table 4.5   *Grants Paid within GIAs and HAAs, 1970–9, England and Wales*

	GIAs	HAAs	All grants	GIAs and HAAs as % of all grants
1970	1,119	—	121,831	1
1971	2,300	—	163,823	1
1972	7,271	—	245,290	3
1973	15,143	—	305,352	5
1974	12,960	—	298,363	4
1975	11,011	189	134,452	8
1976	7,255	1,346	127,675	7
1977	5,359	4,320	120,823	8
1978	10,850	8,545	139,012	14
1979	10,856	7,289	166,400	11

Source: DOE, *Housing and Construction Statistics* and *Local Housing Statistics*, various years.
Note: Changes in the publication of statistics limit comparability. More recent published data are for England only, by financial year, and are based on returns so incomplete that private-sector grant activity is seriously under-estimated.

the early 1980s. Declared areas contain around 173,000 dwellings or about 3 per cent of the pre-1919 stock in England. By comparison, it was originally intended that HAAs should deal with 3–4 per cent of the total national housing stock (Pickup, 1975). On the basis of 1971 Census data it was estimated that about 1,800 potential HAAs might exist in England as a whole. As HAAs were declared at an average rate of 65 a year over the period 1975–82, it would take over twenty-five years to declare all the areas originally targeted for treatment in 1975. Some reassurance was provided by the 1981 House Condition Survey, which suggested that only 408,000 dwellings, 2·3 per cent of the stock, fell within potential HAAs (DOE, 1982a, table 15), but even on this assessment, more than three-quarters of property suitable for potential area action was not within a current programme (DOE, 1983a, p. 23).

If HAAs had been one component of a broader strategy, a different judgement on their contribution might have been made. But, as it turned out, progress was too slow for the scale of the problem. The 1981 House Condition Survey found that deterioration into serious disrepair was significant within potential improvement areas which had not been declared; but even property within GIAs and HAAs had not seen any marked improvement (Table 4.6). Although activity in declared areas had made a significant impact on housing conditions,

this was offset by a deterioration in dwellings not recently subject to action. This deterioration had occurred in both GIAs and HAAs and apparently both immediately prior to and following area declaration.

Thus, notwithstanding the success of many individual areas, the overall result was no improvement in serious disrepair or unfitness by 1981. (DOE, 1983a, p. 24).

Where area declarations had not occurred, the position was markedly worse, with serious disrepair in prospective HAAs doubling over a five-year period to account for nearly a third of the stock in those areas (Table 4.6).

This disturbing evidence on disrepair gave little reason to claim success for area-based strategies. At best, the condition of houses in declared areas had deteriorated less rapidly than houses outside declared areas. Consequently, as the most important vehicle for dealing with older housing problems, HAAs inevitably became the focus of criticism that policy had not been successful in reversing increased disrepair. As this increase in decay and dereliction had been a primary concern of the 1974 legislation, it had to be concluded that policy had failed to influence housing conditions in the manner and scale envisaged.

Table 4.6   *Trends in Serious Disrepair of Dwellings in Areas*

Area action in 1981	Dwellings in serious disrepair		Satisfactory or medium disrepair only	
	at previous survey %	at present survey %	at previous survey %	at present survey %
Declared GIAs	13	14	66	71
Proposed GIAs	4	12	77	73
Prospective GIAs	10	17	69	63
Declared HAAs	22	24	53	58
Proposed HAAs	18	20	69	69
Prospective HAAs	15	31	53	41
Declared or proposed clearance area	32	57	32	11

Source: DOE, 1983a, table 73.

5

Experiment and Innovation

Assessment and Revision

In the years immediately following its introduction there was widespread comment on the shortcomings of the Housing Act 1974, accompanied by various proposals for detailed modification of the legislation. But the Act which eventually emerged was not preceded by any formal examination of urban renewal policy. The review of housing finance, instituted by Crosland in 1974, was transformed by 1977 into a wider study of housing policy, but one which had little substantive to say about older housing. The Housing Policy Review (DOE, 1977a) postponed formal consideration of improvement policy, as it was thought too early to judge the effectiveness of changes made by the 1974 Act. However, because of the increased disrepair identified by the 1976 House Condition Survey, action was proposed to prevent houses deteriorating into unfitness. The review therefore advocated an extension of repair grants to property outside HAAs and GIAs. Apart from this, the emphasis remained one of concentrating improvement resources on bringing the worst property up to a basic though undefined standard.

Background to the 1980 Act
The Housing Policy Review was followed in 1978 by a consultation paper on repair and improvement. Its introductory remarks conceded that proposals for legislative reform were not intended to take the place of a fuller examination of area improvement programmes. Like the 1977 Review it was felt that this would have to wait until the full impact of the 1974 Act could be examined. Again, like the review, the consultation paper made reference to the significant increase in disrepair disclosed by the 1976 House Condition Survey. It was concluded that many of the grants given to private owners since 1971 had done little to improve the worst housing and that there was a risk of accelerating decline in older housing conditions unless there could be some redirection of resources. Given that the 1974 Act had a similar ambition, and that both the Housing Policy Review and the consultation paper conceded that it was too early to judge the effectiveness of this legislation, it was perhaps both premature and ambitious to seek a further redirection.

Though making more detailed proposals, the consultation paper was broadly in agreement with the Housing Policy Review on the need for a change in emphasis, together with a more flexible approach to grant administration. Of the suggestions put forward, most were uncontroversial modifications of the existing legislation, though the proposed extension of repair grants was important in the light of subsequent events. Under the Housing Act 1974, repair grants were available only within HAAs and GIAs. Very few were paid between 1974 and 1980 – partly because they were not actively promoted by many local authorities, and partly because their usefulness was limited by the requirement to prove undue hardship. Like the Housing Policy Review, the consultation paper proposed modifications in their operation to make them more widely available. Faced with the results of the 1976 House Condition Survey, it was felt that a repair grant was necessary in an attempt to check an accelerating decline into unfitness. In justification, it was argued that much disrepair was due to ageing structure rather than the neglect of routine maintenance – a distinction which generated remarkably little political comment.

What did attract attention was the essentially unimaginative nature of the proposals. The Association of Metropolitan Authorities was particularly critical, believing that the government had seriously underestimated the extent of the problem and that their proposals did not go nearly far enough (AMA, 1978, p. 24). In their turn, the AMA recommended the replacement of HAAs and GIAs with a single renovation area; new local authority fabric repair subsidies to tackle improvement on a block basis; increased environmental grants and the abolition of rateable value limits within renovation areas; revision of fitness criteria to include standard amenities and electric lighting; the linking of eligible expense limits to an index of building costs; and greater flexibility to declare clearance areas on the grounds of environmental deficiency. In putting forward these proposals it was recognized that additional expenditure on renovation grants would be involved. This was thought essential if private-sector improvement was to have the effect of halting further deterioration. While not being explicit in advocating increased levels of clearance, the report did conclude that individual local authorities should reappraise the arguments for improvement versus clearance and place improvement policies within the broader context of overall housing strategies (AMA, 1978, p. 27).

The Housing Act 1980

The Housing Bill 1979 emerged in a largely unmodified form from the consultation process, but as in 1974, the Bill fell with a change of government. This time it was the turn of a new Conservative administration to reintroduce a number of former Labour provisions. This Conservative Bill followed a series of consultation papers issued in the autumn of 1979, covering the right to buy, the tenants' charter and improvement policy. Many of the detailed proposals on improvement and repair were the same as the original Labour Bill – the wider availability of repair grants for substantial structural repair, grants to tenants, and flexibility on standards, grant limits and conditions. It was also proposed to increase environmental grants in HAAs, and to introduce subsidies to encourage acquisition, improvement and sale. There were, again, omissions in the consultation paper which were not taken account of in the resulting Bill. With its lack of reference to compulsory improvement procedures, there was no evidence of a willingness to tackle the improvement of tenanted property. The right of tenants to take up improvement grants was not a substitute for an effective attack on poor housing conditions in the rented sector. In this sense, the proposals failed to focus resources on those most in need.

Unlike provisions on the right to buy, sections in the Housing Act 1980 dealing with improvement and repair were largely uncontroversial. Its major simplification was the abolition of priority neighbourhoods, a little used provision of the 1974 Act. The most imaginative part of the Act provided that where local authorities or housing associations acquired dwellings for improvement and sale they would be eligible for an exchequer subsidy if the cost of acquisition and improvement exceeded the sale price. In practice, the bulk of improvement for sale (IFS) was carried out by housing associations using subsidy through the Housing Corporation.

Apart from grants to tenants, the wider availability of repair grants, and the deficit subsidy on improvement for sale, the 1980 Act made a number of detailed changes to the operation of renovation grants which were primarily intended to increase flexibility. For both improvement and repair grants, rateable value limits on owner-occupied houses were removed from property within HAAs. Former tenants who purchased their homes no longer had to wait twelve months before being eligible for grants. And the 1974 Act definition of 'family' was widened to include grandparents and grandchildren – but not brothers and sisters – amongst those eligible to occupy property subject to a grant application. The five-year rule – seven years in HAAs – on the sale of property, which had already been relaxed by circular advice, was loosened further by the provision that, following sale by an owner-occupier, the local authority could only reclaim grant if the new owner did not occupy the house in accordance with conditions in the certificate of occupation (DOE, 1980, para. 15).

While central government made much of its wish to abandon detailed controls, nationally determined criteria under the 1980 Act continued to restrict the ability of authorities to respond to local circumstances. For example, under the 1974 Act works of repair could not constitute more than 50 per cent of the eligible expense on an improvement grant. This allowed authorities to be flexible in their interpretation of repair and improvement. It was common practice among some authorities to describe reroofing as a repair because the new roof had an improved specification. Because these sometimes arbitrary decisions were made simply to balance the grant, many authorities argued for abolition of the distinction. Rather than do this, however, central government decided to retain the 50 per cent limit, while increasing it to 70 per cent in cases where the dwelling was in need of substantial and structural repair (DOE, 1980, para. 44). Given the extremely limited ability of the DOE to exercise control over this type of regulation, proponents of the more flexible approach were left to wonder at the discrepancy between government sentiment and action.

In the area of grants, eligible expense limits and appropriate percentages, the Act provided further powers, subsequently exercised by the Secretary of State, to vary conditions by area, category of area, or category of dwelling. Though this did not extend discretion to individual local authorities, or meet the widespread calls that had been made for protection of cost limits through some form of regional index-linking, the new arrangements were in some ways a more sensitive tool for targeting the poorest property. They were also more complicated. It was calculated that the four grants, together with thermal insulation grants, in combination with the various different grant limits and percentages, meant that there were 90 different permutations of grant aid (RTPI, 1981, p. 22). The basic grant percentage remained at 50 per cent, while grants in GIAs increased from 60 per cent to 65 per cent. Priority properties received grants at 75 per cent – the broad categories being property in HAAs, unfit or substandard dwellings, those in need of substantial or structural repair, and houses in multiple occupation lacking adequate means of escape. To these rates could be applied an extended version of the previous hardship criteria. Appropriate percentages could be increased from 75 per cent to 90 per cent in priority cases, and from 50 per cent to 65 per cent in other cases, where it appeared to the authority that applicants would not be able to pay their share of the cost of works without undue hardship (DOE, 1980, para. 10). Finally, different eligible expense limits applied to priority and non-priority cases, to property in Greater London and elsewhere, and to dwellings and conversion of property consisting of three storeys or more. There were, therefore, four types of grant, four different percentages, and eligible expense limits which were higher in Greater London and, in the case of improvement grants, for priority cases. Table 5.1 summarizes the position in 1984, but there were numerous caveats and exceptions.

In terms of improvement and repair, these changes to the grant system were the most notable feature of the 1980 Act. Critically, while changes were justified in an explicit attempt to direct resources where the need was greatest, the effect was to encourage the voluntary take-up of grants. Higher

Table 5.1   *Renovation Grants[1] under the Housing Act 1980*

| | Priority case | | | Non-priority case | | |
	eligible expense	maximum grant 75%	90%	eligible expense	maximum grant 50%	65%
Improvement[2]						
Improvement in:						
Greater London	13,800	10,350	12,420	9,000	4,500	5,850
Elsewhere	10,200	7,650	9,180	6,600	3,300	4,290
Conversion in:						
Greater London	16,000	12,000	14,400	10,400	5,200	6,760
Elsewhere	11,800	8,850	10,620	7,700	3,850	5,005
Intermediate						
Full standard amenities:						
Greater London	3,005	2,254	2,704			
Elsewhere	2,275	1,706	2,048			
Repairs:						
Greater London	4,200	3,150	3,780			
Elsewhere	3,000	2,250	2,700			
Repair[2]						
Great London	6,600	4,950	5,940			
Elsewhere	4,800	3,600	4,320			
Special						
Means of escape:						
Greater London	10,800	8,100	9,720	10,800	5,400	7,020
Elsewhere	8,100	6,075	7,290	8,100	4,050	5,265
Repair and replacement:						
Greater London	4,200	3,150	3,780	4,200	2,100	2,730
Elsewhere	3,000	2,250	2,700	3,000	1,500	1,950

Notes:
1   As at September 1984.
2   Higher limits apply to listed buildings.

levels of grant for unfit and substandard houses did mean that this benefit was not related only to area declarations, and as such was a welcome response to the problems of isolated properties in poor condition. But there was a sense in which policy had moved back into a more responsive phase. For all their shortcomings, HAAs had been an attempt to intervene in a positive way to tackle identified problems of housing stress. The new grant structure diminished the relative advantages of living in an HAA because, for those who qualified, a 90 per cent grant was available irrespective of location. At the same time, the 1980 Act did nothing which specifically assisted the implementation of HAA policy. In so much as the new legislation helped with the voluntary take-up of grants, this would be reflected in HAA performance. But, apart from more generous grants for environment works, the only legislative change to HAAs concerned the statutory requirement on local authorities to provide information to the DOE. Consequently, as the area approach represented the only effective policy for targeting grant take-up, it must be concluded that, on balance, the 1980 Act represented a marginal shift away from intervention. There remained considerable organizational and procedural arguments in favour of HAAs which were not diminished by the 1980 Act. But, with continued resource constraints, measures adopted in the 1980 Act and extended by subsequent initiatives increased the pressure on local authorities to respond to general grant applications and made it more difficult to target priority areas.

The 1980 Act in Operation

Grant take-up by owner-occupiers began to pick up from 1978, but activity remained well below the 1973 peak. There was no immediate dramatic response to the 1980 Act, with the real rise occurring in 1982 when, for the first time, repair grants were used on a wide scale. The Chancellor's 1982 Budget announced that all repair and intermediate grants would be approved at 90 per cent, initially until the end of 1982, and subsequently extended until March 1984.

This boost was part of a long tradition of Budget announcements. While the incoming 1979 Conservative administration was committed to reducing the public sector borrowing requirement, with housing bearing the brunt of government cutbacks (see Chapter 6), there was a growing concern that capital spending had taken more than its share, and that some form of stimulus was required. In addition, the government was faced with early results from the 1981 House Condition Survey, which focused attention on the increasing problems of disrepair in the owner-occupied stock. With reflationary pressures coinciding with the run-up to a general election, it became attractive to stimulate private-sector grant take-up.

Following the 1983 election, the DOE came under increased pressure from the Treasury to cut back on grant expenditure. The impetus for this was the wish to find further reductions in public expenditure on housing. It was questioned whether the grant system provided good value for money, or whether it subsidized work which would have been carried out even if grants had not been available. This may have been a decisive factor in the decision not to extend the general availability of 90 per cent grants beyond March 1984. It did not, however, suggest a reassessment of grant philosophy, simply a return to the idea of concentrating limited resources on the poorest property. The boom in 90 per cent repair grants for the better-quality pre-1919 stock was over, and with it came the prospect of a lower level of grant approvals in following years.

Renewal and Resources

Despite the special circumstances prevailing between April 1982 and March 1984, the generally higher levels of grant made possible under the provisions of the Housing Act 1980 provided a useful way of helping local authorities to construct a package of works and finance to meet the individual needs of grant applicants. To that extent, it made rehabilitation grants easier to market and, taken with measures to simplify administrative procedures, moved some way towards closing the gap between house improvement in the national interest and the reluctance of individual owners to bear the cost, disturbance and inconvenience of the work. But in the context of evidence on the rate of decay of the housing stock the underlying philosophy of the grant system remained inadequate and ultimately misdirected.

Judged by its share of public sector resources, there continued to be little government commitment to rehabilitation. In 1981, the value of grants to private owners was £149 million, representing about 0·13 per cent of total government planned expenditure. This was less than the cost of one Type 42 destroyer (£180 million) and 8 per cent of the annual research and development budget for defence (£1,833 million). During 1981, under 70,000 properties were affected by grant work – about 0·6 per cent of the privately owned stock. Taking a conservative valuation of £20,000 per house provided an asset value for the privately owned stock of about £240 billion. The replacement cost would obviously far exceed this value. But, as a comparison, government grant assistance represented an annual investment rate at 0·06 per cent of asset value. There was therefore reason to concur with Moore (1980, p. 117) that the level of ideological commitment to improvement far exceeded the level of activity.

There had been a growing sense, throughout the late 1970s, that policy was not sufficiently vigorous in its approach to the problems of older housing conditions. Though there were specific criticisms of the operation of legislation, the broader and more fundamental concern was with the absolute level of resources devoted to renewal, combined with doubts about the ability of approaches and procedures to mount programmes on the required scale even in the absence of resource constraints. Moving into the 1980s, criticism of renewal performance generally carried with it recommendations for increased public-sector expenditure and greater intervention, implying a lack of faith in the government's commitment to private-sector initiatives. Such a message was consistent with experience of urban renewal implementation. Evidence from HAA policy had suggested that success was associated with vigorous public-sector intervention. Instead, the emphasis of government policy was on partnership, private-sector substitution, and the role of the financial institutions. This carried with it an important shift in housing policy. The new emphasis was on reduced government intervention and lower levels of direct public-sector housing provision.

In part, this new policy emerged from a changed understanding of urban problems and of the role of government in reversing decay. During the late 1970s, there was a growing emphasis on the underlying economic processes, reinforced by political, planning and fiscal policies, which were shaping urban problems. Explanations of urban decline increasingly concentrated on the loss of manufacturing employment and the effects of unemployment and lack of private investment. Though older housing was not a problem specific to these declining areas, a focus on the inner city was to influence the course of policy on older housing.

Urban Decline

There has been a national decline in manufacturing industry in recent years. It is not just an inner-city problem, but the depressed industrial sectors are over-represented in the older urban areas. Massey (1983, p. 20) described the geography of decline as the combined result of a long-term contraction in the old basic industries in the development areas, together with more recent loss of employment in the manufacturing sector. Though manufacturing decline was a newer trend, the absolute number of jobs in manufacturing had been shrinking since the 1960s. In ten years from 1965, manufacturing employment in the United Kingdom fell by 12·5 per cent (Department of Employment, 1976). While this decline had a dispersed spatial impact, it tended to have a disproportionate effect on the older urban areas (see, for example, Dicken and Lloyd, 1978; Dennis, 1978; Gripaios, 1977; Lloyd, 1979).

A consequence of disproportionate decline in the older urban areas was a relative shift in employment patterns towards the smaller towns and rural areas, though commentators varied in the emphasis they gave to differential growth. It was generally agreed that closure of plant accounted for a large part of job loss in major urban areas. What was less clear was whether this led to new manufacturing opportunities elsewhere. However, in descriptive terms, the urban-rural contrast in growth appeared to be strong. Over the postwar period the five slowest-growing regions in England contained a conurbation, while the four with fastest growth did not. East Anglia, the least urbanized, grew most quickly (Fothergill and Gudgin, 1982, p. 12). In terms of the growth of employment opportunities it seemed that the larger and more industrial a settlement, the poorer its performance. At least as far as the manufacturing sector was concerned, the picture was not simply one of decline in the city and growth elsewhere. The size relationship meant that small towns grew faster than large towns, just as small cities grew faster than larger cities (Fothergill and Gudgin, 1982, p. 22).

The decline in manufacturing industry presents an essentially structural explanation of growing unemployment in older urban areas. Firms close and local people lose their jobs because the growth industry moves out, leaving inefficient and obsolete firms disproportionately threatened by rationalization. They are disadvantaged by the high cost of sites, by outdated, cramped and inadequate premises, and by the poor quality of the residential environment (Keeble, 1978, pp. 107–11). And their decline is accelerated by planning policies which are insensitive to employment needs because they favour residential use and encourage dispersal (Evans, 1980). However, this simple structural explanation, coherent though it may be, should not be over-emphasized. For example, the Northern Region Strategy Team (1977) argued that demand factors could not account for the persistent economic problems of the north-east. They pointed instead to poor management, low rates of new firm formation and the absence of specialized financial and technical sectors. Fothergill and Gudgin (1979) suggested that it was the performance of indigenous manufacturing industry, rather than industrial structure or the movement of industry, that was the major influence on employment change at the subregional level. Evans (1980) went beyond this and questioned the link between declining job opportunities and high unemployment within older urban areas, because people had been moving out of the cities faster than jobs. He argued that the reduction in population could have caused a decline in the number of available jobs as the demand fell for personal services (Evans, 1980, p. 456). For someone with a given level of skills, age and other characteristics, the chances of being unemployed did not vary much with residential location within the urban area (Metcalf and Richardson, 1980); so high unemployment in the inner area could be associated with high levels of unskilled labour, which had a higher probability of being unemployed than the more skilled. Leaving aside explanations of this concentration, Evans pointed to the importance of labour market characteristics in determining appropriate policy responses. If labour markets were localized, and less skilled workers relatively immobile (Bramley, 1979, p. 89), plant closures would have specific effects which needed to be ameliorated by the creation of new local jobs. The problem was then to persuade new plants to open in what appeared to be a relatively unfavourable environment. Alternatively, if labour was seen to move more fluidly within a single labour market, more emphasis could be given to national employment trends and to solutions which were not tied to the geography of urban areas.

The Inner Area Studies
Though the evidence of urban decline was contradictory, economic factors were increasingly acknowledged to be at the root of inner urban problems. An emphasis on economic decline had been adopted by Shelter's report on their Neighbourhood Action Project in Liverpool (SNAP, 1972). This report anticipated much subsequent debate, arguing

for policies of economic regeneration tied to more favourable treatment under the rate support grant and the co-ordination of service delivery through area management. In the same year, the Conservative government established the Inner Area Studies (IAS). It seems unlikely that the three IAS investigations, in Birmingham, Liverpool and Lambeth, were a specific response to the SNAP report, but their early thinking shared a common interest in a total and co-ordinated approach to urban problems (House of Commons, 1972). The brief which eventually went to the three firms of private consultants was less comprehensive. By then, the central objective was not to obtain a better understanding of inner-city problems, but to discover, in particular, what action could be taken by local government to stimulate the local economy, relieve social stress and improve the social and physical environment. This emphasis on local government was important. While later consultants' reports (DOE, 1977c) underlined the need for public-sector investment, they tended to relate action to the local level rather than emphasizing central government's role in economic planning, investment, unemployment and industrial location (Inner City Working Group, 1977, p. 9).

The evidence from the IAS investigations stressed the importance of employment opportunities and levels of income as primary causes of urban problems. It was no small achievement of these reports that their message was incorporated into political thinking and influenced the formulation of inner-city policy. They introduced a new emphasis on economic decline as well as a recognition that the nature of urban problems varied between and within authorities. Above all, the studies stressed that problems were related to major structural changes in the economy, and that policy should address itself to the creation of employment opportunities. In this sense the IAS reflected a shift in policy concern from social to economic problems; and this focus on industrial decline, the encouragement of small businesses, and promotion of industrial and commercial development were themes continued through inner city partnership programmes, industrial improvement areas, enterprise zones and urban development corporations.

Inner-City Policy
In 1976, anticipating the new inner-city policy, Peter Shore, as Secretary of State for the Environment, began to reverse the postwar policy of job dispersal by talking of the opportunity to attract industry back into inner areas (Shore, 1976a). He acknowledged the disproportionate impact of economic decline on people who lived in inner urban areas and emphasized the need for a policy framework to promote private investment (Shore, 1976b). This message was picked up by the 1977 White Paper (DOE, 1977d), which saw the role of the public sector as one of creating confidence leading to new investment and lending. At the same time, circular advice encouraged local authorities to switch their priorities

to industrial development through sympathetic planning, reduced displacement through clearance, and the provision of suitable premises for small firms (DOE, 1977e).

Because the White Paper recognized the variety of problems affecting inner-city areas, partnership arrangements were proposed to tailor policies to particular circumstances. In so much as this indicated a flexible response, it was widely welcomed. However, it perpetuated the emphasis on area-based approaches and local problems by simultaneously recognizing that urban deprivation was less geographically concentrated than had previously been thought, and then selecting a small number of local authorities for special partnership treatment. What failed to be given any explicit recognition was the need for some inner-city problems to be tackled by national policies for economic growth, employment, education and housing. All these were beyond partnership's emphasis on the local nature of inner-city problems, and the view that they might respond to administrative reforms.

There had been only slight political recognition that public-sector spending was an important component of an urban programme. In his Bristol conference speech, Peter Shore (1977) recognized that resources needed to be redirected to inner-city areas, but regretted that no extra money was waiting and available to be earmarked for that purpose. Following the 1977 White Paper, the rate support grant settlement was redistributed in favour of urban authorities. It was a short-lived redistribution, reversed by the incoming Conservative government at a time when overall levels of local authority capital expenditure were falling after fifteen years of consistent growth. Sensitive to this criticism, the then Environment Secretary, Michael Heseltine, felt it important to emphasize that, at £270 million, the urban programme was at its highest level ever. This was indeed the case, though he omitted to mention that specific government spending in the inner city did not become significant until the financial year 1978/9, when expenditure was increased by £74 million to £114 million (at November 1979 prices). This reflected changes in funding arrangements from 1978, when the urban programme became a generic name and source of finance. Between 1978 and 1981 funding for the new urban programme increased by two-thirds in real terms. This was welcome growth, but it was easily cancelled out by the impact of expenditure cuts on mainstream programmes. Urban programme grants accounted for only a quarter of the total sum lost to urban areas by adjustments to the rate support grant. Lansley (1982) estimated that in 1981/2 alone the partnership authorities designated under the Inner Urban Areas Act lost £275 million in Whitehall aid through reduced rate support grant, housing subsidies and urban programme grants. Home (1982 p. 119) remarking on the marginal contribution of inner city partnership spending compared with mainstream spending programmes, noted that Liverpool's inner city partnership programme annual allocation was less than the total unemployment benefit paid out in the city in one week.

Partnership and the Private Sector
After the Toxteth riots in the summer of 1981, Michael Heseltine made it clear that he recognized the inner-city problem. But the role of government spending continued to be tempered by the government's desire to cut public expenditure. Hence the political attraction of extending the idea of partnership arrangements to embrace the private sector, a device which Peter Shore had previously and unsuccessfully floated. In this sense the Conservatives continued the partnership approach to inner-city problems, but the emphasis on economic regeneration moved even further away from social programmes towards the generation of private wealth.

The task force device initiated in Liverpool, together with the introduction of urban development grants, gave an increased emphasis to the role of private-sector financial institutions. Michael Heseltine visited Liverpool, seconded managers from the private sector to form the Financial Institutions Group (FIG), and gave them the brief of formulating initiatives for attracting private capital into older, inner-city areas. The emphasis on partnership with the financial institutions appealed to a simple political pragmatism. For government, it promised high-profile activity with minimum calls on public-sector capital expenditure. The financial institutions also found the arrangement convenient. Provided the level of public-sector investment was sufficient to remove risk, they could make quite ordinary commercial investment decisions while enjoying the benefits of government approbation and free publicity.

Leaving pragmatism aside, there was nothing new in the attraction of pump-priming – the idea that small amounts of public-sector investment could attract substantially larger amounts of new private capital. Neither was there much disagreement about the need to involve private-sector investment through the financial institutions. The Wilson Committee drew attention to the fact that as personal savings increased personal investment had declined as more and more people passed their savings, either voluntarily or compulsorily, to professional fund managers (Wilson Committee, 1980). These fund managers, acting with the caution of trustees, had replaced the diversity of personal investment decisions with the uniformity of financial institutions (Cadman, 1981). They had been prepared to invest in commercial property, which out-performed equities and gilts between 1971 and 1981. But they were only prepared to invest in prime sites. Tertiary property had not attracted investment, contributing to the decline of older commercial areas. Investment there had been seen to involve high risk and low return, contrary to the objectives of financial institutions to maximize returns on minimum risk. This was the dilemma for any policy aimed at redirecting private-sector funds towards the older urban areas. A report by the Property Advisory Group (1980) concluded that financial institutions would only become involved in schemes which offered growth of income and asset values comparable with those available from alternative investment opportunities:

> It is therefore unrealistic to hope that any large part of the growing income of the financial institutions can be channelled towards property investment in locations of low demand and high risks as an act of social responsibility towards declining areas. Some relaxations of institutional criteria are possible, but these are more likely to result in investment in schemes where there is confidence that an environment conducive to economic growth is being created. (Property Advisory Group, 1980, p. 23)

The basis of Michael Heseltine's FIG initiative, beyond its immediate publicity impact, was to explore further the opportunities for institutional involvement in older urban areas. No truly new ideas emerged, but some existing ones were given more weight by the group's direct access to the minister. Urban development grants were imported from the United States, with pump-priming given fresh impetus by the term 'leverage'. But, behind the veneer of private sector enthusiasm, FIG reports were stressing the need for continued public-sector investment. It was emphasized that the financial institutions were not philanthropic bodies. They had a social conscience at the margins, but they were not in existence to promote social policy. This was unremarkable, but there was also a suspicion that the commercial nature of the financial institutions did not extend to taking risk. Investment which did not measure up to their rigorous and conservative criteria demanded public-sector underwriting or guarantees. Older urban areas were not an attractive market unless investment opportunities were expanded by public-sector action. In this singular definition of partnership, the private sector was looking for profit; risk was for the public sector. The danger for older urban areas was that in the process of underwriting private-sector risks, limited public-sector funds would be shifted away from direct spending programmes, with no guarantee that investment in partnership ventures would benefit the most seriously disadvantaged sections of the urban population.

Proposals for Urban Renewal
A direct link between general economic performance and improved housing conditions was a clear theme of government thinking: 'improved national economic performance is the most important single key to ensuring that the condition of our housing stock improves rather than deteriorates' (Stanley, 1983). Unfortunately, behind this bland truism,

there was no link between aim and impact. Just as the creation of jobs, even jobs in the inner city, need not benefit the poor who lived in the inner city, there could be no certainty that improved economic performance would lead to higher levels of investment in the poorest housing stock. The shortcoming of inner-city policy was that economic regeneration could not be linked with physical investment or social welfare. Jobs created in the inner city, for example, might not go to people living in the inner city; and, if they did, these people need not necessarily choose to spend any increased discretionary income on maintaining their homes. Consequently, while there was nothing wrong with the analysis of inner-city problems as those of structural economic decline, the emphasis on economic regeneration carried with it no certainty that programmes would benefit people actually living in the poorer, older urban areas.

In the absence of any coherent policy for older housing, the focus of debate began to swing back to more direct ameliorative intervention. By the early 1980s, considerable pressure had built up for a broad review of approaches to urban renewal. Professional groups and local authority organizations continued to put forward proposals which looked for increased levels of activity, and these were paralleled by various experiments aimed at the perceived shortcomings of area approaches to voluntary improvement. The point was made repeatedly that the pendulum had swung too far in favour of renovation, resulting in levels of clearance which were inadequate. At the same time, improvement policy was seen to be over-dependent on the voluntary take-up of improvement grants, which, when concentrated on the worst housing conditions, imposed too high a cost on low-income groups, increasing the problems of implementing policy and leading to high resource costs in return for low capital investment.

Three reports published in 1981, by the Royal Town Planning Institute (RTPI), the Institution of Environmental Health Officers (IEHO), and the Association of Metropolitan Authorities (AMA), all showed a considerable degree of unanimity in their analysis. All were looking for changes in unfitness criteria, for a simplified unitary grant, for increased levels of clearance, and for modifications to the area approach. And all three reports called for extra resources. The IEHO was not specific about the scale of programme they had in mind, but the AMA was looking to expand annual HIP expenditure by at least £1,640 million with a programme of nearly 300,000 public and private sector improvements in addition to a larger clearance programme (AMA, 1980, p. i). The RTPI was slightly more ambitious, looking to improve and clear about 400,000 dwellings a year (RTPI, 1981, p. 5). Underlying these recommendations was a general concern about the condition of the housing stock. None of the reports argued for abandoning the area approach, but they were worried about rates of progress and presented the view that lack of impact had been the result of too little action too late. At the same time, they argued that more effective area action could not occur without systematic block improvement and integrated programmes of environmental upgrading.

Area-Based Policies

Proposals for the reform of area-based policies took place in the context of a wider debate about their effectiveness. All small-area approaches assumed that problems were geographically concentrated and were in some way capable of solution by focusing attention through subsidies, extra resources or special organizational arrangements. The justification was variously described in terms of increased accountability, improved service delivery and social control. In housing, a nineteenth-century preoccupation with slum housing began a tradition of area-based policy which was maintained by GIAs and HAAs. In GIAs, which were based on assumptions later extended to HAAs, it was intended that local authorities should direct their effort towards the improvement of whole areas (MHLG, 1968, para. 11). It was recommended that:

> The effort and resources devoted to improvement provide a much better return when directed to the upgrading of whole areas – the houses and the environment. People are more likely to find it worth their while to cooperate, and to maintain their houses after improvement; and the remaining useful life of whole residential areas is extended by many years. (MHLG, 1969, para. 3)

There were two ideas implicit in this recommendation. First, that it was necessary to carry out rehabilitation on an area basis so that 'neighbourhood effects' did not prevent a long-term improvement in housing conditions. And, second, that the declaration of an improvement area was likely to prevent the further decline of an area within the wider housing market, and might possibly improve its market status. This link between house condition and externalities argued that concerted action generated investment confidence and reversed market decline, with the rate of obsolescence of an area capable of accelerating or decelerating the natural rate of obsolescence of individual houses (Pickup, 1975). The area effect recognized that spatial problems were characterized by externalities, uncertainty and interdependence, and suggested that co-operation would be more productive than competition (Richardson, 1978, p. 358). Consequently, area improvement hoped that the market effects of externalities would be compressed by concentrated action, thus discouraging the economic advantages of non-investment.

Arguments about market externalities, and what might be thought of as a regenerative dynamic resulting from investment confidence, were therefore an important if untested assumption lying behind a justification of the area approach. To a lesser extent it was also suggested that there were cost benefits arising out of the concentration of staff resources, and possible economies of scale for the building industry. But the greatest weight was attached to the concentration of physical and social problems within identifiable areas. Against this rationale were ranged various criticisms: that housing problems were not particularly spatially concentrated; that policies were ameliorative, with the underlying economic problems not capable of solution on an area basis; that there was an over reliance on private capital; and that there was a political motive to show maximum concern at minimum cost.

The Academic Debate

During the 1970s, the effectiveness of area-based policies became the focus of increased attack. It was suggested that deprivation was not as spatially concentrated as had been assumed (Craig and Driver, 1972; Hatch and Sherrott, 1973); that the majority of those suffering from deprivation lived outside small areas of spatial concentration (Donnison, 1974); and that fundamental causes could not be tackled on a small area basis (CDP, 1977). It was conceded that the logic of a spatial component to policy was partly determined by the nature of the problem, and that there was a spatial dimension to the distribution of poorer housing. But even here there was evidence that properties in need of improvement were not concentrated in well defined geographical areas. One of the factors leading to the 1969 Act was the scale of unfitness revealed by the 1967 House Condition Survey. But it was one of the inconsistencies of policy that the legislation sought to achieve significant levels of improvement on an area basis when the survey had shown that about 700,000 unfit dwellings were widely scattered and would have to be dealt with individually rather than within clearance areas (MHLG, 1968, para. 4). Further evidence of a lack of spatial concentration came from the 1976 House Condition Survey. This showed that of nearly 800,000 unfit dwellings 56 per cent could not be dealt with in clearance areas; and that of 2·2 million dwellings requiring repairs costing over £1,000, 86 per cent were outside potential clearance areas (DOE, 1978a, paras 13–14 and table 21). The 1981 survey confirmed that it was the growing problem of disrepair that was less suited to the area approach. Half of all unfit property was assessed as suitable for potential HAAs, and together with GIAs, accounted for three-quarters of all unfits. But disrepair continued to be less spatially concentrated. Of property requiring repairs costing over £2,500, only a quarter fell within potential GIAs or HAAs (DOE, 1982a, table 25).

Evidence concerning the spatial concentration of poor physical conditions was only one component of a wider critique of area housing policies. The concern was with a combination of factors which might act together within a defined geographical area and so constitute a range of social, economic and environmental characteristics consistent with ideas of multiple deprivation. The counter arguments remained, however, that combinations of deprivation were not spatially concentrated; that where there was a concentration people may not be especially disadvantaged by the fact of concentration (they might be no worse off than people of similar age and class living elsewhere); and that, even if priority areas could be identified, conventional programmes rather than area-based policies might be a better way of delivering help (Donnison, 1974). The case was often summed up in terms of 'most poor people do not live in poor areas; and most of the people in poor areas are not themselves poor' (Barnes, 1974). This critique of spatial concentration led Townsend (1979) to support an attack on poverty through policy at the national level.

While conceding the importance of national policy, there continued to be justification for area policies. Holtermann's analysis (1975) showed that housing stress was more spatially concentrated than many other aspects of deprivation. The majority of studies had been concerned with single measures of deprivation. There was little evidence on multiple deprivation, or on the effects of neighbourhood externalities: whether people were worse off for living surrounded by other deprived people – perhaps because of high crime rates, a stigmatised address, or lack of social services (Holtermann, 1978). Deakin (1983, p. 169) pointed to the misleading antithesis between local and national initiatives, with some housing and environmental programmes being necessarily spatial and local in their emphasis. Perhaps of most significance, pragmatic analysis continued to see the administrative and political advantages of a priority area approach, if only because the problems of multiply deprived areas appeared impervious to the efforts of conventional services (Donnison, 1974). They also had a demonstration effect, provided a learning experience and offered an effective way of spending scarce resources (Hall, 1981, p. 62).

The administrative efficiencies and capital economies of scale promised by area policies were advanced by Holtermann (1978, p. 37), who argued that these occurred if programmes were designed, like GIA and HAA policies, to provide a collective good. If environmental improvements, for example, were undertaken in an area where there were large numbers of deprived people, the same resources would increase the aggregate welfare of the deprived more than if the resources were scattered. Consequently, Holtermann concluded that, in focusing on the needs of the multiply deprived, housing policies aimed at improving the physical environment were particularly suited to an area approach given the potential cost savings and externalities involved. Area policy could result in higher take-up amongst the most deprived, thereby being more effective in reducing inequality than looking for the most deprived on a non-area basis (Holtermann, 1978).

The Professional Response
It is in the context of this academic debate that the professional bodies and local authority organizations presented their recommendations on the future of renewal strategies. All were critical not of the approach but of the scale of resources devoted to the problem. Programme spending was described by the IEHO (1981, p. 4) as totally inadequate when viewed in the wider context of the overall housing problem. In the fullest critique, the RTPI maintained that criticism of area-based approaches was misplaced in that the resources had never been made available to allow them to work effectively. There was a spatial component to substandard housing, but it was one which covered sizable tracts of inner urban areas. There was a case for concentrating effort on these areas, but the rate of declaration of area programmes had been insufficient to include all the eligible houses within an effective programme. Consequently, the 'highly selective application of the area approach ... created a complex and divisive hierarchy of priorities within priorities' (RTPI, 1981, p. 8). In effect, the report was suggesting that the area component of a renewal strategy could only operate if the areas were declared and the resources devoted on a scale to match the problem, while also responding to the needs of householders living in poor conditions but who were geographically dispersed.

There was therefore a need for effective allocation of resources to individual households in the worst housing conditions irrespective of location. But where there were concentrated housing problems there remained four main advantages in the area approach. First, it provided an efficient and effective method of achieving public and private investment. It helped to overcome the reluctance of individual owners to invest in the face of uncertainty about the future of the area and, by influencing judgement about the future of the area, encouraged lending by the financial institutions. At the same time, the concentration of effort helped to safeguard public-sector investment. Neither local authority nor housing association investment would be a proper use of public funds if the expenditure had to be written off because improved houses were affected by the deterioration of surrounding property, leading to the need for future clearance action. Second, to be effective in their ambition of creating confidence, environmental improvements need to be carried out on an area basis. Third, and linked to this, environmental improvement needed the maximum possible resident support. There were conflicts of interest and priority which could only be identified through discussion and negotiation with local residents. Finally, the area approach promised an efficent use of local authority staff resources through economies of scale, easier co-ordination and more effective public involvement.

Within this broad support for the small-area approach as a component of renewal strategies, reports by the RTPI, IEHO and AMA all proposed modifications to the existing legislation. The RTPI recommended replacement of HAAs, GIAs and clearance areas by a single housing renewal area. By abandoning the idea of a separate clearance area, demoliton could be integrated more effectively within general renewal action, encouraging a combination of clearance and block improvement. The RTPI did not envisage any limitation on the size of housing renewal areas; there would be no secretary of state powers of intervention; but there would be additional powers of acquisition, clearance and reformed compensation procedures.

In a very similar set of proposals, the IEHO also advocated the replacement of GIAs and HAAs with housing renovation areas, which again would involve more clearance and improvement on a street or block basis, together with similar recommendations for simplified compulsory improvement and revised compensation procedures. Unlike the RTPI, the IEHO report did not acknowledge the problems of dealing with property which might fall outside an area-based strategy; but in turn the RTPI did not offer specific proposals aimed at targeting isolated properties. The IEHO made reference to the special needs of housing in London – by implication, the lack of spatial concentration – but asserted that their concept of a housing renovation area provided a sufficiently flexible framework to deal with the problem (IEHO, 1981, p. 4).

This was not enough to convince the AMA, who were alone in their proposal for two types of area approach. The GIA was to be abolished, with the HAA retained and strengthened – again with more clearance, improvement on a block basis, compulsory improvement and a review of compensation arrangements (AMA, 1981). However, to tackle the problem of poor housing where there was a lack of spatial concentration, the AMA advocated the use of housing improvement zones (HIZs) along the lines proposed by Hammersmith and Fulham. These were areas substantially larger than typical HAAs which merited intervention but did not need intensive treatment. The approach envisaged was essentially voluntary, but with back-up powers to deal with pockets of poor physical condition.

Housing Improvement Zones
The concept of housing improvement zones arose out of a local need for an area approach more suitable than HAAs or GIAs, combined with a public-sector pump-priming role to bridge the gap between capital needs and public resources. The London Borough of Hammersmith and Fulham contained large areas of housing which were not thought suitable for statutory area declaration, but which contained quite high proportions of substandard housing. The HIZ was designed to promote the improvement of housing over a larger area than would be the case in an HAA, while recognizing the management advantages of an area strategy and the need for such an approach if the policy was to receive the support of the private sector. Based on the Greater London House Condition Survey (GLC,

1981) the private sector repair bill in Hammersmith and Fulham was £107·5 million at 1979 prices, compared with the authority's HIP allocation in 1982/3 of £18·6 million for all purposes. Simply to service a debt equivalent to the private-sector repair cost would require £14·4 million a year (Hammersmith and Fulham, 1981). With this disparity between problems and resources, the local authority – like many others – was forced to look at initiatives which could harness additional private-sector resources. With their emphasis on voluntary improvement, HAAs and GIAs had always sought to encourage investment by residents, but in the climate of the 1980s authorities like Hammersmith and Fulham became interested in the more active support of building societies and banks, and in the involvement of local builders, architects and surveyors. In slightly different forms, each component of this strategy had been tested elsewhere. In Hammersmith, as in other parts of the country, building societies were happy to announce special allocations and put out some free publicity. Detailed technical advice for grant applicants through an agency service could be offered through private architects and housing associations, to supplement the local authority's own service working as part of the project team. The problem was to make these additional resources available over a substantial area. The size of an individual HIZ raised questions about the ability of the local authority to intervene on the required scale. Compared with the potential ability of GIAs and HAAs to achieve effective and efficient use of resources, the danger of larger areas was that they might dissipate the impact of resources to the point at which special status was effectively meaningless.

In selecting an area where the HIZ concept could be introduced, the authority was looking for conditions rather better than a typical HAA, but with more problems in the privately rented sector than might be found in a GIA. It therefore sought an area with at least 60 per cent of households having exclusive use of amenities, an equal number of owner-occupiers and private tenants, and at least half of all properties in single occupancy. Combined with this, the area was to exhibit evidence of improvement activity and characteristics which would encourage building society investment. The HIZ, by definition, was not seen to require the level of public sector capital investment needed in HAAs – in terms of acquisition, rehabilitation and compulsory action. Instead, the local authority's role was to direct public and private resources towards the people and houses in greatest need. In this sense, the authority was to co-ordinate a range of people and agencies involved in the improvement process, providing a framework for action within which to create a partnership between the public and private sectors.

The first HIZ was in Fulham, selected because it was likely to attract private-sector investment, and an area where house prices were increasing very rapidly. With the purchase price of small unimproved terrace houses coming on the market at nearly £50,000 in early 1984, any success in operating a HIZ in Fulham did not mean that the approach would work elsewhere. In fact, the early years of the first HIZ achieved a relatively slow rate of improvement, with no startling evidence that substantial private-sector finance had been drawn in. Though admittedly a relatively crude measure, public-sector grants totalled more than four times building society lending on improvement loans. There were no evidence that the activities of the financial institutions had been influenced by the existence of the HIZ, or that housing conditions for existing residents could be improved in less propitious circumstances by a combination of reduced public-sector intervention and more active promotion of loans and reverse mortgaging by the banks and building societies.

Neighbourhood Housing Services
In its careful selection of areas which were potentially attractive to private investment, combined with an emphasis on co-ordinated action in a partnership between public and private sectors, there was common ground between Hammersmith's HIZ and that of Neighbourhood Housing Services (NHS). Introduced in America, NHS represented a partnership between residents, local government and private financial institutions to revitalize a local neighbourhood. Their primary concern was with the improvement of the environment, and with fostering self-help and owner-occupation. A central organization, the Neighborhood Re-investment Corporation (NRC), was responsible for setting up NHS programmes, assisting with staff training functions and servicing the revolving loan fund. This provided finance for those people considered unbankable propositions. The NRC established a revolving fund for each NHS project, withdrawing once the programme was in operation, leaving a local self-supporting organization. Considerable emphasis was given to these revolving funds. They were under the control of individual NHS programmes, with each loan vetted by a subcommittee of the NHS board. There was some suggestion that the criteria adopted were at least as strict as those of the lending institutions. In practice, the default rates on the revolving fund were very low, and while this seems to have encouraged the conventional lending institutions to reappraise their own criteria it questioned the flexibility and utility of a high risk fund.

The NHS concept stemmed from a successful experiment in Pittsburgh in the early 1970s (Ahlbrandt and Brophy, 1975). Each NHS was established as a private non-profit corporation having a board of directors, a full-time staff and a prospective life of about five years. Residents formed a majority on the board, together with representatives from local government and the private sector – banks, savings and loan associations, and credit unions. The local financial institutions involved with NHS agreed to make loans at market rates to all owners who met normal lending criteria. They were asked to take into account the fact that the area was likely to improve, and therefore to be more flexible in their lending policy. The financial institutions contributed to the operating costs of the NHS, with these contributions being tax-deductible. Financial support also came from the NRC and relevant local authority (Huntley, 1980, pp. 17–21).

The intention of NHS, therefore, was to bring together all those with an interest in improving the neighbourhood's housing conditions, environment and social facilities. Local finance and insurance institutions were represented because their willingness to lend money was central to the area's future. And residents were seen as the key to promoting neighbourhood identity in a way which could encourage and sustain the physical and financial efforts being made to revitalize the area. This was the meaning of 'turning round' the neighbourhood: reversing not only its physical but its psychological decline. As for 'leverage', NHS were seen to be effective in using a small amount of public funds to encourage a larger amount of private investment. As with the British notion of pump-priming grants within an area programme, the willingness of the public sector to invest in an area was seen to promote confidence in the neighbourhood's continued improvement, and so make it attractive for private-sector investment.

As part of an NHS programme, staff provided three main services to local residents: first, technical advice on rehabilitation, covering survey and design, through tendering, to the supervision of work on site; second, financial advice to residents on the availability of improvement loans; and, third, the promotion of community involvement designed to strengthen 'neighbourhood pride'. Each of these elements had its parallels in British initiatives, but this did not lessen the enthusiasm with which the NHS concept was greeted by those searching for a high-profile response to urban problems which promised a private-sector involvement. As with other American policies, however, there was good reason not to adopt them uncritically in Britain. The role of local authorities in British urban renewal was much more firmly established than in the United States, making it more difficult to construct a convincing case for a new, non-governmental agency. To justify such an agency, there would have to be a real expectation that dramatic new impetus could be provided, with a better chance of achieving voluntary co-operation than through a local authority urban renewal team, and of achieving new forms of investment beyond those which could be devised by partnerships between local authorities and building societies. Here too, there were differences. Locally based savings and loan organizations in America were more susceptible to pressures for community reinvestment than were the national building societies and banks in Britain.

Of all the lessons arising from housing action areas under the 1974 Act, perhaps the most important was that voluntary improvement was a resource-intensive activity, and that it was generally those local authorities who devoted the necessary resources who achieved successful implementation. It was in the context of resources being unavailable on the required scale that approaches were sought which offered intensive support and action within a local area without drawing exclusively on the public sector. Perhaps the main reason to be cautious of these approaches was not at the ideological but at the practical level. It would take more than co-ordination to secure investment in an unfavourable area. But the thinking behind NHS could not be dismissed out of hand. Its strength was that it drew attention to the small-area, single-faceted character of British urban renewal. The American programme made the point that the inter-relationship between the local economy, the housing market and the community's achievements were very important, and needed to be considered together rather than as separate and isolated elements.

Increased Clearance

In their calls for a single type of housing renewal area, both the IEHO and the RTPI envisaged an increased level of clearance as part of an approach which recognized the need to integrate clearance and improvement programmes. The RTPI saw the need to adapt a process which had originally been designed for comprehensive area clearance on public health criteria. It was suggested that the new aim should be to achieve sensitive demolition of small groups of property, either on the criteria that the houses could not be improved to the ten-point standard at reasonable cost, or that the land was needed for the benefit of local residents. The IEHO recommended the need to look closely at current clearance procedures with a view to devising policies which were capable of speeding up the process. They were particularly concerned that selective clearance had become very difficult under the provisions of Circular 13/81 (DOE, 1981a). This had indicated that government did not intend to confirm CPOs where owners declared an intention to carry out improvements. It was felt that such a policy would have a disastrous effect on clearance programmes. Like the RTPI, the IEHO wished to achieve clearance on a broad range of criteria, pointing out that the change of emphasis from clearance to retention had made this impossible. Its report argued the need to take action based on the obsolescence of a group or area of houses, taking into account factors like fitness, the possibility of improvement to the ten-point standard, their planning arrangement and level of congestion, and their environment and services (IEHO, 1981, para. 5.11). So both reports were broadly consistent in proposing that clearance in a renewal area should be on the basis of physical obsolescence, site assembly for redevelopment, or for environmental improvements or community facilities.

Related to clearance proposals, the RTPI, IEHO and AMA reports all proposed changes in unfitness criteria to include basic amenities and electric lighting. The IEHO's proposals were more comprehensive and involved thermal insulation, noise insulation and facilities for space heating. All three reports also proposed revised compensation procedures. The RTPI argued there was a strong case for market value compensation to speed up acquisition and to minimize the use of compulsory purchase (RTPI, 1981, p. 48). The IEHO (1981, para. 5.12) proposed compensation for tenanted property on the basis of existing property value, separate disturbance payments for owner-occupiers similar to those received by tenants, and the scrapping of well maintained payments, with tenants receiving instead a proportion of compensation assessed in relation to the investment they had made in improvement and repair. The AMA (1981, p. 14) combined these views with a call for a single system of compensation for owners and tenants, based on market value, and providing associated payments for disturbance and standards of maintenance.

While all three reports argued for more clearance activity, and the need for this to be sensitively managed, there were no detailed proposals to achieve these aims. The call for varying levels of clearance within a new form of renewal or renovation area was consistent with ideas for gradual renewal put forward at the time of the 1974 Act. It was this theme which was explored by the RTPI report, drawing a distinction between cellular renewal, which was considered to have 'several practical limitations given the urgency and scale of bad conditions', and community-based redevelopment, which was thought capable of meeting housing and social objectives within clearance areas (RTPI, 1981, p. 4).

Gradual Renewal

The mounting opposition to slum clearance during the 1960s influenced the switch of policy towards improvement. But the idea of clearance was not abandoned by the 1974 Act. Instead, the circulars made reference to gradual renewal – the management of a continuous process of small-scale change within older housing areas. The 1973 White Paper preferred this notion of gradual renewal to the existing policy of comprehensive redevelopment. There were implicit criticisms of large-scale slum clearance in the White Paper's view that gradual renewal could solve bad housing conditions without disrupting communities or leaving large areas of land derelict for long periods of time. Continuous small-scale clearance would not cause distress through compulsory acquisition, destroying people's familiar and comfortable environment, and diminishing the choice of house type, tenure and price (DOE, 1973b, para. 15). In a circular accompanying the 1974 Act, local authorities were urged to pursue a policy of flexible and co-ordinated renewal involving rehabilitation, new building and small-scale clearance with a continuous process of gradual renewal sustaining and reinforcing the vitality of a neighbourhood in ways which were responsive to changing social and physical needs (DOE, 1975a, paras 5 and 23). As an approach, gradual renewal saw housing renovation operating flexible standards, with clearance and redevelopment scheduled for those properties considered to be beyond improvement. Proceeding on a small-area basis, it was envisaged that initial plans would usually identify a short-term programme of firm commitments, while being less specific about rebuilding in the medium term, and with later clearance related to the impact of improvement programmes (Gibson and Langstaff, 1977).

In the history of ideas, attribution is surrounded by uncertainty. Moore writes that within central government the concept was first suggested in 1966 (DOE, 1975c, p. 2) and put forward in the plan for Greater Peterborough (Hancock and Hawkes, 1967). Credit has also been given to Frieden (1964), Schoor (1964) and Greer (1965) in the United States for their work in developing the concept of gradual renewal as a way of accounting for user objectives. Others have pointed to the writings of Geddes and his description of 'conservative surgery' (Gibson and Langstaff, 1982, p. 104). Whatever the source, however, in the immediate build-up to the 1974 Act, the debate was influenced by McKie (1971; 1974) and Moore (1971).

In 1971, McKie expanded the idea of cellular renewal developed with the Peterborough planning team. His paper investigated the economic function of twilight housing, and advocated that improvement and small-scale redevelopment should be matched to demand so that marginal households would not be pushed out of the market. The concept was to restrict the role of purely physical planning to that of providing a broad framework within which neighbourhoods could be regenerated through the management of social and economic forces. The loose planning framework would ensure that present redevelopment did not prejudice the ultimate redevelopment of other sites in the area, while encouraging the inflow of private investment for infill development (McKie, 1971, p. 61). Unlike Taylor (1973) this did not imply the orderly phasing of redevelopment but, as with Habraken (1972), derived from a physiological analogy of urban form as an organic structure. McKie (1974, p. 282) saw regeneration corresponding

> to the spontaneous pursuit of economic advantage, corporate welfare and individual expression within a set of social rules which created the medieval English market town ... The natural pattern of redevelopment must occur in pockets rather than sequential blocks if it is to follow functional changes rather than attempt itself to impose change ahead of demand.

In the same year as McKie's contribution, Moore published a short paper on progressive redevelopment. This was based on work in Leicester over the preceding two years. As originally outlined, the concept involved a greater degree of forward planning than was envisaged by McKie. Moore (1971) was proposing that a procedure combining rehabilitation and enviromental improvement with a phased infiltration of new housing could enable physical renewal to be implemented while still encouraging the development of an existing social fabric. Thus, while both papers were proposing that redevelopment of an area should be phased over a long period of time, they differed on the extent to which this redevelopment could be planned. Moore initially suggested a future life for groups of property according to their tenure distribution, physical condition, potential for improvement and their relation to other development proposals.

There were problems with the implied rigidity of a long-term strategy based on an assessed future life for property, and subsequent formulations emphasized the need for a continuous process of monitoring. As unimproved or partly improved houses came on to the market, they could be re-surveyed and either further improved or demolished. This was not seen as a *laissez-faire* approach. The neighbourhood plan would set out the broad framework for any long-term changes in the infrastructure of the area: major traffic reorganization, parking provision, the creation of sites for large community or commercial buildings, or provision of open space. Within this framework, piecemeal incremental renewal could take place bearing in mind local design guidance and the compromising of future development.

McKie, on the other hand, always avoided any reference to the need to assign a future life to property. He proposed that analysis of the plan area would identify functionally 'soft' areas where change or redevelopment would be appropriate, while improvement would occur in functionally 'hard' areas. Once this process had begun, implementation would become a cyclical process in which changes in the pattern of hard and soft areas were established and appropriate responses devised. McKie went into some detail on the criteria for hard and soft areas and his general philosophy suggested that soft area redevelopment would be for immediate action, while hard area property would not be blighted by any forward planning proposals. However, it is not clear how the practical conflicts would be resolved - for example, the treatment of a functionally hard area influenced by long-term planning proposals.

In recognizing the unresolved aspects of detailed implementation, McKie accepted that cellular renewal was little more than a research concept in search of a pilot study (McKie, 1974, p. 283). In many senses, this remained the case ten years later. Despite circular guidance, the type of fine-grained approach to clearance and rebuilding anticipated by both McKie and Moore had rarely been implemented. The reasons for this seem to have been largely practical. To prepare and continually revise detailed proposals implied a substantial resource input and questioned whether such an individualized approach was a feasible response to the scale of housing problems being faced. While its advocates reached for ecological metaphors in advancing their ideas of 'watchful management', the scale of continuous input and daunting problems of co-ordination made the implementation of more traditional clearance or improvement areas simple by comparison.

Faced with this kind of complexity, the clearance element of gradual renewal continued to be associated with a more coarse-grained approach than envisaged in cellular renewal. In Rochdale, for example, the local authority's non-statutory 'community-based action areas' were a planning tool devised to provide a comprehensive approach to urban renewal across a relatively large geographical area. GIAs and HAAs were just two of the tools of implementation across a range of possible action covering the provision of services, employment and traffic management. Clearance action was determined early in the programme to avoid any blighting effects. For people affected by clearance, the policy was that residents should have the opportunity to be rehoused within the action area and to have a choice of tenure, implying the need for public-sector new-build provision as well as private-sector and housing association development. This emphasis on local rehousing was an important response to criticism of earlier clearance programmes, and was a component of various community-based approaches to redevelopment.

Community-Based Redevelopment

There was nothing new about the search for more sensitive clearance procedures. Phased demolition and redevelopment to rehouse existing residents was being discussed in the 1930s (Barnes, 1931). In the 1960s, social dislocation attributed to comprehensive redevelopment was responsible for a re-examination of the community-based approach and its application in projects like Swinbrooke (MacMurray, 1973; Redpath and Chivers, 1974), Rocheford (Gibson and Langstaff, 1982), Byker (Malpass and Murie, 1982) and Glodwick (Barr and Urwin, 1977). Arising out of these projects came some idea of the difficulties of phasing clearance and rebuilding programmes to accommodate the demand for local rehousing.

The Byker experience in Newcastle was an example of incremental policy-making, with the idea of community rehousing gathering momentum as the 1960s clearance programme proceeded, but arriving too late to achieve the revised objectives. In 1960 the area's population was estimated at about 17,500. By 1967, at least 5,000 had been rehoused outside the area, with no new houses under construction in Byker itself (Malpass and Murie, 1982, p. 126). It was not until 1970 that outline proposals were put forward for the construction of about 2,400 dwellings for a rolling programme of local rehousing. In the event it is reported that the phasing was designed to produce a steady supply of new housing, rather than to maximize local rehousing opportunities. This problem of phasing, increased by delays in new-build completion and accentuated by people moving away from the area, meant that the Byker population fell to nearly a third of its 1960 level by the end of 1975, while in 1979 there were 10,000 dwellings under construction or planned, with only about fifty local people remaining to be rehoused (Malpass and Murie, 1982, pp. 129-30). The conclusion drawn from this experience was that community rehousing was a policy added on to redevelopment objectives, and that while it was a genuine goal throughout the 1970s it was in conflict with early decisions to allocate a significant area of land for a proposed motorway, to reduce residential densities and, later, to achieve rapid redevelopment and continuity of work for contractors. To maximize local rehousing would have required a more deliberately phased approach and a much extended development period (Malpass and Murie, 1982, pp. 129-31).

Phasing for local rehousing was more central to the implementation of clearance in the Glodwick area of Oldham. Within Glodwick a clearance area containing nearly 250 dwellings was confirmed in 1974. A local action group gave evidence at the public inquiry on the basis of a survey carried out with the help of CDP. Their case was not opposition to clearance action, but that people should have the opportunity for Council rehousing in the immediate area through a programme of phased redevelopment and priority allocations. This was subsequently accepted as council policy for the area, and a three-phase programme devised to release the land necessary for new housing. In the absence of cleared sites for a local programme, residents affected by phase 1 demolition required temporary rehousing over a period of several years while waiting for their new homes. Meanwhile, families in phases 2 and 3 were also faced with the prospect of perhaps a three-year wait in rapidly deteriorating environmental conditions. Some consequently changed their minds and accepted permanent rehousing outside the area.

The reduced number of people wishing to stay in the area was a fortunate outcome, as there were doubts about the ability of lower density redevelopment to provide for all those initially requiring local rehousing. Nevertheless, the phasing problem associated with lower density redevelopment created difficulties comparable to the Byker experience. The scale of phase 1 clearance had to be relatively large in order to meet the anticipated need to rehouse residents in later phases. This meant that more than half the residents who needed to be rehoused from the area were in the first phase, for whom rehousing was the most difficult to achieve (Barr and Urwin, 1977, p. 15). One solution was seen as the use of short-life property, involving temporary repair and improvement by a local housing association. Where administrative difficulties and delays could be overcome, this was thought to be a means by which the impact of blight could be considerably reduced. Another emerging approach involved an extension of the phasing principle to encompass inter-CPO programmes. Residents in a later clearance area within Glodwick were able to benefit from rehousing in the earlier clearance areas without having to accept a temporary decant.

There were similarities here with pre-allocation policies in Leeds, which were linked to a co-ordinated programme of clearance and new housing starts. This was thought to be valuable as a way of reducing uncertainty amongst people affected by clearance proposals and of allowing some flexibility in allocation (Gibson and Langstaff, 1982, p. 268). In Rocheford, the first pre-allocation experiment in Leeds, an assessment by the tenants' association concluded that the experiment was a success, though problems remained in relation to compensation and blight. It was feared that pre-allocation might encourage early agreement of compensation and disturbance payments, which would prove inadequate as a result of inflation when moving perhaps two years later. And while pre-allocation reduced uncertainty, the physical problem of clearance remained. Some families still had to be the last to move, experiencing the isolation and vandalism of an area with a high proportion of vacant and derelict houses (Rocheford Tenants' Association, 1976).

Experience in places like Oldham and Leeds brought together the three elements identified as characteristic of community-based renewal: a commitment to rehouse on site all those who wished to remain; redevelopment in small phases to reduce the impact of demolition and to allow rehousing from one phase to the next; and a programme of public involvement in the redevelopment process (Frost and Sharman, 1975). By adopting this response to criticisms of the redevelopment process it was argued that rehousing could be made more sensitive to the needs of residents, preserving the social continuity of the area and identifying the changing needs of the community through their involvement in the redevelopment process. In this way, and on the basis of the limited number of schemes which had been implemented, the 1981 RTPI report concluded that 'in circumstances where substantial area clearance is considered essential in housing stock terms, community based redevelopment enables social objectives to be met' (RTPI, 1981, p. 14). Compared with traditional methods, however, it was more staff-intensive and required more careful programming. It was not therefore offered as the solution to urban renewal problems in the absence of adequate resources.

Grant Reform

The reports of the RTPI, IEHO and AMA all called for a unified or unitary grant to replace the existing fragmented and overlapping structure. As part of a general plea for consolidating legislation, the grant system was seen to have grown incrementally since 1949 in response to changing patterns of ownership and reassessments of standards, resulting in a complex structure of grants and legislation. The proposed unitary grant was intended to give local authorities discretion on eligible works and grant percentages for any expenditure to bring private houses up to a full standard, the emphasis being to secure the fabric of the dwelling. The RTPI was particularly opposed to the idea of basic improvement standards, as a kind of holding operation, because of the difficult choices it presented for the future. They rejected the 'more for less' approach of the 1977 Housing Policy Review and subsequent legislation, proposing instead that the ten-point standard should be treated as the acceptable minimum. It was recognized that this presented problems, with an insistence on high standards leading to limited grant take-up. The lesson of experience was that comprehensive improvement could only be achieved if adequate public funds were devoted to provide more substantial assistance to private owners, or to sustain major programmes of social ownership (RTPI, 1981, p. 14). The report was less specific, however, on means of resolving an emphasis on high standards with its recommendation on local authority discretion.

While the IEHO also supported renovation to a full standard, their proposals implied less radical changes to the legislative framework (IEHO, 1981, para. 5.20). The RTPI report proposed that local authorities should be given complete discretion on work eligible for grant and over the interpretation of standards. The majority of conditions governing eligibility criteria would be removed, and replaced by a set of model rules which local authorities would be free to adapt to local circumstances (RTPI, 1981, p. 44). In principle, similar arguments applied to grant percentages and cost limits, given that central government had global control over local housing expenditure. If this proved too radical, the report concurred with the IEHO in recommending the need for flexibility in awarding grants of up to 100 per cent, depending on income. The index-linking of cost limits was also advocated, because these had been dogged by infrequent reviews, eroding the real value of grants over the intervening periods and leading to similar houses being improved to different standards.

On the improvement of tenanted property, all three reports felt that new powers were needed to require landlords to install amenities and carry out repairs. These procedures needed to be quicker and to permit higher standards of improvement in certain circumstances. There was a common concern that the problems of tenanted property continued to be tackled with legal provisions which had their roots in the sanitary legislation of the nineteenth century. In its current form this was complex, cumbersome and largely ineffective. It had been calculated that an astute landlord could drag out compulsory improvement procedures by up to thirty months (RTPI, 1981, p. 22). One route to reform was seen to be through the proposed redefinition of unfitness to include basic amenities and a supply of electricity. This would bring more property within the scope of 1957 Housing Act repair notice procedures and marginalize the value of the

1974 compulsory improvement procedures. The RTPI proposed that the 1957 Act procedures should be remodelled to include improvement to a ten-point standard and allowing the landlord to serve a purchase notice on the local authority. If the landlord did not serve a purchase notice or a 'notice of intention to improve the property' within a specified time, this failure would be deemed a purchase notice (RTPI, 1981, p. 49). In some ways, the IEHO's proposals were more far-reaching. While being equally critical of the complexities associated with compulsion, the report argued that a statutory obligation on owners to improve their property should come automatically with area declaration, linked with the availability of 100 per cent grants in certain cases (IEHO, 1981, p. 9).

Enveloping
The broad consensus emerging from the reports was that comprehensive house improvement on an area basis was difficult to achieve, with legislation restricting the operation of voluntary improvement, while making public-sector intervention through compulsion and acquisition difficult to achieve. A view stemming from Birmingham, and influential in the RTPI and IEHO reports, was that the promotion of improvement grants on a one-off basis was not the way forward, and that there was a need for a more radical approach which dealt with the fabric of properties in a comprehensive manner while still retaining the flexibility for individual improvement. All three reports recommended powers to improve property on a block basis along the lines of Birmingham's envelope experiment.

The background to urban renewal policy in Birmingham has been described elsewhere (see, for example, Paris and Blackaby, 1979; Gibson and Langstaff, 1982). By 1978, the city had declared twenty-seven HAAs containing 13,800 dwellings, but progress in achieving improvement was very slow. Of the 10,000 properties in private ownership, only 6 per cent had received grants after nearly five years of work by eight area-based renewal teams. A massive amount of time and effort was being expended for relatively little return. It was felt that the urban renewal teams were trying to sell grants which were fixed at an inadequate cost level, were offered with restrictive legislative conditions and were aimed at the poorest people living in the worst housing, requiring high levels of expenditure by those least able to afford their share of the contribution. At this stage, Birmingham concluded that an emphasis on one-off voluntary improvement was ineffective, and that the main thrust of their renewal programme required a more radical solution. It was decided that the problem needed to be tackled on an area basis dealing with large blocks or streets at a time. The problem was initially approached by trying to assemble and co-ordinate individual grant applications, but this proved to be resource-intensive and time-consuming. A solution was seen in the simplified administration of contracts, requiring no owner's contribution, and thereby minimizing the time taken to assemble a programme. The starting point was Operation Face-lift, financed by the inner city construction programme announced in the 1977 Budget. Under this programme, loan sanction for expenditure of £2·3 million was obtained for work on just over 750 houses within two HAAs. Government subsidy was at 75 per cent, with average expenditure running at £1,900 a house for repairs to roofs and external frontages. This was all carried out at no cost to property owners on the assumption that external renovation would encourage grant take-up for internal works.

With the face-lift scheme under way, the idea was extended to cover complete external structural renovation. This programme became known as enveloping and was originally financed through the inner city partnership programme. The first project went on site in January 1980 as a £1·4 million contract, with final unit costs at around £4,000. Pre-contract delay occurred because the DOE did not approve the original ICPP submission. Their reservations included the lack of an owner's contribution and a concern for the public expenditure implications of an expanded programme. It was the incoming Conservative government who approved the scheme on an experimental basis in August 1979. This was for a total of £6 million over three years, with the annual programme running at around 500 dwellings a year.

Because of delays on the first ICPP envelope contract, the programme was actually preceded by Birmingham's first block improvement scheme. This was an extension of enveloping to include internal and external work within a single contract. The owners' contributions were restricted to their share of the grant up to the eligible expense limit. Most owners were treated as hardship cases, meaning that their contribution was £500 – under the grant limits prevailing until 1980 – for a full improvement scheme costing about £12,000 per house. Subsidy was limited to improvement grants and environmental grants, with the residual amount not attracting a government contribution.

Encouraged by early progress on face-lift, the city actively campaigned for a specific exchequer subsidy to support a proposed expansion of the enveloping programme to include around 2,000 properties a year. The approach seemed to have found favour with other local authorities, and answered professional concern about the scale of housing deterioration. In this sense, enveloping was not principally a response to social problems and housing need, but an attack on physical conditions. It offered a political response to evidence of increased disrepair disclosed by the English House Condition Survey. It also offered a high-profile capital programme without an overall increase in government spending. The DOE was initially reluctant to concede the principle of an owner's contribution to grant work in the context of enveloping – partly, perhaps, because as a precondition of the availability of traditional grants an owner's contribution effectively reduced levels of public spending. There was no such precondition on public spending for enveloping. Consequently, the 'capacity for the rapid deployment of public sector funds ... is almost awesome in comparison with the much lengthier process of municipalisation' (Gibson, 1979). However, because most local authorities were coming out of subsidy, it was possible for government to contribute to capital works while total housing expenditure continued to decline in real terms. It also had the political attraction of helping owner-occupiers, while much of the capital spending was directed at private builders. For this reason, a construction industry which was experiencing high levels of unemployment and was looking for reflation through capital programmes actively joined local authorities and professional bodies in supporting the enveloping approach.

Following the DOE's own evaluation of Birmingham's approach, together with additional envelope experiments in Leeds, Leicester and Hull, the Minister for Housing announced a national programme of enveloping in October 1982. The circular following this announcement ended the experimental funding of enveloping under the Urban Programme, and permitted all authorities to carry out this type of work in HAAs with an exchequer contribution of 75 per cent (DOE 1982c). The circular envisaged a wide variety of schemes, from small groups of dwellings to entire blocks. The subsidy was to be made available through increased cost limits on environmental works. The early announcements were unclear about the nature of expenditure control, but reference was made to a £750 million programme over ten years, with £60 million allocated in 1983/4. However, the early response of local authorities was slow, with the bulk of a projected incurred expenditure of £45 million accounted for by Birmingham's own programme. The city's total expenditure on improvement grants and various forms of enveloping increased from £8·2 million in 1978/9 to £23 million in 1980/1, and £75 million in 1983/4.

The initial lack of response from other local authorities was surprising given their earlier enthusiasm. A partial explanation was that some authorities saw enveloping as a solution which had emerged out of the special problems of Birmingham, and was not applicable to housing conditions within HAAs in other parts of the country. This was said by smaller urban authorities without large areas of nineteenth-century terraced housing, and by inner London boroughs faced with substantial multi-occupied property. Perry (1983) pointed out that Birmingham's size limited the direct applicability of their programme, arguing that other cities would naturally want to begin with small contracts on selected difficult blocks. For this reason, and because of the higher element of central government subsidy for repair grants, some authorities preferred to carry out smaller-scale block schemes using 90 per cent repair grants in co-ordinated contracts. This approach had also been used in Birmingham but, though unit costs were found to be competitive, any savings were thought to be outweighed by the cost of administering the individual grants and separate contracts.

Early lack of progress was also attributed to central government delay. Procedural and administrative restrictions surrounded the early stages of HIP-funded enveloping, and might explain the small number of schemes approved in the first year (Perry, 1983). Because the enveloping programme was funded through the environmental grant, the minister could vary the percentage and the cost limit in special cases, but only with Treasury consent. By choosing to introduce enveloping without new legislation, the DOE adopted a special power for general use, and by placing the Treasury within the approval procedure, increased the paperwork, the scrutiny and the delay. Birmingham proceeded with work on submitted envelope schemes in advance of formal approval. Most other authorities did not, and found their proposals delayed for several months. Birmingham, in its turn, experienced the administrative consequences of mainstream funding. As the DOE began to tighten up their envelope procedures, the familiar conflict emerged between public accountability and scheme implementation. Rapid and relatively informal procedures, adopted by Birmingham in order to maximize the scale of their capital programme, sat uneasily with central government concern with value for money and overall control of public expenditure. With an apparently inverse relationship between administration and capital spending, the success of Birmingham in promoting a national enveloping programme through government subsidy threatened, in turn, to undermine the city's original concept of a speedy, large-scale programme with a minimum of pre-declaration administration.

Though these threats were very apparent by 1984, the ideas behind enveloping remained important. As practised in Birmingham at the time of Circular 29/82 (DOE, 1982c), enveloping demonstrated a significant shift in approach and attitude to urban renewal. The justifications for the approach were wide-ranging, covering scale and economies of operation, standards of work, structural coherence and market externalities.

The first justification for enveloping was that it was carried out at no cost to owners, and was therefore capable of achieving urban renewal quickly and in a way commensurate with the scale of the problem. Enveloping could be used in a selective way to deal with a difficult group of properties within a programme of voluntary grant take-up. But perhaps its main attraction remained the potential ability of enveloping to tackle renewal problems quickly. It enabled resources to be concentrated in an area through a planned and controlled investment programme, rapidly implemented on a street-by-street basis. It was difficult to envisage any other way in which such large-scale investment could be directed at the existing housing stock. It was administratively far simpler than processing the equivalent value of improvement grants; the resource costs were substantially lower; and in programming terms it gave a much greater level of control over the success of renewal policy. Implementation was no longer dependent on the uncertainty of voluntary grant take-up.

Enveloping therefore promised the opportunity to embark on a more ambitious and predictable urban renewal programme, which was easier for local authorities to implement. However, this simplicity was relative, as the block approach had its own complexities. Contract management could present problems, and circumstances could be imagined in which well managed clearance would be a better experience than poorly managed enveloping. In public meetings prior to enveloping work, residents in Birmingham were usually warned of the discomfort which faced them. Though realistic, this highlighted problems facing residents living on what was effectively a building site for periods of several months. Survey evidence suggested that about half the residents in an envelope area encountered serious or slight difficulties with mess and disruption. More worrying, perhaps, was the apparent lack of a learning curve. Compared with initial enveloping contracts, later schemes did not show a lower incidence of operational problems or higher levels of resident satisfaction (McCarthy and Buckley, 1982, p. 19).

Early work in Birmingham provided experience and well documented guidance on enveloping procedures (Community Forum, 1983) which stressed the need for a project manager, a local office and good communications with residents. Confidence, understanding and mutual respect were all said to have a vital role to play (Brunt et al., 1982, p. 133) in a processs which involved great upheaval and numerous opportunities for problems to arise out of poor communications.

The second point advanced in favour of enveloping was that it was cheaper than municipalization. Birmingham's first five years of urban renewal affected only 6 per cent of privately owned property within declared HAAs. In the city's review of options in 1978, reduced standards of improvement were rejected because they might increase uncertainty and discourage building society investment. Equally, while acknowledging that the pendulum had swung too far in favour of improvement, an increased programme of clearance was not thought to be feasible. Not only was council new building inadequate for the rehousing which would be required, but there was likely to be opposition from people who had already improved their homes as a result of grant activity encouraged by the project teams. The final option was a large-scale programme of municipalization. But this implied bringing property into public ownership on a scale which had massive capital implications. The city already had a stock of 34,000 interwar council dwellings requiring modernization; there was little enthusiasm for extensive use of cumbersome compulsory purchase powers; and, in contradiction of policies to promote owner-occupation, it could leave the inner-areas dominated by public-sector ownership.

Consequently, the policy of enveloping emerged as a way of achieving physical improvement while not involving a change of tenure. The cost was estimated to be half that of municipalization and subsequent public-sector improvement. But while enveloping was, at least initially, cheaper than municipalization or clearance, it still represented a relatively expensive policy when compared with the traditional grant approach. Envelope was, in effect, a 100 per cent grant on external repair. Together with the wider availability of 90 per cent grants, it represented the most generous framework of financial assistance to be offered to home owners, and raised issues about the appropriate level of capital subsidy to property owners in the absence of other reforms of housing finance. There was criticism of a policy which aimed subsidy at bricks and mortar irrespective of people's ability to pay. Enveloping was a physical process blind to tenure or income distinctions. It was a costly way of supporting private ownership in older urban areas, but it emerged from an analysis which suggested that programmes of social ownership were even more expensive.

Though the lack of an owner's contribution to enveloping changed the 'investment partnership', there was some evidence that grant take-up increased following envelope work. With the external fabric secured, internal improvements were more likely to fall within eligible expense limits, while the investment might seem more secure and worthwhile. Of enveloped areas surveyed in Birmingham, 70 per cent of owners living in unimproved property said they intended to carry out internal work following the envelope contract, with about 40 per cent of respondents attributing this intention to the fact that external work had been done. There was an inverse relationship between the pre-enveloping condition of property and the propensity to carry out internal work. The worse the original condition of property, the more likely owners were to say that enveloping prompted them to carry out internal improvements (McCarthy and Buckley, 1982, p. 47).

The third argument for enveloping concerned possible economies of scale for administration and building work. Given a concern for the ratio of resource costs to capital works, traditional area improvement policy was seen as a way of utilizing staff more effectively. But, as authorities tried to target grant take-up towards the areas and people most in need of help, the operation became more staff-intensive. Hence the justification for enveloping: that the higher levels of capital support to home owners could be offset by lower staff costs through savings in grant promotion. The strength of this case was difficult to quantify in the absence of adequate manpower budgeting within local authorities. The general argument was persuasive, but an assessment of costs would need to include follow-up work on internal improvement. If this was to be achieved through voluntary grant take-up, the full armoury of grants, advice and support needed to be employed, which carried with it additional resource implications.

On the contractual side, the argument was that larger contracts attracted the larger builders, with volume resulting in lower costs per unit. Evidence on this was difficult to obtain without systematic control of the main variables: size of contractor, size of contract, standard of work and size of property. Where local authorities had targeted enveloping at smaller groups of particularly difficult property, unit costs were relatively high compared with the Birmingham experience, where large block programmes averaged costs over a wider range of property condition. However, anecdotal evidence suggested that Birmingham's programme was relatively expensive in terms of costs, and that a more economical programme could be obtained through small contracts let to local builders, or directly to specialist subcontractors.

There was little empirical evidence to illuminate the debate, but the information there was did nothing to dispel the impression that economies of scale were cancelled out by higher overheads. Through enveloping contracts, larger builders were theoretically able to take advantage of economies of scale through bulk purchase and efficient programming of work sequences. In an operation which remained labour-intensive, however, small local builders could compete on unit costs because of their lower overheads. What they could not do was compete on volume, and perhaps a more persuasive justification for enveloping was as an approach which made possible the involvement of large contractors in private-sector renovation. The value of this lay in the possibility of increased capacity, but was determined by the impact of subcontracting practices. In the past, expansion of rehabilitation programmes increased the demand for small builders and exposed the inelasticity of skilled resources. In this sense, the involvement of larger contractors suggested a way in which to tackle an expanded programme of urban renewal. But, as subcontracting was common, it might be that the operations were being carried out by the same workforce, irrespective of the size of the main contractor. If this was the case, an advantage only accrued if the main contractor performed effectively on project management.

The fourth argument concerned standards of work. A familiar criticism of grant-aided rehabilitation was that people found the whole administrative and technical process difficult to understand. Consequently, a great deal of thought was given to ways of helping people through the process. Various types of agency service were devised to provide design guidance, advice on grants and loans, help with administration, and then with the supervision of building work. In a sense, enveloping was a form of agency service which relieved owners of all technical and financial responsibility in a programme of comprehensive external repair. As practised in Birmingham, envelope was a large-scale package which inevitably provided a less personalized service than offered by the one-off agency. But the well managed envelope contract was capable of taking individual requirements into account. And it promised a higher standard of work than was generally achieved through voluntary grant take-up. Unlike most grant work, enveloping was carried out under a building contract, while the scale of the programme could justify a clerk of works. In the absence of good small builders concerned with their local reputation, there was much to be said in favour of careful specification and close supervision as a way of achieving high standards of work. The problem was to obtain the necessary level of supervision on large contracts. Early programmes of enveloping were characterized by marked variations in contractor performance which were largely determined by the ability of individual managers.

The fifth argument for enveloping related to visual and structural coherence. Tackling an entire block avoided pepper-potting and unnecessary material junctions between separate contracts. With work in progress, perhaps the most satisfying feature of enveloping, for politicians and local authority officers alike, was the sight of scaffolding down the whole length of a terrace. The finished product could reassert the visual uniformity or individual character of the original street. With good reason, residents were often more ambivalent. With the contract in progress, they were living in a noisy, dirty and sometimes dangerous environment. But, having survived this, the majority of residents in Birmingham seem to have been pleased with the end product. The DOE survey showed a generally favourable reaction. Over 90 per cent thought the scheme a good idea, and nearly three-quarters of owner-occupiers thought it increased house prices significantly (McCarthy and Buckley, 1982, pp. 13–16). Indeed, a new form of enveloping blight began to assert itself, with residents anticipating the programme and applying political pressure to gain priority.

There were problems which arose from the visual and structural logic of tackling entire terraces. First, the ability of enveloping to carry out rehabilitation on a large scale was limited by the nature of older housing problems. The logic of the approach was particularly clear when disrepair was concentrated within a defined area rather than dispersed throughout the stock. Second, because the aim was to repair entire terraces, there was a tendency to select groups where a limited amount of improvement work had taken place. Too high a proportion of improved houses, and the logic of enveloping began to disappear. But pepper-potting was so widespread that it was difficult to find unimproved terraces. It was possible to tackle small blocks or even isolated properties, and this was a valuable technique, which was employed most flexibly through the co-ordinated use of 90 per cent repair grants. In this way, enveloping began to emerge as a tool of HAA implementation rather than a policy in its own right. Third, the drive to achieve complete envelope affected people who had potential difficulty coping with the upheaval. Internal damage almost inevitably occurred given the type of work being carried out, with first-floor ceilings being especially at risk in bad weather. In these circumstances the elderly were particularly vulnerable. Even where their homes were omitted from the scheme, they would still be surrounded by building work, which might affect their own property and create nearly as much noise and general disturbance. Decanting was the only other option but, even assuming that appropriate accommodation was available, the elderly were often reluctant to face even a short move.

The final argument used to justify enveloping was that it secured confidence in the area and thereby encouraged private investment. In this sense, it was an extension of the logic used to promote area policies, where the concept of externalities was advanced to describe patterns of investment decisions. Concentrating on the rapid improvement of relatively small areas was intended to restore market confidence in a way which would then encourage private-sector investment. The early implementation of publicly funded environmental works was designed as a visible statement of local authority confidence in the area which was directed both at property owners and the financial institutions. Prior to enveloping, Birmingham was encouraging this confidence within HAAs by a major programme of environmental improvements, including new walls, fences, improved rear access and minor landscaping. But the city was acutely aware of the absurdity of building new garden walls around decaying houses in the hope that it might give owners the confidence to carry out improvements they could not afford. Compared with the uncertainty of carrying out environmental works to stimulate grant take-up, enveloping provided a more reassuringly direct route.

While enveloping was a very effective way of achieving capital investment, the market implications of the policy were largely unknown. In terms of confidence, survey evidence showed that residents in enveloped areas expressed greater optimism about the future of the area than residents living in 'traditional' HAAs. Almost half the sample living in enveloped property thought their area would be a better place to live in five years time, compared with a national average of 40 per cent and an inner-city average of about 25 per cent (McCarthy and Buckley, 1982, p. 16). In terms of property values, prices might rise as a result of enveloping, or of increased building society willingness to lend in the area. But the scale of Birmingham's enveloping programme made it difficult to predict the impact on local market prices, while reliable empirical data were scarce in the absence of information on the general selling price of property. Concern about the speculative advantages accruing from enveloping needed to be balanced by evidence of lower population turnover. A survey of HAAs throughout the country showed that only 37 per cent of original residents were living at the same address at the end of the period (Niner and Forrest, 1982, p. 22). By comparison, two-thirds of the original population remained in enveloped areas (McCarthy and Buckley, 1982, p. 51). This might be partly explained by variations in the characteristics of HAAs, but it did suggest that, compared with other approaches, enveloping was better able to maintain existing community and tenure patterns. Assuming, however, that enveloping did bring a rise in property prices, there was the possibility of a knock-on effect, with low-income home owners being channelled towards other areas of low-cost housing and perpetuating the relationship between poor people and the worst housing, with its consequent implications for continued under-investment in maintenance.

These concerns apart, there remained fears that enveloping placed a 'premium on neglect'. Areas were selected largely because houses had a poor maintenance history, but it was not clear whether enveloping had an impact on general levels of investment. The immediate prospect of a scheme was likely to affect grant take-up, but this was a relatively short-term impact. Beyond this, it would be speculative to suggest that general patterns of maintenance behaviour were influenced by the simple existence of enveloping procedures. It would depend on the scale of enveloping programmes whether people were likely to postpone maintenance work because, at an unknown time in the future, their houses might be part of an enveloping scheme.

The broader implications of enveloping related to the costs of owner-occupation. With poorer households concentrated in the worst housing stock, they could not afford their share of the costs of traditional grant work. Enveloping was a solution to the problem; but it was another subsidy benefiting home owners, unrelated to need, and carrying with it future maintenance implications. If existing owners could not afford to maintain their homes, they might also be unable to maintain the enveloped property. There was nothing in the 'proper functioning' of the bottom end of the owner-occupied housing market which did anything for the regular maintenance of property.

Revising the Context
When the RTPI, IEHO and AMA published their separate reports in 1981, each presented sensible proposals for reform. If these proposals were not radical, it could in part be attributed to their terms of reference. The RTPI recognized a 'deepening housing crisis' but focused specifically on the future role of area renewal, rather than a wider analysis of older housing problems. The IEHO similarly focused on the performance and shortcomings of area improvement. The AMA had a wider brief, and was the only report to provide an estimate of the scale of unfitness and disrepair. All three reports argued that prevailing policies and levels of resources were having little impact on the problem, and indeed that the position was deteriorating. Perhaps predictably, they all called for extra resources to increase the rate of improvement. But, even if these resources became available, there was little in their respective proposals to give confidence that performance could be improved significantly. All three settle for tinkering with the framework of grants while accepting in

principle the view that more clearance was necessary. Within the context of extra resources for HIPs, renewal activity was to be increased by a combination of simplified grants, revised clearance procedures, and the wider application of enveloping. In themselves, these proposed reforms were largely sensible and worthy of support. But the question remained whether the problem could be tackled on the required scale through the kind of mechanisms being discussed. In addressing themselves to the symptoms of under-investment, no attempt was made to secure adequate and sustained capital spending on regular maintenance of the housing stock.

Fifteen years of emphasis on area-based improvement policies had provided a number of useful lessons. They helped to concentrate local authority resources, provided a framework for environmental improvements and could encourage the kind of confidence necessary for private investment. Various techniques were developed to implement HAAs and GIAs, and these reached a degree of sophistication. But area policies, pursued through the public sector, were not in themselves sufficient. This was partly because problems of disrepair had been seen to affect a broad range of the housing stock which was not particularly concentrated within discrete areas, emphasising the need to help individual households in the worst housing conditions, irrespective of their location. But attempts to achieve this carried with it the danger that local authority resources would be dissipated in an inefficient and ineffective manner – pepper-potting on a grand scale. For this reason, the underlying approach to the problems of older housing needed to come not through grant mechanisms, but through a more general stimulation of capital investment. The problems of older housing stemmed from a cumulative lack of maintenance only partly attributable to the initial inadequacies of construction, amenities and design. An effective policy approach needed to encourage continuous investment in the maintenance of property throughout its life. It followed from this that central government needed to move away from the treatment of symptoms, through major but intermittent injections of public capital, towards the concept of progressive investment in the maintenance of the whole housing stock. This was an objective which could be achieved only by going beyond traditional housing policy boundaries and asking fundamental questions about the relationship between housing subsidies and housing consumption.

6

The Investment Contradiction

Capital Spending

Despite the rehabilitation policies pursued during the 1970s, levels of capital investment in housing repair and improvement were never sustained on the required scale, and projected rates of new building and rehabilitation throughout the 1980s indicated that conditions would continue to deteriorate as lower investment was channelled towards an ageing housing stock. At the same time, various estimates suggested a growth in the demand for mortgage finance. There was a contrast between declining capital investment in housing and the buoyant demand for funds to sustain the private housing market. Two particular concerns were prominent. The first was that the growing demand for housing finance was being used not for new production but for the consumption and exchange of existing assets. Additional personal-sector funds were required to finance a growing owner-occupied sector and to replace capital leakage on property exchange. And, while there was a continuing demand for mortgage funds to finance the growth and exchange of houses, there had been a decline in capital investment in new building and maintenance. This was reflected in the way the bulk of mortgage finance was directed towards existing houses and to existing owners, leading the Housing Centre Trust to comment that a bigger slice of the nation's credit was funding a smaller volume of new capital formation and a higher volume of transfer, with each transfer carrying an exchequer liability in the form of tax relief (Housing Centre Trust, 1975, p. 43). The second concern was that, looking at the wider economic implications, housing had performed relatively well as a form of investment. A consequence of this favourable performance was that some other sectors of the economy had been less successful in attracting investment.

In the general debate about housing subsidies, the focus tended to be on neutrality – both between tenures and on the attractiveness of investment in housing compared with other uses of savings. However, the concern of policy on older housing was not with the issue of neutrality but with the more specific question of capital spending. Though this did not ignore the relationship between housing investment and other uses of savings, it was in the context of determining a balance – within total housing expenditure

– between the financing of consumption and the level of capital investment necessary to build and maintain an adequate housing stock.

Various assessments had been made of the levels of investment actually required to achieve improved housing conditions. The estimated bill for outstanding repair presented in the 1981 English House Condition Survey was around £35 billion (Chapter 2). To tackle problems of this size, the Association of Metropolitan Authorities (1981) proposed to increase annual HIP expenditure by at least £1,640 million to achieve a programme of nearly 300,000 improved units a year, while the RTPI (1981) were looking at a renewal programme of 400,000 units (Chapter 5). A more modest programme, designed simply to arrest the rate of deterioration, was put forward by the Housing Centre Trust (1981). This proposed the rehabilitation of just over 200,000 units a year at an additional cost of £364 million (1979 prices), nearly half this expenditure being offset against lower levels of clearance. It was the work of Kilroy, however, which presented a more comprehensive analysis of investment priorities within government expenditure. In 1977, Kilroy assessed actual housing output in the public and private sectors at £5·5 billion. Of this, £2·5 billion was going on the replacement, improvement or maintenance of existing houses, with the outstanding £3 billion on additions to the stock (Kilroy, 1979). Putting forward an investment model based on the work of Stone (1970), Kilroy proposed that expenditure on stock renewal should be increased by nearly 70 per cent to £4·2 billion.

Following Kilroy's approach, Figure 6.1 shows output expenditure at 1980 prices together with two estimates of spending requirements. Total housing investment in Great Britain in 1980 was approximately £8·5 billion. This figure was based, like Kilroy's, on construction industry output figures for new building, repair and maintenance in the public and private sectors (DOE, 1981b, table 9), and as such could substantially under-estimate total repair and maintenance work. The centre column suggests the level of expenditure required to prevent further deterioration of the housing stock, based on the Housing Centre Trust's proposals to build new houses at a rate of just over 200,000 a year, together with the renovation of a similar number. To achieve this would imply an increase in capital expenditure of about 8 per cent to £9·2 billion. However, the Trust's proposals were relatively modest and, indeed, were drawn up to identify priorities within existing expenditure plans. Inevitably this placed constraints on the rates which could be proposed for public-sector new building and grant activity. The right-hand column gives an alternative estimate based on an assessment of housing need. The latest available official estimate suggested that new building should run at around 300,000 houses a year, based on a forecast demand for owner-occupation, and maintaining prevailing rates of progress in meeting housing need (DOE, 1977a, tech. vol. 1, table III.29). As for a renovation programme, to tackle existing substandard houses in England suffering from substantial disrepair implied a target of over 200,000 a year for ten years (Table 2·3). Taking a figure of 275,000 for Great Britain as a whole would give a total capital programme approaching £11 billion in 1980, similar at constant prices to Kilroy's estimate.

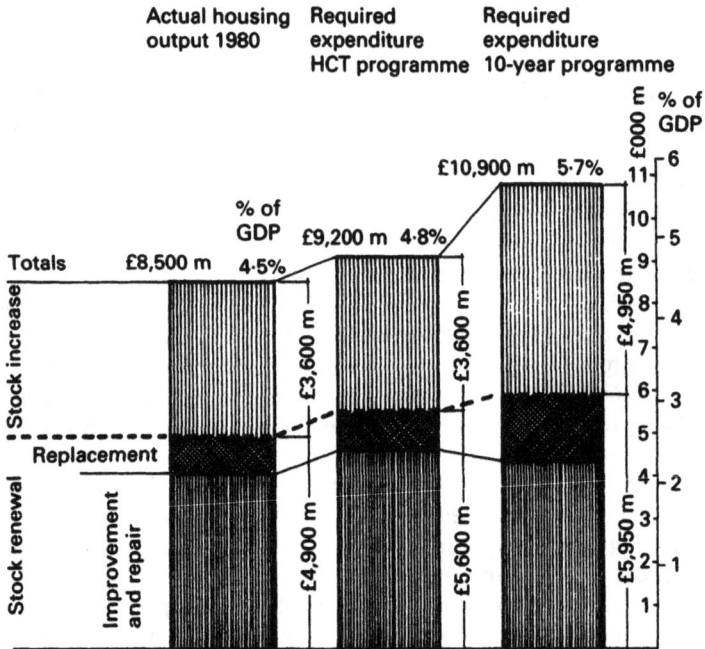

Figure 6.1   *Achieved output and estimated required expenditure,* 1980.
Source: Adapted from Kilroy, 1979; DOE, *Housing and Construction Statistics,* 1980.

While a more sophisticated investment model could be constructed, it was the principle of the approach which had fallen from favour by the end of the 1970s. Despite arguments from the House of Commons Environment Committee that expenditure plans should be considered in the light of changing housing needs, the impact on employment levels, and the social effects of a given level of expenditure (House of Commons, 1980, paras 8 and 22), housing plans continued to be determined on the basis of a view of what the country could afford (see, for example, Michael Heseltine's evidence to the Environment Committee, House of Commons, 1980, p. 3). It was easy to sympathize with the view of a later Environment Committee report that 'in the field of housing ... the Government has, as a matter of policy, deprived itself of information which is necessary for sound decisions to be taken' (House of Commons, 1981a, para. 5). Crucially, the creed of 'what the country can afford' denied a political debate about desirable levels of expenditure and how this might be achieved.

Public-Sector Expenditure
it is easy to over-emphasize the level of consensus characterizing postwar housing policy. There have been varying levels of political commitment to intervention. But the context has been one which assumed that more could be spent on housing by individuals and government as the level of national income tended to rise (Ball, 1983, p. 7). This orthodoxy was overturned by the new Thatcher administration in 1979. Lower public expenditure became a central target of economic policy. But this strategy was intermeshed with a political conviction which resisted the idea of intervention, searching always for a market-based approach. It was consistent with this philosophy that the government's role in housing should be restricted to that of encouraging markets to operate effectively. This view, which had the apparently enthusiastic support of the Treasury, implied that intervention distorted consumer choice, and should therefore be restricted to the absolute minimum. The logic of this approach threatened to sacrifice the holy cow of owner-occupation, as tax relief on mortgage interest payments could be presented as a significant distortion of the market. However, the early objectives were rather easier political targets. Public-sector spending on housing was to be reduced, and the immediate victim was capital expenditure.

The scale of cuts in housing expenditure was massive. By 1985/6, the programme was planned to run at about a third of its level ten years previously. Commenting on the government's expenditure plans for the period 1980/1 to 1983/4 (Great Britain, 1980) the Environment Committee noted that 92 per cent of the planned £2·8 billion reduction in public expenditure had been found by the reduced housing provision of nearly £2·6 billion (House of Commons, 1980, para. 3). Table 6.1 shows that, in the last year for which the government's programme was expressed at constant prices, total expenditure was planned to fall by 2·3 per cent between 1979/80 and 1983/4, while housing expenditure was planned to fall by 55 per cent. From 1982, housing programme expenditure was redefined, and all expenditure programmes were expressed in cash terms. On this recalculated basis, planned housing expenditure in 1985/6 was to be a third lower than in 1979/80 (Table 6.2), its share of total expenditure falling from 5·9 per cent to 2·4 per cent. Planned expenditure for 1985/6 was higher than 1983/4, but again expressed in cash terms. There was an allowance for projected rates of inflation, though the assumptions were not made explicit. However, assuming an annual rate of inflation of 5 per cent from 1983/4 onwards implied that housing programme expenditure was due to fall by 65 per cent in real terms over the ten-year period from 1976/7 to 1985/6.

Housing's share of public expenditure savings was substantial, but the

Table 6.1 Total Public Expenditure by Programme, 1980 Survey Prices £ million

	1975–6 Outturn	1976–7	1977–8	1978–9	1979–80	1980–1 est.	1981–2 Planned	1982–3	1983–4
Housing	6,072	5,880	5,093	4,728	4,928	4,256	3,143	2,720	2,230
Defence	9,436	9,287	9,082	9,026	9,294	9,746	9,750	10,050	10,350
Industry and employment	4,850	4,328	2,854	3,530	2,929	3,899	4,023	3,080	2,460
Law and order	2,572	2,629	2,571	2,596	2,698	2,833	2,886	2,960	3,000
Education and arts	9,421	9,393	9,011	9,171	9,236	8,909	8,544	8,360	8,190
Health and social services	8,618	8,700	8,746	8,973	9,003	9,067	9,234	9,400	9,480
Social security	15,737	16,246	17,093	18,644	19,106	19,775	21,161	21,600	21,400
All programmes	81,283	79,202	74,375	77,951	77,776	79,245	79,225	77,900	76,000

Source: Great Britain, 1981, table 1.7.

Table 6.2 Total Public Expenditure by Programme, Cash Prices[1] £ million

	1976-7 Outturn[2]	1977-8	1978-9	1979-80	1980-1	1981-2	1982-3 est.	1983-4 Planned	1984-5	1985-6
Housing	3,805	3,418	3,572	4,514	4,457	3,137	2,579	2,792	2,990	3,110
Defence	6,183	6,821	7,496	9,227	11,180	12,606	14,411	15,987	17,290	18,330
Industry and employment	3,093	2,233	3,036	2,881	4,011	5,319	5,854	5,622	5,490	5,410
Law and order	1,678	1,791	2,036	2,579	3,167	3,774	4,284	4,583	4,820	5,040
Education and science	6,982	7,039	7,755	8,946	10,901	11,828	12,628	12,560	12,910	13,340
Health and social services	5,937	6,542	7,425	8,899	11,362	12,751	13,879	14,608	15,380	16,070
Social security	11,603	13,917	16,437	19,417	23,458	28,510	32,473	34,394	35,940	37,900
All programmes	54,649	56,789	65,734	76,939	92,815	104,684	113,007	119,568	126,370	132,260
Housing as % of total	7·0	6·0	5·4	5·9	4·8	3·0	2·3	2·3	2·4	2·4

Sources:
1 Great Britain, 1983, Vol. 1, table 1.7.
2 Great Britain, 1982, Vol. 1, table 1.9.

Table 6.3 Public Expenditure on Housing £ million (cash)

	1976-7[1] Outturn	1977-8	1978-9	1979-80	1980-1	1981-2	1982-3 Planned	1982-3 est.	1983-4 Planned
Current Expenditure	1,125	1,147	1,396	1,834	2,134	1,598	1,196	1,295	949
Capital Expenditure									
Local authority									
New housing	1,318	1,263	1,105	1,078	978	726		625	
Improvement of public stock	340	374	510	761	695	649		750	
Land and acquisition	271	182	179	173	147	132		100	
Lending to housing associations	215	225	184	189	170	142		110	
Improvement grants	66	66	98	134	144	218		430	
Mortgages and loans	183	122	173	260	116	47		55	
Total local authority gross expenditure	2,393	2,231	2,249	2,595	2,250	1,915	2,471	2,070	2,488
Gross new town investment	180	147	130	161	165	115	73	84	61
Net Housing Corporation lending to housing associations	254	288	324	397	495	492	530	680	630
Less sales and replacements[2]	-282	-394	-525	-472	-587	-983	-1,090	-1,550	-1,336
Total capital expenditure	2,545	2,271	2,177	2,680	2,323	1,539	1,984	1,284	1,843
Total Programme	3,670	3,418	3,572	4,514	4,457	3,137	3,180	2,579	2,792
Capital expenditure as % of total programme	69	66	61	59	52	49	62	50	66

Source: Great Britain, 1982, 1983.
Notes:
1 Excluding option mortgage scheme subsidy.
2 Net of Housing Corporation schemes for first-time buyers and other lending.

consequences for capital expenditure were even more serious. Capital spending by the public sector on new and renovated houses fell dramatically after 1979, though the trend had begun earlier under a Labour government. Capital expenditure as a proportion of the total housing programme had already fallen from 69 per cent in 1976/7 to 59 per cent in 1979/80, and fell to 49 per cent in 1981/2 (Table 6.3). Real capital expenditure on dwellings by local authorities in 1981 was only 15 per cent of that in 1976 (Ball, 1983, p. 8).

It was easy to see why capital spending carried a disproportionate burden of cuts. Compared with recurrent costs, capital savings were relatively easy to make through postponed or cancelled projects. Indeed, the temptation to find savings in capital programmes was seen as a product of imposing cash limits on public spending (CSD, 1981). But the balance of priorities within current expenditure programmes gave rise to anxiety. The Treasury and Civil Service Committee expressed repeated concern about the falling share of fixed investment in the overall expenditure total. This had declined from 13·1 per cent in 1978/9 to 10·4 per cent in 1982/3, and, while planned to rise during 1983/4, was still likely to be 2 per cent below the 1978/9 figure (House of Commons, 1983 para. 19).

Levels of Public Spending

Public expenditure on housing fell because government chose to reduce its spending on social programmes in order to meet political commitments to defence and law and order while reducing the total level of public-sector spending. Among the advocates of an alternative approach were an alliance of those looking to stimulate economic recovery through capital investment programmes and those who adopted the multiplier effects of capital spending as a justification for increased public-sector housing expenditure. These advocates of increased public spending contradicted the government's monetarist policy, which had led to planned lower levels of public borrowing and a resulting squeeze on housing programmes.

Under the government's medium-term financial strategy, the public sector borrowing requirement (PSBR) was planned to fall because government borrowing was held to be inflationary. The argument seemed to centre on the public sector's two main sources of borrowing. It is able to sell gilt-edged securities to the banks, but this is usually seen to increase the money supply, as gilt-edged securities represent an increase in bank assets and therefore allow an increase in liabilities. Alternatively, it is generally held that raising funds by selling National Savings or Treasury gilts to the pension or life assurance companies does not increase the money supply. But the government's belief was that it imposed upward pressure on interest rates.

The government's medium-term financial strategy therefore sought to reduce public borrowing as a proportion of GDP. In 1982/3 the borrowing requirement was around £9·2 billion compared with £13·2 billion in 1980/1. The government's programme planned a fall to £7 billion in 1985/6 (cash terms). This was around 2 per cent of GDP, approaching a balanced budget and, according to the government's economic theory, bringing a dramatic reduction in interest rates. The immediate price for this theoretical advantage, however, was an excessively restrictive fiscal stance. Just to finance the higher benefit payments and lower tax income of increased unemployment, it was estimated that with respect to unemployment in 1977/8 PSBR in 1982/3 should have been £17·6 billion (Devereux and Morris, 1983). Instead, it was held constant in real terms, well below the level inherited in 1978/9, and representing a small and declining proportion of GDP. The PSBR in 1981/2, at about 3·5 per cent of GDP (Treasury, 1983), was about half the proportion it represented in the mid-1970s, with government borrowing in 1982 lower than countries like the United States, Germany and Japan (Price and Choraqui, 1983). Far from being a profligate borrower, figures from the Bank of England suggested that, when allowing for inflation, government had generally been a net lender from 1967 and was in near balance between 1975 and 1977 (Bank of England, 1979), the peak years for PSBR (Alexander and Toland, 1980, p. 90).

Public Expenditure and Employment
The importance of the debate on levels of government borrowing lay in the perhaps over-simplistic but nevertheless highly illustrative point that government revenue effectively covered current (non-capital) spending. Douglas Jay pointed out that in 1980/1 capital expenditure in the public sector exceeded PSBR, which could therefore be seen as borrowing to create capital (House of Commons, 1981c). Capital expenditure plans for 1983/4 were £11·4 billion (Great Britain, 1983, vol. 1, table 1.8), just £3·2 billion larger than planned PSBR. Because PSBR might be described as borrowing for investment, it was suggested that it be referred to as the 'public investment borrowing requirement' (PIBR). In this way, an expansion of PIBR could be seen as a way of financing capital projects, not current spending, and indeed might tend to reduce current spending through the employment multiplier.

Kilroy was a leading proponent of these reforms. He suggested that capital programmes had been harshly treated in the budgetary process because the government failed to make a normal accounting distinction between capital and current accounts, treating all expenditure as a potential increase in its borrowing requirement (Kilroy, 1981b, p. 46). Proposing that there should be separate capital and revenue accounts within the government's expenditure programme, the Housing Centre Trust pursued this accounting reform with the aim of distinguishing capital spending from public expenditure on transfer payments. These were described as mainly subsidies to users to assist them with current expenditure on the interest charges to pay for the sums borrowed, and were properly paid for through taxation. In contrast, public-sector capital expenditure was an allocation of real resources and could be legitimately financed through borrowing in the same way as was private housing investment (Housing Centre Trust, 1981, p. 6).

The importance of the Trust's argument was in the weight attached to investment reform as a means of tackling the problems of older housing. The framework of grant policy and area-based strategy were implicitly rejected as peripheral to the need to secure massive housing reinvestment on a scale commensurate with the original Victorian programmes. The call was to concentrate housing resources on capital spending and to revise traditional methods of financing investment and consumption in a way which did not emphasize unreal distinctions between the public and private sectors. Proposed reforms embraced the need to reform subsidies to owner-occupiers, but emphasized the importance of safeguarding public-sector expenditure as a means of sustaining capital expenditure in housing both through direct intervention and by stimulating private investment.

Though the Trust proposed to make an accounting distinction between public investment and current liabilities for subsidy, capital investment even under these arrangements would continue to register as public spending. This was clearly in conflict with a powerful combination of political ideology and economic dogma opposed to any increase in government-funded housing programmes. However, the early 1980s saw persuasive arguments launched in favour of reflationary policies. As always, the economists were divided, but there was support for the view that capital spending could increase without unduly inflationary effects. A Treasury model, for example, showed that increasing capital investment by 1 per cent of GDP would increase growth by between 0·6 per cent and 0·9 per cent a year while increasing the annual rate of inflation by just 1 per cent (Lipsey, 1983a).

The debate was not only for economists. It was uncertain whether increased investment could provide the economic growth necessary to finance social programmes, or whether any reflation would be neutralized by inflationary pressures. But there was some feeling that social programmes should not be defined exclusively by economic theory. Faced with growing unemployment, there were widespread calls for economic policy to be given a social dimension.

For those who wished to create employment opportunities by increasing capital spending, urban renewal programmes were an obvious vehicle for reflation. It was widely agreed that boosting the housebuilding industry was an effective way of increasing employment. Spending went largely on home-produced materials, as there was a low, though growing, level of import penetration, while the building process itself was relatively labour-intensive. An expansion of this sector was therefore advocated to provide extra employment with minimal inflationary consequences. Looking at the impact of spending £500 million of government money, one study showed that an expanded housing programme would produce an additional 64,000 jobs. This was fewer than direct employment subsidies, but more than in civil engineering, or across a wider spread of public spending, or by a reduction in income tax (Cambridge Econometrics, 1982).

The capacity appeared to exist within the building industry for this type of reflation, with published statistics suggesting that the number of unemployed building workers rose from about 190,000 in February 1980 to 400,000 by the end of 1981, a rate of unemployment around double that affecting industry as a whole. The construction industry repeatedly drew attention to these figures, estimating that the cost of unemployment benefits represented over a third of the savings made on public housing expenditure (Housing Centre Trust, 1981, p. 5). A reflationary strategy through increased public sector capital expenditure was proposed by successive TUC policy documents. Within an overall plan for economic growth (TUC, 1981a), a five-year £24 billion programme of public investment was proposed, half of it to be spent on house building and repair (TUC, 1981b). In 1983, a revised five-year programme of reconstruction totalled £30 billion, involving an additional £3·2 billion of public sector spending in 1983/4 to create over half a million new jobs (TUC, 1983). The AMA (1981b) also put forward a public-sector capital programme designed to create 300,000 jobs. And in February 1982 it was reported that the Department of Industry had called for a boost to the building industry in the Budget, launched through a programme of house improvement rather than large-scale capital projects (*Sunday Times*, 21 February 1982).

Such programmes were advocated not only on the ground that high unemployment was socially undesirable, but that they made sense in economic terms. It was variously estimated that, including the cost of benefits and loss of tax income, the cost of keeping someone unemployed for a year was about £5,000–£6,000. A Shelter report suggested that on the basis of jobs created and unemployment costs saved a £100 million boost to housing construction would save the Treasury between £71 million and £82 million. They would get three-quarters of their money back, and see 3,000 new homes, or the equivalent in improved units, for a net cost of about £20 to £30 million. The effect of expenditure on job creation was argued to be even more dramatic if it was concentrated on repair and maintenance, which was said to generate about 40 per cent more jobs than the average for all housing work. On these terms, a programme of capital spending on rehabilitation would almost pay for itself in savings on benefits (Shelter, 1981). The AMA were more cautious in their claims, but nevertheless made the point that part of the increased cost of public investment in housing could be saved through the employment created. Based on a net increase in HIP expenditure of £3·3 billion in 1985, it was estimated that between 248,000 and 313,500 new jobs would be created, depending on the multiplier adopted. Assuming an unemployment cost of £5,000 per person, the new jobs would lead to public expenditure savings of between £1·24 billion and £1·56 billion, reducing the net HIP cost to between £1·74 billion and £2·06 billion. In other words, between 38 per cent and 47 per cent of additional HIP expenditure could be offset through the employment created, while gaining an extra 50,000 new homes, 40,000 renovated council houses and 70,000 private-sector grant improvements (AMA, 1982, p. 23).

Keynesian economists were presumably not alone in recognizing the social and economic costs of an unemployed population costing around £14 billion a year, while housing and infrastructure lacked a capital programme which would provide large numbers of valuable jobs. However, the government argued that the extra public-sector borrowing required by these proposals would destroy at least as many jobs in the private sector through the higher interest rates which would inevitably follow (House of Commons, 1981d). The credibility of this assumption again depended on views about the relationship between government borrowing and interest rates. While general interest rates had tended to fall from 1981 onwards, a 1983 House of Commons Committee showed that total public-sector expenditure had risen in cost terms by 6·2 per cent between 1978/9 and 1982/3, and was likely to rise by a further 2 per cent by 1985/6 (House of Commons, 1983). Despite its stated aim of reducing the Budget deficit through reductions in public spending, the government had experienced the same difficulties as other countries, and had similarly relied on increased revenue through taxation to bring the deficit under control (Price and Chouraqui, 1983, p. 41).

Given the failure of government to reduce public expenditure, the burden of cuts imposed on the housing budget could only be explained as the transfer of resources to other programmes. Two factors were operating. First, there was a deliberate shift in government priorities in favour of spending areas like defence, where planned expenditure in 1983/4 was nearly £7 billion higher than 1979/80 in cash terms. Second, there was the unemployment cost of economic policy. At constant prices, the cost of unemployment increased from £5·8 billion in 1977/8 to nearly £14 billion in 1982/3 (Devereux and Morris, 1983, table 5). Expressed in these terms, there was no irrefutable economic logic determining the case for housing cuts; it was simply the ordering of political priorities. A case remained that even within the government's own public expenditure programme a different ordering of priorities could have achieved a more satisfactory result from the point of view of employment and capital investment.

Private-Sector Investment

In terms of a programme for urban renewal, it is all too easy to concentrate on arguments surrounding the government's housing expenditure plans. To do this would be to take a very limited view of overall investment patterns. Direct capital grants and subsidies from government form a small proportion of total investment. Therefore, while the balance of public-sector capital investment is important in determining overall levels of improvement and replacement activity, a potentially more profound influence is exerted on urban renewal programmes through the broader structure of housing subsidies and tax incentives.

This chapter is concerned with a paradox: that the housing stock appears to be falling into disrepair for lack of capital investment, while there is a continuing growth in demand for finance to facilitate the exchange of what is apparently a deteriorating asset. It has been seen that public-sector housing programmes have been reduced, and that with this has come a marked fall in the scale of capital programmes. At the same time, government policies have continued to increase subsidies to owner-occupation (Ball, 1983, pp. 9–10).

Others are better qualified to assess the effect of these subsidies on capital investment. But, for a variety of reasons, the balance of subsidies has encouraged the growth of owner-occupation. As a result, home ownership has become an important means of accumulating wealth. It has also led to a rise in the outstanding mortgage debt. The need to finance this increased demand for mortgages has raised a number of questions. In particular, there has been speculation that the performance of housing as an investment, combined with the demand for mortgage funds, has been in some way responsible for low levels of economic growth in Britain.

Arguments such as these are considered at this stage in a deliberate attempt to widen the boundaries of debate which, in the past, have limited discussion of older housing issues to traditional areas of grant policy and slum clearance programmes. These are concerned with treating symptoms. If approaches are to look for ways of achieving regular capital investment in housing, the starting point has to be with an understanding of the factors which might encourage such an objective. The way in which owner-occupation is financed then becomes centrally important. It asks whether the subsidy system is doing all that it might to encourage capital investment in the housing stock. Is it perhaps favouring consumption at the expense of investment? And, if so, might the desirability of stimulating capital investment be represented in debates about the reform of housing subsidies, the reform of taxation and the treatment of housing in relation to other forms of investment?

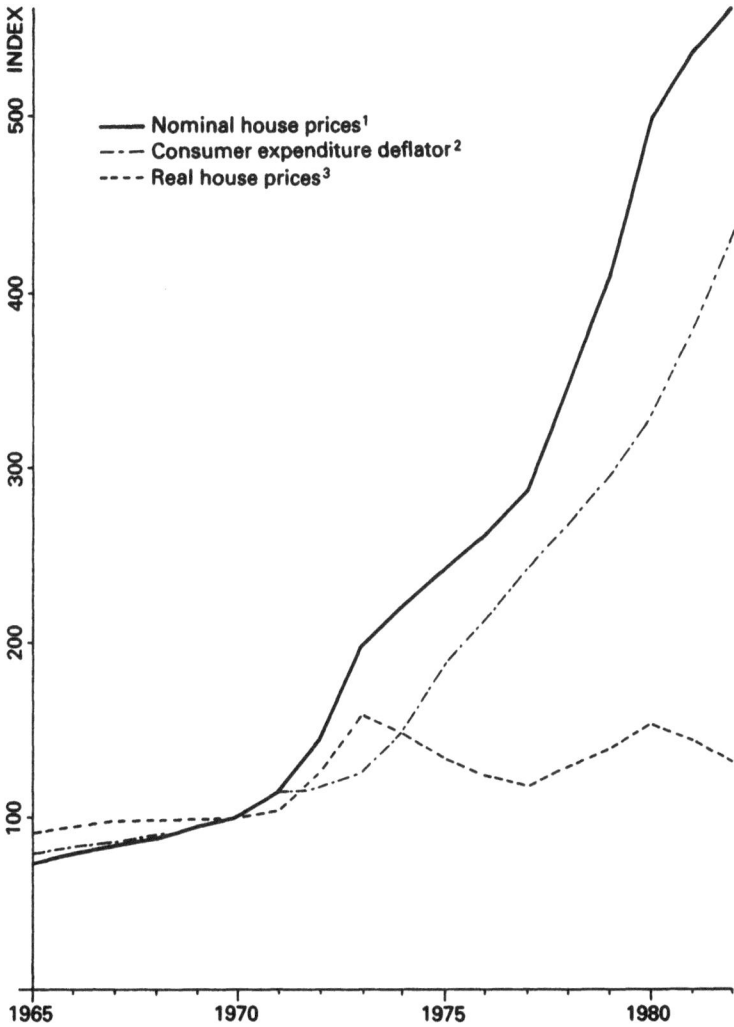

Figure 6.2   *Real and nominal house prices.*

Source: Updated from Farmer and Barrell, 1981.
Notes:
1   New houses mortgaged by building societies: *Housing and Construction Statistics.*
2   Monthly Digest of Statistics.
3   New house prices deflated.

Housing Wealth
Since the Second World War, home ownership in Britain has functioned
as an important way to accumulate wealth. House prices have tended to

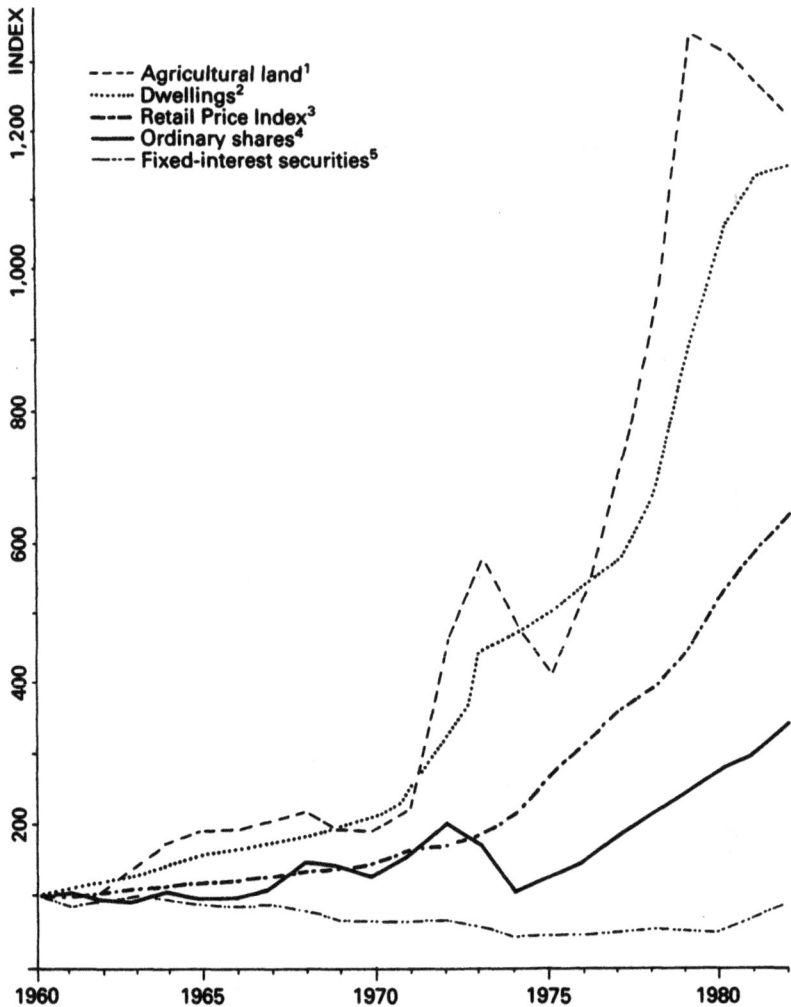

Figure 6.3   Trends in prices of selected assets.

Sources: Updated from Great Britain, 1979.
1   Ministry of Agriculture, Fisheries and Food.
2   Housing and Construction Statistics (DOE, 1983b, table F).
3   Economic Trends.
4   Financial Times Actuaries All Share (CSO, 1983, table 13.7).
5   Financial Times Fixed-Interest (debenture and loan stock) (CSO, 1983, table 13.7).

keep ahead of the overall price level of consumer goods, and, while the rise
has not been regular (Figure 6.2), between 1965 and 1982 the real price of
houses rose by a third, with only a small part of this increase being

attributable to improvements in the stock (Farmer and Barrell, 1981, p. 312). Figure 6.3 shows how house prices out-performed other indicators from 1960. Indeed, in the period 1945–80, retail prices increased by a factor of 9; stocks and shares by 6; and house values by 16 (McIntosh, 1982). During the 1970s, in particular, home ownership performed outstandingly well as a form of personal savings. Gough and Taylor (1980) looked at the best investment strategy for an individual with a £1,000 to invest in January 1969. Their calculations showed that only housing was able to show a constant rise in real value over the period (Table 6.4). Building society and local authority investments showed a fall of about a quarter in real terms, investment in the Trustee Savings Bank a fall of a third, and in commercial banks by as much as 40 per cent. Though some shares and unit trusts performed much better than average, investments in the stock market generally showed an even more marked fall of almost 60 per cent. Only investment in dwellings showed a rise, by nearly a third over the ten-year period.

Table 6.4   *Real Value*[1] *of £1,000 Investment,*[2] *1969–78*[3]

Year ending	Building society (share account)	Commercial banks	Deposits with local authorities	Trustees Savings Bank	Equities	Unit trust	Housing
1969	1,081	1,009	1,040	1,014	809	796	1,018
1970	1,004	979	1,035	997	659	718	1,027
1971	995	928	1,015	985	864	885	1,146
1972	987	892	1,002	978	833	1,005	1,551
1973	963	860	996	940	515	631	1,633
1974	891	787	936	849	235	340	1,416
1975	802	682	840	746	417	454	1,254
1976	762	629	805	690	355	383	1,149
1977	767	600	791	679	428	441	1,154
1978	775	582	789	667	417	443	1,340

Source: Gough and Taylor, 1980, table 2.
Notes:
1   Deflated by General Index of Retail Prices (all items) to base 1 January 1969 = 100.
2   Gross of tax.
3   Date of investment, 1 January 1969.

The work of Gough and Taylor was based on the return from a single investment of £1,000. Farmer and Barrell (1981) considered the scope for investment return through regular movement and re-borrowing to take advantage of higher income through inflation. Over the period 1965–79, if someone had moved every three years and maximized their borrowing, they would have made over 15 per cent per annum in real terms. The authors concluded that few entrepreneurs could have done better elsewhere. An average pre-tax yield on the stock market was under

10 per cent. As a measure of returns from productive enterprises, post-tax real returns to the Bank of England ran at below 5 per cent throughout the 1970s.

The relative performance of housing as an investment was reflected in the increased importance of physical assets as a component of personal wealth. Between 1960 and 1974, there was a doubling in the proportion of personal wealth held in land and dwellings (Great Britain, 1977, table 34). Between 1969 and 1980, housing as a proportion of total personal-sector assets increased from 28 per cent to 41 per cent (Table 6.5). Total outstanding loans for house purchase held relatively steady as a proportion of total assets: 6·3 per cent in 1969 and 7·2 per cent in 1980. However, this was largely because the rapid increase in liabilities accounted for by house purchase (+412 per cent) could be offset by growth in total physical assets (+532 per cent). Consequently, physical assets accounted for 44 per cent of total assets in 1969 and 62 per cent in 1980. The increase in personal wealth represented by housing was the reason that mortgage lending did not grow significantly as a proportion of total personal-sector assets. But financial assets grew more slowly. While liabilities for house purchase as a proportion of financial assets had fluctuated from 1975, they increased from 11·2 per cent in 1969 to 19 per cent in 1980 (Table 6.5). This growth in the proportion of personal wealth held in housing, and of outstanding mortgage debt – £10·2 billion in 1969, £52·2 billion in 1980 (table 6.5) and £75·8 billion in 1982 (BSA, 1983a, table A7) – was paralleled by a debate about the implications of sustaining an increased demand for mortgage finance.

The Demand for Mortgage Finance
Growth in mortgage lending was caused by three factors: house price inflation, net growth in mortgaged property and increased capital gearing. The refinancing of this mortgage debt, as home owners traded up and first-time buyers entered the market, was shown to mean a steady growth in the housing sector borrowing requirement (Kilroy, 1979, p. 38). This represented an increasing demand for finance, most of which went not into capital or productive investment but to finance consumption through property exchange. If owner-occupiers accumulated wealth through the ownership of property, this had to be paid for in some way. Various explanations were offered. First, that owner-occupation was a means of enforced savings, with a financial gain arising from the reduced discretionary income of home owners. Second, that the gain was supplied as a result of subsidy, from savers, or through favourable tax treatment, some of these benefits having been capitalized to represent higher housing costs for incoming home owners. And, third, that it was financed through demands for additional personal-sector funds and reflected in the cost and availability of finance in general.

Table 6.5   *Personal-Sector Balance Sheet*

	1969 £bn	1975 £bn	1976 £bn	1977 £bn	1978 £bn	1979 £bn	1980 £bn
Total physical assets	71·6	209·6	237·5	268·6	335·8	412·2	452·3
of which dwellings	45·6	137·5	153·0	167·8	218·4	270·9	300·7
Total financial assets	90·8	140·5	152·5	186·9	207·1	237·5	274·8
Total assets	162·4	350·1	390·0	455·5	542·9	649·7	727·1
Total liabilities	18·2	39·5	44·6	50·9	59·4	70·1	81·7
of which loans for house purchase	10·2	25·0	28·8	33·1	38·5	45·0	52·2
Net wealth	144·2	310·6	345·4	404·5	483·5	579·7	645·4
	%	%	%	%	%	%	%
Total assets	100	100	100	100	100	100	100
Housing	28·1	39·3	39·2	36·8	40·2	41·7	41·4
House purchase loans	6·3	7·1	7·4	7·3	7·1	6·9	7·2
Net wealth	88·8	88·8	88·6	88·8	89·0	89·0	88·8
Total financial assets	100	100	100	100	100	100	100
Loans for house purchase	11·2	17·8	18·9	17·7	18·6	18·9	19·0

Source: CSO, *Financial Statistics* (London: HMSO), various years.

Housing as Enforced Saving

The real gain enjoyed by owner-occupiers was seen by Saunders (1980, p. 87) to represent their own enforced savings. His abstract model saw owners extracting the equivalent of what was paid to the building society over and above the real rate of interest, defined as representing the charge for the use of the loan rather than the repayment to cover erosion of the value of the loan as a result of annual inflation. However, Saunders then proceeded to demolish this model, demonstrating that the assumptions on which it was based were not empirically valid. The assumptions were that the general level of house prices inflated at the same rate as overall inflation, including wages; that interest rates charged on credit for house purchase adjusted to take account of the true rate of inflation; and that interest payments were met entirely out of the owners' own resources. Contrary to these assumptions, it was clear that house prices had not increased at the same rate as other prices and wages. Interest rates charged on mortgages had not taken account of the overall rate of inflation; indeed, lending had been at substantial negative real rates. And owners' interest payments were subsidized by the exchequer, ensuring that 'house owners gain more through increased house prices than they lose through increased interest payments' (Saunders, 1980, p. 92).

Tax subsidy

The second explanation rested on higher housing costs resulting from favourable subsidy treatment. Tax relief on mortgage interest repayments and the non-taxation of both imputed rent and capital gains had demand effects which included a tendency to encourage trading up and the maximizing of mortgages. Households were encouraged 'to become owner-occupiers and once owner-occupiers to trade up by purchasing more expensive housing with the assistance of a larger, subsidized mortgage, and to realize greater capital gains' (Doling, 1982, p. 33). There were mixed financial benefits in trading down, but the overall effect was an inefficient use of the housing stock, with a substantial incentive to invest in housing rather than in other assets (Hughes, 1980, p. 71). Owner-occupiers also enjoyed credit advantages. The security of a house, even one with a substantial mortgage, provided a route to credit not open to tenants. It was not unknown for owner-occupiers to enjoy tax relief on loans which were only notionally for house improvements – the so called kitchen on wheels: a car that came complete with a builder's receipt (Lipsey, 1983b).

A consequence of the favourable investment treatment enjoyed by housing was that existing owner-occupiers had accumulated wealth through the ownership of fixed assets. In 1960, the proportion of personal wealth held in dwellings and land was the same as the proportion held in company securities. Within fifteen years the former doubled while the latter was halved (Great Britain, 1977). The cost of this was borne partly by offering relatively low returns to investors. Purchasers throughout the 1970s benefited from not having to pay a market rate of interest on their mortgage. Allowing for inflation and tax relief, the real rate of mortgage interest was negative from 1967 (Farmer and Barrell, 1981, p. 315) – achieved by offering low rates of interest to investors and causing wealth to be redistributed from savers to borrowers. However, it was argued that the main cost was borne by charging higher entry costs to first-time buyers. Wealth accumulation was achieved at the expense of incoming owner-occupiers because purchase represented a transfer payment, a premium paid for the right to replace someone else in the sector. The capital gain of the individual leaving the sector was therefore matched by the increased indebtedness of the new entrant (Clarke and Ginsburg, 1975, p. 19). Kemeny characterized the 'capital gain' of existing owners as 'a sort of levy on householders who are entering the owner-occupied sector for the first time' (Kemeny, 1981, p. 37).

To sustain this argument required evidence that housing had been getting more expensive in real terms. Compared with general prices, housing had become relatively more expensive since 1945. But a broad relationship had been maintained between general house prices and average earnings. For just two periods during the 1970s (1971–3 and

1978–9), the ratio of house prices to earnings rose significantly above its long-term average figure of 3·5. In 1973 the ratio rose to 4·95 and in 1979 to 3·82 (BSA, 1981). However, in terms of the hypothesis, what was more important was the price of housing to first time buyers. Building society statistics gave no suggestion that this housing had become more expensive. Indeed, the price to income ratio was lower in 1980 than in 1969 (BSA, 1982a, table 12). It is possible that the price of dwellings purchased by first-time buyers could be related to income rather than to house prices generally. If so, it might be expected that, if housing had become relatively more expensive, there would be a divergence between average house prices and the average price of houses purchased by first-time buyers. The available data were inconclusive, mainly because a time-series was not available over a sufficient period of time. Table 6.6 shows that the ratio between average house prices for first-time and former owner-occupiers tended to increase over the period 1969–80. However, the data were drawn only from houses purchased with a building society mortgage.

Table 6.6   Average House Prices, 1969–80

	Average house price first time buyer[1] (A) £	Average house price former owners[2] (B) £	Average price all houses[3] (C) £	Ratio C:A	Ratio B:A
1969	4,097	5,418	4,850	1·18	1·32
1970	4,330	5,838	5,190	1·20	1·35
1971	4,838	6,666	6,130	1·27	1·38
1972	6,085	8,965	8,420	1·38	1·47
1973	7,908	11,900	11,120	1·41	1·50
1974	9,037	13,049	11,300	1·25	1·44
1975	9,549	13,813	12,119	1·27	1·45
1976	10,181	15,160	12,999	1·28	1·49
1977	10,857	16,246	13,922	1·28	1·50
1978	12,023	18,792	16,297	1·36	1·56
1979	14,918	24,074	21,047	1·41	1·61
1980	17,533	28,959	24,307	1·39	1·65

Sources:
1   BSA Bulletin, No. 29, table 12.
2   BSA Bulletin, no. 29, table 13.
3   BSA Bulletin, no. 27, p. 19.

The 1977 Housing Policy Review provided additional information on the increased housing costs of new owner-occupiers. This showed that, for mortgagors as a group, average interest repayments increased from £88 in 1938 to £160 in 1975 (at 1970 prices). It was not clear whether these figures were adjusted to account for increased real incomes. However, the Housing Policy Review showed that costs to the entrant owner-occupier rose very much more; from £85 a year in 1938 to £325 in 1975, nearly four times as large in real terms (DOE, 1977a, tech. vol. 1, pp. 44–5). The review also looked in more detail at outgoings net of tax relief for first-time buyers over the period 1970–6. This showed a worsening relationship between net outgoings and net income of 25 per cent, over the period, for purchasers in non-manual occupations, and 20 per cent for those in manual occupations. A reduction in interest rates in 1976 eased the position, but the relationship between first-year housing costs and income was still unfavourable compared with 1970, which in turn seemed to have represented a worsening position compared with the situation ten years earlier (DOE, 1977a, tech. vol. 2 pp. 55–6).

There was limited but contradictory evidence, therefore, to support the proposition that capital gains had been financed through higher entry costs for incoming owner-occupiers. There remained the more general point, however, that house prices were higher than they would otherwise be as a result of tax concessions to owner-occupiers:

> ... investment in housing is very favourably treated relative to investment in other kinds of asset. As a result, house prices are higher than they would otherwise be. This means that the interest and capital repayments being made by current house-buyers are substantially greater than they would be if there were no tax concessions, and hence the concessions are of little net assistance to them. (Kay and King, 1980, p. 12)

Because of tax-stimulated demand, therefore, house buyers benefited little from tax concessions. The tax system favoured owner-occupation not owner-occupiers (Kay and King, 1980, p. 53). But house purchase remained the best investment for most people. The principal beneficiaries were the descendants of those who had owned housing in the past. The principal losers were those who rented and those who were forced, through lack of choice, to own when they could not easily afford the mortgage repayments. The other main loser was the national Exchequer. The cost of mortgage interest tax relief was estimated at £2·15 billion in 1983, with the cost of housing's exemption from capital gains tax costing a further £3 billion (Great Britain, 1983, vol. 2, p. 121). At the same time, the accumulation of housing wealth through house price inflation had to be financed by an increased mortgage debt. Consequently, over the period 1956–78, net loans for house purchase quadrupled as a proportion of GDP, from 1 per cent to 4 per cent (Kilroy, 1979, p. 39). In cash terms, this meant that loans for house purchase increased by over £7,000 million a year during the period 1976–80 (at 1980 prices), giving a total housing-sector borrowing requirement similar in size to the PSBR (Kilroy, 1981, p. 115). This growth was mostly to finance the exchange of houses already built, with a relatively small increase in houses produced.

Increased Demand for Mortgage Finance
The third way in which housing gain might be paid for is through an increased demand for mortgage finance. The 1977 Housing Policy Review estimated that building society finance for house purchase would need to increase by about 50 per cent in real terms by 1986, assuming modest increases in house values and without taking into account any net increase in owner-occupation (DOE, 1977, tech. vol. 2, p. 127). The building societies' own estimate included provision for a net increase in owner-occupation, forecasting that the total demand for building society loans could more than double from £8·9 billion in 1979 to £19·4 billion in 1985 (BSA, 1979a, p. 2).

Table 6.7 *Net Advances, Forecast and Outturn*

	1976 £m	1977 £m	1978 £m	1979 £m	1980 £m	1981 £m
DOE forecast[5]	3,647	3,770[4]	3,894	4,018	4,141	4,265
Outturn price						
RPI[1]	3,647	4,231	4,867	5,706	6,957	8,018
Av. house price[2]	3,647	4,034	4,790	6,348	7,619	8,231
Net advances[3]						
Building societies	3,618	4,100	5,115	5,271	5,722	6,331
Total net advances	3,928	4,362	5,530	6,592	7,399	9,617

Notes and Sources:
1 All item Retail Price Index.
2 All house average prices at mortgage completion stage (BSA *Bulletin*, no. 29, table 17).
3 BSA, 1983 table A7.
4 Figures for 1977–80 are interpolated.
5 DOE, 1977a, tech. vol. 2, p. 127 (at 1976 prices).

Table 6.7 compares the Housing Policy Review forecast with outturn values. Demand in 1981 was estimated in terms of trends for new mortgage lending and flows of mortgage repayments. Net advances were forecast at £4,265–£4,290 million (1976 prices) – an increase of around 17 per cent over the period 1976–81. Translating this into outturn values on the basis of actual inflation rates, the estimates implied a net increase in advances of between 120 and 126 per cent. Compared with this, actual building society net advances grew by only 75 per cent; but total net advances from all sources grew by 145 per cent. Over the period 1976–81, therefore, what appeared to happen was that net advances by building societies did not increase at the forecast rate, but that advances from other sources, notably the banks, made a contribution to total lending at levels not anticipated in 1976. Over the period 1976–8, building society lending accounted for over 90 per cent of net advances (Table 6.8). In 1982 their share had fallen to 57 per cent, while the banks, with their high proportion of new lending, accounted for over a third; but this had reverted to a more familiar distribution by 1984.

Table 6.8   Net Advances, All Sources   Outturn Prices

	Building societies	Local authorities	Insurance and pension funds	Banks	TSB	Other public sector	Total
	£m	£m	£m	£m	£m	£m	£m
1976	3,618	67	103	80	—	60	3,928
1977	4,100	4	119	120	1	18	4,362
1978	5,115	-43	166	270	5	17	5,530
1979	5,271	293	357	590	7	74	6,592
1980	5,722	461	376	500	93	247	7,399
1981	6,331	252	239	2,265	182	348	9,617
1982	7,855	541	161	4,927	—	325	13,809
	%	%	%	%	%	%	%
1976	92	2	3	2	—	2	100
1977	94	—	3	3	—	—	100
1978	92	-1	3	5	—	—	100
1979	80	4	5	9	—	1	100
1980	77	6	5	7	1	3	100
1981	66	3	2	24	2	4	100
1982	57	4	1	36	—	2	100

Source: BSA, 1983, table A.7.

Financing Owner-Occupation

It has been seen that housing performed relatively well as a form of investment during the postwar period, but that to offer these returns, through the refinancing of a growing owner-occupied debt, meant a growing demand for mortgage finance. This demand had an impact on the savings sector. Table 6.9 shows the transformation of the personal deposit market. Between 1968 and 1978, a period of rapid house price inflation, the share of personal sector deposits held by building societies rose from 30 per cent to 49 per cent, while there was a fall in the market share held by banks and National Savings (BSA, 1979b, p8). In 1968, building society deposits were £7·7 billion, or 13 per cent less than total bank deposits. By 1978 they had increased to £36·6 billion, or 51 per cent more than total bank deposits. The total value of bank deposits in 1978 was less than the increase in building society deposits over the previous decade. This was almost certainly one reason for the temporary increase in bank lending for house purchase which occurred in the late 1970s. From 1978, building society deposits continued to rise, increasing by over 80 per cent during the period 1978–82; but bank deposits increased even more sharply (Table 6.9), as did the market share of National Savings.

Table 6.9   *Selected Assets of the Personal Sector*[1]

Year ending	Deposits with building societies £bn	%	Deposits with banking sector £bn	%	Deposits with savings banks[2] £bn	%	Total amount outstanding £bn	%
1968	7·7	30	8·9	35	1·5	6	25·6	100
1970	10·1	35	10·1	35	1·8	6	29.1	100
1972	14·2	38	12·9	34	2·4	6	37·5	100
1974	18·3	38	19·3	40	2·6	5	48·2	100
1976	25·8	44	20·5	35	3·2	5	58.6	100
1978	36.6	49	24·2	32	4·5	6	74·7	100
1980	49·6	46	36·6	34	7·7	7	107·4	100
1982	67.0	48	50·0	36	—		140·7	100

Source: CSO, *Financial Statistics* (March 1979 and September 1983) (London: HMSO), various years.
Notes:
1   Personal sector holdings of national savings certificates and banks, excluded from the table, grew only gradually in cash terms, from £4·2bn in 1968 to £7·3bn at the end of 1978.
2   National Savings Bank and Trustee Savings Bank.

The growing demand for building society funds and the level of building society deposits led to considerable debate about the impact of a larger housing-sector borrowing requirement on the wider economy: its effect on interest rates, and on the tendency of people to invest in housing rather than in other parts of the economy. It was argued that:

Capital and effort have become increasingly tied up in own-home ownership, and have not therefore been available for 'productive', but possibly riskier (and less lucrative purposes). (Farmer and Barrell, 1981, p. 312)

The major restructuring of the personal savings market as a result of increased building society penetration was accompanied by warnings from the banking sector that housing finance was beginning to take a disproportionate share of personal savings, and that bank lending for industry was suffering as a result (Croham, 1979; Leigh-Pemberton, 1979). The Wilson Committee (1980), examining the workings of financial markets, provided a public forum for this debate, and much of the discussion took place in the context of submissions made to the committee.

Housing Investment and the Wider Economy
In their evidence to the Wilson Committee, the BSA (1978) considered the proposition that the low level of industrial investment and economic growth in Britain was partly attributable to the success of building societies in attracting funds. Their defence was based on two main points. First, that building society activities were largely neutral, with industry not being denied money directed away from the banks; and, second, that industry did not suffer from a lack of capital.

It was central to the building societies' argument that their lending activities did not influence the availability of funds for investment; that the low-level of industrial investment was a product of poor competitiveness rather than shortage of finance, and that mortgage funds were recycled, with aggregate lending not constituting a call on savings. In their competition for funds the building societies emphasized that the personal savings market was not a fixed size, but could be expanded at no expense to the interests of other institutions. In the personal sector, physical and financial assets could be acquired through savings – disposable income not spent on the consumption of goods and services – or borrowing, usually from financial institutions. In 1982, savings from income ran at £22.5 billion, accounting for 56 per cent of total capital funds available to the personal sector. Borrowing for house purchase was also an important component, accounting for 35 per cent of private-sector funds (Table 6.10). On the other side of the balance sheet, 23 per cent of funds were used to acquire fixed assets and stock (largely the purchase of houses); 43 per cent went into short-term liquid assets (of which nearly three-fifths went to the building societies); and 33 per cent in life insurance and superannuation. Because personal-sector savings were only one of the sources of funds available for investment, the building societies argued that their lending activity was essentially neutral.

However abstract the concept of a personal-sector balance sheet, the argument was that borrowing in the personal sector created funds available for the acquisition of assets (BSA, 1981b). Loans for house purchase from the building societies accounted for £7·8 billion of the total amount of funds available for investment in 1982. When a building society made a loan, it increased the funds of the personal sector, and some of these funds came back to societies in the form of deposits (Boleat,

Table 6.10 Sources and Uses of Personal-Sector Capital Funds, 1982

Sources of funds	£m	£m	Uses of funds	£m	£m
Saving		22,463	Taxes on capital and transfers		1,216
Capital transfers		1,652	Investment in fixed assets and stock		9,406
Borrowing for house purchase			Acquisition of liquid assets		
Building societies	7,841		Deposits with building societies	10,059	
Banks	5,041		Deposits with banks	3,836	
Other	1,033		National savings	3,445	
Total		13,915	Other	-242	
			Total		17,098
Other borrowing		5,484	Acquisition of public sector and company securities		-921
Accruals and balancing items		-3,450	Acquisition of life assurance and superannuation funds		13,265
Total		40,064	Total		40,064

Source: CSO, Financial Statistics (July 1983) (London: HMSO), table 9.2.

1982, p. 16). As a result of a building society mortgage, a house was purchased, and the vendor was in a position to acquire either physical or financial assets. Many vendors became the purchaser of another property. A last-time seller could invest in liquid assets, possibly in the form of building society deposits if interest rates were attractive. Extending this argument, in a perfect system, additional mortgage finance would only be required to fund increased value in the owner-occupied sector: new building, transfer from other sectors, and improvement work.

But the system was not perfect. On property exchange, vendors would not necessarily reinvest all the capital in a new purchase; apart from transaction costs, cash might be taken out and used for the consumption of goods and services. All the capital value of an end-of-chain sale might be disposed of in a similar way. Because of the nature of housing life-cycles, many legatees would already be owner-occupiers in their own right. Their use of capital released by property sales might involve a substantial injection of consumer spending.

The term 'leakage' was used to describe this process of cashing in some or all of the market value of a house. Levels of leakage were important because they influenced the demand for house finance. But attempts to quantify leakage floundered on the problems of inadequate data. A Bank of England estimate (1983) suggested that about £7 billion of mortgage lending during 1983 went to finance spending on goods or other real or financial assets, rather than additions or improvements to the owner-occupied stock. While concentrating on the difference between new lending and the estimated value of new additions to the stock, the analysis confirmed earlier work by the Bank (Davis and Saville, 1982) that a substantial part of mortgage lending was available for the acquisition of other assets or other spending. In the absence of data on sellers rather than purchasers, the destination of mortgage flows remained uncertain, with an unknown proportion returning as bank and building society deposits. However, the Bank of England argued that people were obtaining relatively cheap loans on the security of their homes in order to maintain their spending.

Looking at levels of leakage on a range of different indicators, Kemeny and Thomas (1984) suggested that the figure in 1980 fell into the range £1·4–£2·5 billion. Quite conservative assumptions were made, producing an upper figure below the Bank of England's estimate for 1980 of £3 billion (1983, p. 333). These limits represented the best available estimates of the scale of equity withdrawal. In relative terms, the figures were not very large – about 1 per cent of the total value of personal-sector dwellings, valued at £243·1 billion in 1979 (CSO, 1980). But it represented 20–25 per cent of net total advances on house purchase in 1980. Expressed another way, capital extracted in that year averaged around £2,000–£3,700 per sale. This was a problem in so much as the loss had to be refinanced, thus expanding the demand for mortgage finance faster than the growth of owner-occupation would otherwise justify. Rather than mortgage lending being neutral, therefore, leakage did occur, with real resources being used to finance transaction costs and consumer spending at property exchange and end-of-chain sales.

By taking out a capital gain in return for a higher mortgage, owner-occupiers were receiving the equivalent of tax relief on a personal loan. This was because a non-housing purchase was made using a capital gain which had been assisted by housing subsidies. Not only was this an expensive and ineffective form of housing subsidy which tended to increase inequalities between tenures, but it also had the effect of expanding the mortgage debt and thereby increasing demand for housing finance from the personal savings sector. Because of capital gains made from exchange or by last-time vendors, additional mortgage finance had to be attracted into the market. In this sense, leakage could be seen as an important reason for the growth in mortgage demand, and had some impact on the personal savings market. The extent of this impact depended on the proportion of funds available for reinvestment. But, given that leakage occurred, the refinancing of house purchase required some additional funds. While subsidy arrangements continued, buyers would be encouraged to maximize their mortgage debt. This would be reflected in trading up, an interest in continued house price inflation, and an expanding demand for resources from the personal sector to finance the housing sector borrowing requirement.

The call on the personal sector influenced the cost of borrowing. While building societies were active in a personal savings market which was not fixed in size, their operations were not self-sustaining. They were in competition with banks and other financial institutions to attract savings, and their activities could not be neutral. Indeed, receipts from investors were a very important source of funds for building societies, and the attraction of savings was essential to their operation (Boleat, 1982, p. 14). On a variety of measures the building societies had been very successful in expanding their market share. As a proportion of net wealth, building society shares and deposits doubled from 4.1 per cent in 1957 to 8·2 per cent in 1978; as a proportion of financial assets from 5·5 per cent to 17·6 per cent; and of liquid assets from 16·1 per cent to 43 per cent (Boleat, 1982, table 2.4). To meet the growing demand for mortgages meant that in 1983 new funds needed to be attracted at the rate of about £700 million a month. Hence the large number of savings schemes designed to attract new investors and the entry of building societies on to the wholesale money market to supplement private deposits with the funds of large corporate investors. The 1977 Housing Policy Review had suggested that these sources would have to be tapped if an adequate flow of mortgage finance was to be made available (DOE, 1977a, tech. vol. 2, p. 140).

If pursuit of housing consumption caused the building societies and banks to look beyond the personal savings sector, more expensive money on the wholesale market threatened to force up the relative costs of a mortgage. In competing for savings, the rates of interest offered by the building societies had a possible influence on the general money markets, with demand factors having some impact on the cost of borrowing despite the more important role of exchange rates. There was also a danger that these funds might be attracted at a cost to other sectors of the economy (Bassett and Short, 1980a, p. 296). In considering their impact on the capital needs of industry, the BSA's case to the Wilson Committee was that industry had not been suffering from a lack of capital. Rather, there had been a lack of demand for capital from the corporate sector, with industry suffering from low level of profitability, allied to low levels of demand in relation to the level of capital utilization (Wilson Committee, 1979a, p. 22).

This conclusion was only partly accepted by the committee, who were concrned that demand was influenced by the conditions of supply (Wilson Committee, 1980, p. 257). The impact of building society activity on the availability of funds for industry therefore remained a contentious area of debate. In considering whether building societies took deposits away from banks, Llewellyn (1979) came to no firm conclusion. Kilroy (1981, p. 115), however, was clear that remortgaging meant higher interest rates and higher exchange rates, both of which were detrimental to industry. Kay and King (1980, p. 56) described the high proportion of personal wealth held in houses, life insurance and pension funds as 'civil servant' rather than 'entrepreneurial' assets; they were all highly illiquid, and might explain low levels of investment in the small business sector and the rapid growth in the importance of institutional investors.

Expanding on the Wilson Committee's conclusion, critics pointed out that the demand for capital would be influenced by the terms on which finance was made available: the length of loan and rate of interest, which in turn influenced the climate of investment decision:

> If investment credit is provided to industry with little credit for consumption and government budgets, then economic growth will be of poor quality, the social infrastructure investment will be unsatisfactory, and personal savings will be high. That is Japan. If, at the other end of the scale, credit is provided to households and governments, while investment credit for industry is restricted, then there is a high level of public amenity and good housing, with a low productivity industrial sector. That is Britain. (Lever and Edwards, 1980)

In considering the low profitability of industry, what counts is the relative returns after tax, with a link between these rates of return and investment decisions. The favourable performance of housing as an investment coincided with a reported decline in the provision of entrepreneurial funds supplied to businesses by private investors (Wilson Committee, 1979b, pp. 12–13). Though the connection was not proved, Farmer and Barrell noted that low growth rates for small enterprises were experienced in the United Kingdom and United States, where housing subsidies were open to exploitation. In France, Germany and the Netherlands, where it had been more difficult to make entrepreneurial gains in housing, growth rates in the small business sector had been high. The housing subsidy system was not seen as the sole factor explaining differential performance, but it had a more disruptive effect on the efficiency and growth of productive capacity in the economy than might occur through other possible forms of subsidy (Farmer and Barrell, 1981, pp. 328–9).

In a debate more notable for assertion than evidence, the balance of opinion tended to support the view that a financial and tax structure favourable to housing investment had diverted capital away from industry. The National Economic Development Office (1975, p. 134) characterized Britain as having a relatively poor record of investment in manufacturing industry, arguing that the part of the capital market which serviced industry suffered from discrimination against it and in favour of finance for government spending and housing consumption. Boddy (1980, p. 86) pointed out that the 'investment diversion' argument paralleled criticisms of institutional investment in the commercial property boom of the early 1970s, with the flow of funds through the building societies being on a considerably larger scale than through property companies, and thus demanding serious attention. He noted that there was little evidence of a demand for capital from industry, but commented:

> ... this in no way removes the possibility that a revival in profitability and demand for funds could bring finance for house purchase and industrial investment into more immediate conflict, raising questions about the use of finance and resources within the economy as a whole and, more specifically, the efficiency of loan-finance house-purchase as a form of housing provision.

In their own deliberations, the Wilson Committee had found no evidence of any general shortage of finance for industry, but pointed out that the conditions attached to the price of finance would influence potential borrowers. The committee concluded that 'the market's ability to clear at the prevailing price does not necessarily mean that either the price or the demand for funds are at desirable levels in a macro-economic sense' (Wilson Committee, 1980, p. 371). Carrington and Edwards (1979) took this further, arguing that there was a shortage of the right type of funds for industrial investment. They saw the length of term of loans determining the cash flow required to service the loan, demand being a function of the cash flow cost of borrowing rather than simply conditioned by interest rates. To increase industrial investment, they argued that capital needed to be cheaper, and the amount of investment funds increased. This, they suggested, should be achieved through the banks becoming lenders of long-term capital, in line with their counterparts in Germany, France and Japan. To facilitate this, banks would have to attract longer-term savings, for which they would have to compete in the personal savings market, partly by stemming the flow of money to building societies by offering long-term savings accounts with tax-free interest (Carrington and Edwards, 1979, p. 231). The authors preferred to see this competition stemming the long-term trend of money away from the clearing banks towards the building societies. Their argument implied that an imbalance had developed in the use of personal sector savings, which had been utilized by the building socities to extend home ownership, with no similar industrial credit bank to offer long-term investment finance.

If this was the case, support for the owner-occupied housing market, in a way which continued to increase demand for mortgage finance, was in conflict with the need to release long-term finance to industry. However, the arguments remained largely speculative because the flow of capital released from housing investment had an impact which was not straightforward. Some capital was recirculated in the form of savings and investment which might benefit the formation of new businesses. An unknown proportion went on consumer durables and services. If the expenditure was on goods and services produced in the United Kingdom, this could re-enter the economy as investment. However, industry in general would not benefit if spending increased the flow of imported goods. Also, the inducement to maximize mortgaging could be argued to minimize certain forms of discretionary spending, with implications for patterns of expenditure at different points in the family life-cycle. Whether either personal consumption or productive investment was influenced by higher levels of interest as a result of competition in the personal savings market was an argument which was likely to continue. It was leading economic indicators like the US exchange rate that had an immediate impact on market rates, which meant that any influence exerted by mortgaging activity would occur through more difficult to determine effects on the economy.

Housing investment and the Housing Market
Though there was argument about the impact of increased demand for mortgage finance, there was more general agreement concerning the favourable tax treatment of housing, and the stimulus this provided to consumption while failing to encourage capital investment. When investment gains were cashed, they were balanced by an increased debt load borne by the incoming owner, or in the form of higher capital gearing for the continuing household. Not only did this increase the demand for

mortgage finance but it required a higher Exchequer subsidy in the form of tax relief on interest repayments. Because interest charges on debt were the basis for tax relief, an increase in mortgage debt meant that mortgage tax relief would continue to rise. Evidence to the House of Commons Environment Committee showed a projected fall in subsidies on the housing revenue account, while at the same time tax relief on mortgages was tending to increase (House of Commons, 1980 pp. 28, 34–5).

Criticisms of the housing subsidy framework were familiar. The existing system of tax relief was indiscriminate, expensive and inequitable; it had an inflationary effect on prices; and it encouraged housing to be used as savings. Mortgage tax relief gave greater subsidies to the rich – the higher the tax rate the greater the tax relief. Home owners had a vested interest in high house price inflation, and were not particularly sensitive to high interest rates – higher mortgage costs were outweighed by the combined impact of higher tax relief and large tax-free gains on the value of most houses. And too much money was invested in housing, because the investment was encouraged by relatively low-cost loans and was generally free of capital gains tax. The Clare Group therefore argued that home buyers were encouraged to spend and borrow as much as they could, rather than as much as they needed (King and Atkinson, 1980).

Housing consumption might be damped by concentrating tax relief on first-time buyers and lower income groups, by tapering off tax relief on those paying surtax, and modifying tax relief on the exchange of homes, possibly through a single annuity (Housing Centre Trust, 1975). But there did seem to be attractions in a more thoroughgoing reform which sought to treat owner-occupied housing as any other investment. Reforms which taxed imputed rental income, or eliminated mortgage interest tax relief, or applied capital gains tax, had been discussed by a number of observers (see, for example, Goss and Lansley, 1981; Grey, Hepworth and Odling-Smee, 1981). Reforms such as these could not be achieved overnight. Gradual reform of mortgage subsidies had been proposed by failing to increase the maximum mortgage limit eligible for relief, by restricting this relief to the basic rate and by offering the relief on the single annuity principle (Housing Centre Trust, 1975, p. 13). Beyond this, considerable political courage was needed to apply capital gains tax to property exchange. There would be difficulties if it applied to all transactions as it might force people to trade down, while if it applied only to a realized capital gain the encouragement to trade up would be maintained. As for the introduction of tax on imputed rental income, the idea hardly figured on the political agenda.

Because mortgage interest tax relief was a regressive subsidy, its abolition might reduce both inequalities in the housing market and levels of over-consumption. But it was difficult to predict the price and supply-side implications. If the initial tax subsidy was capitalized in the form of higher housing costs, prices might fall if the subsidy was abolished.

Ermisch (1981, p. 45) predicted this effect, while implying that any resultant hardship could be offset by the tax reductions permitted by the removal of mortgage tax relief. Alternatively, price might be sustained by demand through the substitution of income and savings. Hughes (1979) argued that the removal of tax relief on mortgage interest would bias the investment decision of households with non-housing wealth in favour of housing by encouraging them to reduce their mortgage debt at the expense of other financial assets. The Clare Group was uncertain about the demand side effects, but suggested that if the demand for housing were to become less dominated by the investment motive the pattern of investment might change in a way which was more attuned to social priorities (King and Atkinson, 1980, p. 15).

In practice, there was little apparent political willingness to tackle the general case for housing finance reform. Even the expedient course of leaving unchanged the £25,000 limit for mortgage interest tax relief was breached in the 1983 Budget. In these circumstances, a possible pragmatic response was that of a direct limit on capital leakage at exchange. This would take the form of upper limits on percentage advances to purchasers at second and subsequent transactions, or through a requirement to reinvest the asset value of the existing home. Such direct limits could be achieved through voluntary action by building societies. Indeed, similar mechanisms had been known to come into operation during periods of mortgage famine. But building societies were unlikely to accept voluntary restraint on their lending activity in periods when funds were adequate, while government control would prove difficult. The need, for example, to allow elderly owners to trade down would create a series of exceptions which others would exploit to maximize gains. This argued for more careful consideration of the suggestion from Kay and King that housing be taxed at the point where it was passed on to legatees. Their argument was founded on the inequalities of wealth caused by inheritance, leading to a justification of taxing the transfer of wealth through some form of lifetime expenditure tax. They maintained that to tax the value of owner-occupied property transferred by gift or – more usually – at death was a relatively painless way of recouping revenue and could be offset by lower rates of tax on earned income (Kay and King, 1980, p. 167).

As part of a package of taxation reform, the reintroduction of Schedule A had been advocated as a means of improving maintenance investment. If imputed rent income was taxed, it would once more be possible to offset against tax any expenses on repair and maintenance. While such a tax scheme might draw new groups into the tax net, it had a high yield which could easily pay for special allowances or even the abolition of domestic rates (Shelter, 1982, p. 22). While this raised wider taxation issues, it was debatable whether setting maintenance costs against tax was an effective and appropriate way to proceed. It was questionable whether the facility would lead to a better maintained stock, and it was difficult to avoid the conclusion that, on the objective of maintenance investment alone, the abolition of VAT might represent a simpler device. However, this issue of maintenance emphasised a special feature of the housing subsidy debate. There had been a range of policy proposals in response to shortcomings in the existing structure of housing subsidies. In summarizing the main contributions, Kemeny (1983, pp. 2–3) commented on their remarkably narrow conception, with no attempt to rationalize the housing subsidy system as a whole, or to propose a set of subsidies which could be justified in terms of explicit housing objectives. He made special reference to the failure of subsidy reform to consider the relationship between tenure policy and other aspects of housing such as urban renewal, and gave the specific example of housing maintenance as an element of interaction between subsidy and other aspects of the housing system (Kemeny, 1983, p. 30).

While the immediate political difficulties surrounding any change in the taxation of housing were formidable, the momentum of housing subsidy reform was nevertheless present. Subsidies were being reduced in the rented sector, and the government continued to have difficulty in financing its own spending programmes while controlling PSBR and seeking to reduce direct taxation. Elimination of mortage interest tax relief and the imposition of capital gains tax looked politically more attractive when seen in terms of the substantial revenues they would release. It has been seen that the cost of mortgage interest tax relief and capital gains exemption is around £5 billion a year. Reducing this subsidy would offer a number of options. One choice would be to increase direct spending on capital programmes. An alternative would be to reduce overall levels of taxation. Any increase in income as a result of lower taxation, though available as discretionary spending, would not necessarily go on increased capital investment. Nevertheless, it would create the option, while existing subsidies offset expenses incurred in owner-occupation without either encouraging or accounting for investment in repair and maintenance.

While the justification for housing subsidies is founded on the failure of the unmodified market to make adequate and fairly distributed provision, in operation intervention is incoherent in its plethora of grants and subsidies, ineffective in achieving new capital investment, inequitable in its treatment of different tenures and potentially harmful in terms of its impact on other areas of the economy. So there is a need to reform housing finance in a way which reduces the attractiveness of housing as an investment; and to stimulate capital spending to maintain the housing stock.

Because of the growing scale of resources devoted to exchange, there is neither the available funding nor the incentive to encourage this investment. There is a need to finance housing in a way which concentrates resources on new building, renewal and maintenance, rather than on indiscriminate subsidy of consumer demand. The reduction of subsidies on consumption could make it possible to expand capital subsidies on property maintenance. In this way, it would be possible to encourage investment in regular repair and maintenance – thus reducing the need for infrequent but massive injections of capital through the grant system. If the public-sector capital investment programme could be protected, and the growth of the housing sector borrowing requirement shifted from exchange to production, there is a possible recipe for investment on something like the scale which is required.

7

The Future of Urban Renewal

It is not inconsistent to argue for the fundamental reform of housing finance while recognizing the continued need for special assistance through measures such as grant and area-based policies. There is a need for tax reforms which improve the incentives to invest. But tax reforms only help certain groups. Changes in mortgage interest relief only affect people with outstanding mortgages, while reductions in the standard rate only increase the discretionary income of those people paying tax. Many of those currently living in the worst housing conditions are outright owners or live on low incomes which are below tax thresholds. These groups, in particular, would not be helped in the immediate future by indirect tax reforms aimed at increasing housing capital investment.

The impact of such reforms on new housing supply and the maintenance of the existing housing stock would be long-term, if they had any impact at all. It is therefore necessary to continue with policies which address themselves directly to the problems of housing decay and disrepair. While it may be a long-term goal to encourage higher levels of capital investment in the repair and maintenance of the privately owned stock, immediate policies will have to continue the tradition of grant-aided rehabilitation. This will be conditioned by levels of public expenditure devoted to housing programmes, and needs to be balanced against more sensitive policies of clearance. This in turn seems likely to demand different organizational approaches and changing roles for building societies, housing associations and local authorities.

The Role of Building Societies

Because the problems of older housing are associated with patterns of uneven development, disinvestment and an unequal distribution of wealth, special policies will sometimes be required to ameliorate the operation of market processes. For example, arguing that the nature of housing subsidies should be reformed, to encourage private capital investment, presupposes that institutional finance, particularly from the building societies, will be available in declining urban areas. This is no small assumption. There is nothing inevitable about the building societies' involvement in the older housing market. A concern for the long-term interests of prospective mortgagors is a justification for cautious lending policies. But the proper caution of building societies does not necessarily protect the prospective home buyer. People's need for housing, and to borrow money to finance its purchase, may push those on lower incomes towards riskier investments and fringe finance, increasing their housing costs and making it even more difficult for people to improve their homes. Hence the need to remedy any divergence between the concerns of building societies and the policy goals of urban renewal.

The possible consequence of any reluctance to lend in certain older areas can be seen in terms of spatial disinvestment and a polarization of both wealth and income between the inner city and suburbs. Survey data in Birmingham suggested that the relative increase in inner-area property values resulted in capital gains less favourable than for suburban owner-occupiers (Kemeny, Karn and Williams, 1981). This evidence gave support to the view that property values were polarizing, increasing wealth and income gradients between inner areas and the suburbs. It is a trend which has been the implied concern of all inner-city policies aimed at restoring 'social mix', in order to reverse what are generally seen to be undesirable economic and social trends. In the American context, Grigsby commented:

> In both the central city and the suburbs, the residential real estate market works in such a way as to produce a degree of income separation that society finds increasingly objectionable, that even upper income families may not strongly prefer, and that seems to aggravate the problems of poverty, inequality and neighborhood decay. (Grigsby *et al.*, 1977, pp. 112–13)

In many British cities the picture is more complicated, due to the impact of inner-area slum clearance and suburban public-sector developments. But the simple USA spatial model is one of the factors which resulted in policies aimed at minimizing income gradients by encouraging reinvestment in the inner city.

The same inner-city policies have been concerned about the spatial impact of building society lending. Through their allocation practices, the building societies play an important role in determining who can buy houses and where. By controlling access to mortgages, they function with other urban managers who have an impact on the workings of the housing market and influence how certain types of household are allocated certain types of housing (see, for example, Norman, 1975; Williams, 1978, 1982). In this role, individual building society managers have a degree of autonomy, but their actions are highly constrained. Collectively, building societies do not create scarcity. Neither do they act corporately, despite their co-operation on matters like interest rates. They have no knowledge of the combined spatial impact of their lending activities. But the outcome of these combined actions does have consequences for the people or areas affected by allocation practices. Williams, for example, showed how an increase in house sales in Islington during the 1960s and early 1970s was associated with an expansion of building society activity in the borough (Williams, 1976).

It has been argued that local building society managers generally have little understanding of how their lending activities affect other aspects of housing. In concentrating on growth-oriented policies, they have tended to disregard their impact on the housing market, or to find it convenient to see building societies reacting to changing market conditions rather than being an important element affecting these processes (Housing Monitoring Team, 1978, p. 47). This is not to suggest that building societies are the cause of inner-city housing problems. But, for whatever reason, the problems of poor housing can be seen in terms of low capital investment and, because building societies are such an important source of finance, their lending has an influence on the spatial pattern of investment (Bassett and Short, 1980b, p. 76).

Older housing areas require a sustained level of building society commitment and investment, which will not be forthcoming on the necessary scale unless it is seen to represent a sound financial proposition. To achieve this, various government support and guarantee schemes have been advocated to insure private sector risk. With continuing political pressures to extend assistance to first-time buyers, support and guarantee schemes may be used more widely. But in practice they probably have limited effectiveness. Mechanisms designed to benefit specifically inner-city residents, for example, will tend to inflate inner-city house prices, providing windfall profits for existing owners and disadvantaging potential low-income purchasers. If it is a general, rather than an area-specific mechanism, outer-area residents will receive greater advantage, because competition for limited funds will remain. To avoid such competition would require a scheme so successful in attracting new funds that it would tend to act to the disadvantage of other forms of investment.

Rather than looking simply for special schemes of inducements, subsidies or guarantees, it may be possible to link the interests of residents and building societies in a way which improves the housing stock and secures the investment value of property. For this to be achieved requires building societies to extend their commitment to lending in older urban areas and to make available new forms of service and assistance to the owners of older houses. In looking at the justification for a move towards social lending practices, it can be argued that lending in the older urban areas is consistent with the best interests of the building society movement, and, by looking at the credit needs of the local community, will generate growth through the link between savings and mortgages. Also, having moved through a period of sustained growth, the future of the building societies might be seen specifically in terms of housing-related services if their special position is to be maintained against competing financial institutions.

Local Lending Policies
The idea that building societies might generate investment through an awareness of community credit requirements stemmed from a concern about the spatial distribution of mortgage lending and experiments which discriminated in favour of local residents.

There was growing evidence throughout the 1970s on the lack of building society lending in inner-city areas (Boddy, 1976; Duncan, 1976; Weir, 1976). Some investors had a poor chance of obtaining a mortgage, even with substantial savings. In Leeds, research between 1974 and 1979 showed that minority ethnic groups were disadvantaged by building societies' attitudes towards inner-city housing in relation to the operation of the support lending scheme (Harrison and Stevens, 1983). Evidence of this nature was responsible for focusing attention upon the performance of building societies, and led to criticisms of red-lining practices. In the United States, this emerged as an explicit manifestation of capital exportation, with a spatial disjunction between investors and borrowers (Boyer, 1973; Harvey, 1977). In Britain, similar comments were made about investment exceeding mortgage commitments in inner areas (Harloe, Issacharoff and Minns, 1974), though an assessment of the area distribution of investment and mortgaging could not be attempted on any scale due to the lack of spatial information. In the United States, this type of information was made available as a result of the Home Mortgage Disclosure Act, and was influential in assisting the community tactic of green-lining. This involved a commitment from all residents to specify how much money they had in particular local savings and loan institutions, with the threat to withdraw or redeposit in other institutions if there was evidence of any failure to reinvest in areas where depositors lived (NCC, 1981, p. 55). Though the relationship between building societies and investors in Britain differed from the more area-specific role of savings and loan organizations in the United States, the idea of green-lining was taken up and applied by Shelter in their Bradford project. There were two linked objectives. First, to persuade a mainly Asian local community to save with building societies with the expectation of seeking funds for house purchase; and, second, to persuade local building society managers that a commitment to local lending would actually be good for business, while encouraging them to lend money on properties which they would normally be reluctant to consider (Young, 1979). Some success was claimed for the experiment. A Shelter survey suggested that, on unchanged conditions, about eleven mortgages would have been forthcoming in the first year of the project:

In fact, twenty-nine mortgages were granted by the five participating building societies and forty-one new savings accounts were opened in the first eleven months of the project. This suggests that the level of building society activity in the project area has increased at least threefold. (Wintour, 1980)

It was reported that new accounts increased building society savings by 50 per cent, leading to the conclusion that the building societies taking part in the experiment gained an advantage (NCC, 1981, p. 55). It also suggested that if building societies were seen to be willing to lend in an area new investors would be attracted. These people might be opening savings accounts in the expectation of obtaining a mortgage, but this could be associated with further saving activity in the future.

The Bradford experiment was small and despite the interesting questions it raised there remains a lack of empirical evidence to establish the nature of any links between investment and mortgaging activity. Though the Abbey National Building Society argued that their closer involvement with local communities brought in more savings (Thornton, 1981a), it is open to doubt whether building society activity in the inner areas leads to a significant increase in investment with building societies. However, societies will have to compete for the savings of potential investors who see themselves as future borrowers, and any suggestion of poor building society performance in meeting these expectations might deter potential investors. The prospective borrower has not been a major source of building society funds, but these investors are young, and are potentially the larger savers of the future. Evidence from a 1979 survey of the savings market (BSA, 1979b) confirmed two main points. First, that a majority of young investors were looking for a mortgage, and were saving in anticipation that this would be an advantage when applying for a mortgage. Second, that if building societies began to lose these young investors in the face of competition from the banks, they might in future lose other categories of saver – the two-thirds of mortgagors who were also investors and the outright owners who continued to save with their building societies from convenience, habit or loyalty. In this type of analysis, the potential mortgagor is an important source of future investment, and argues the need for building societies to adopt a more 'locally responsible' attitude which recognizes that if they do not act on behalf of local depositors these savers may look for more sympathetic options, perhaps through the banks or the growth of local credit unions. It is an analysis which is open to challenge by those who see commercial dangers accompanying increased lending at the lower end of the market. But, for those who feel that building societies should aim to satisfy local housing needs, the emphasis on a more direct relationship between depositors and lending has references to the community origins of the building society movement.

The Direction of Building Society Growth

After a long period of sustained growth, the early 1980s saw building societies considering their future development. As legally defined, the objectives of building societies were relatively narrow and limited: simply to raise by the subscriptions of the members, and by accumulated deposits, a fund for the purpose of making advances to members on the security of freehold or leasehold property. The growth of building societies was achieved within this narrow area of operation. Proponents of change suggested that in the future societies would be facing increased competition in the market for both savings and mortgages. This had already led to a proliferation of special investment schemes attracting premium rates of interest on relatively short-term money. At the same time, while clearing bank competition for mortgage lending had been variable, the building societies might reasonably assume that the major banks would follow their counterparts in other countries and become more active in the general mortgage market as they pursued their objective of providing a comprehensive financial service.

On this analysis, if building societies were to sustain past rates of growth, they would have to widen their objectives in a way which adapted to changing patterns of demand. A report by the Building Societies Association (1983b) suggested that societies should be permitted to undertake a wider range of functions related to their mainstream business in the housing and financial fields, or which enabled them to make more effective use of their assets.

Reaction to the report focused on the wisdom of abandoning the specialist housing and saving functions of building societies. This resulted in a second report, which dropped the proposal that societies should be able to own subsidiary banks and finance houses, suggesting instead that building societies should be allowed to offer directly a wider range of financial services (BSA, 1984).

Unsurprisingly, it had been the move towards 'bank-like' activities which concerned the Governor of the Bank of England, who warned that diversification in that direction would expose the building societies to the full rigours of the Banking Act 1979 and would raise basic questions about the ownership and accountability of societies (Richardson, 1983). Neither was it a direction which the government would necessarily favour. There had been earlier indications that the extension of building society activities into banking, insurance and hire purchase would not be welcome (Lawson, 1980). There was therefore a case for building societies to maintain a distinct identity from other financial institutions and to demonstrate a unique role in the market place. The most obvious way of achieving this would be to concentrate on housing-related activities, an area of growth which received the support of the Chief Registrar as a sensible and logical extension of building societies' involvement in housing policy (Brading, 1981). It was also a line down which individual building societies were already moving. Hence the interest in direct housing provision and new forms of private-sector development finance. It also argued for greater involvement in urban renewal. Through lending for both the purchase and improvement of older property, in co-operation with local authorities, and perhaps in partnership with a development function for housing associations, a role could be seen for building societies which emphasized their housing concerns, safeguarded their position in the financial markets and linked their savings function back to local communities.

Housing Services
It is not difficult to identify new areas of building society lending which are consistent with these urban renewal objectives. Societies have an established role in providing development finance for builders and housing associations which might be dramatically expanded through index-linked mortgages and schemes to help first-time buyers. The starting point for index-linked mortgages is low-interest, long-term institutional finance and the use of rental income to finance the interest charges. The debt would be allowed to increase in line with inflation, so giving a constant real rate of return. The repayments can be met because income is also increased in line with inflation.

A further area with obvious growth prospects is lending for house renovations. Again, building societies have been involved in various experiments to provide financial help and advice within HAAs. But there remains a more general market for improvement loans and maintenance services. Though the likely scale of future effective demand is uncertain, it is already a substantial market. One estimate suggested that total lending for all forms of home improvement was around £1,220 million in 1979, compared with total building society lending for house purchase in the same year of £10,000 million (Cantle, 1981). At the same time, there is clear evidence of need. For owners of property which requires improvement, cost remains a central constraint, but in a survey of six HAAs it was found that building society improvement lending was surprisingly low. In one West Midlands HAA, for example, 56 per cent of owners financed improvement through savings, 17 per cent through friends, 10 per cent with a bank loan, and only 4 per cent with help from a building society. And in an inner London Borough building society mortgages were used on 54 per cent of house purchases, but on only 4 per cent of improvement loans (Niner and Forrest, 1982, p. 63).

One area where lending seems particularly likely to increase is to elderly owner-occupiers. Various schemes have been devised which realize the asset value of property owned by the elderly. This is principally for the purchase of annuities, but capital could be released to assist in the maintenance or improvement of property. It seems likely that competition will increase to lend to the elderly owner-occupier, with most financial institutions developing some form of home income plan based on the security of property.

Interest-only or maturity loans are another area of potential growth, allowing the elderly to improve or repair their homes at modest cost. In appropriate cases, the DHSS is able to pay the interest charges on the full loan through supplementary benefit. It might also be possible for building societies to make a loan without requiring repayment of capital or interest. Given a low ratio of loan to property value, a building society could allow interest to accumulate on the mortgage account without threatening the loan's security. Anchor Housing Trust made a recommendation along these lines in respect of local authority maturity loans. It was suggested that these could be offered with the option of rolled-up interest: a loan on which the interest is rolled up with the capital and repaid only when the mortgagor dies or when the house is sold, whichever is the earliest occurrence (Anchor Housing Trust, 1980). As these ideas are unlikely to be practised on a substantial scale, building society income would not be significantly affected by reduced repayment income in the short term, and over time, income and deferred payments would balance out.

For those who are not elderly, equivalent financial options have received less attention, though in principle there is the possibility of expanding the idea of rolled-up interest to include any property with a suitable loan to value ratio. There seems little scope for schemes which offer preferential or low-start interest rates on the improvement loan element, though building societies need to be more competitive in terms of interest rates when an improvement loan is added to an existing mortgage. At the same time, there are opportunities for building societies to make it easier for people to purchase and improve older property, tying a purchase and improvement loan package to available grants in a way which avoids bridging finance.

While this type of lending represents the relatively straightforward end of the improvement market, it remains uncertain whether more ambitious aims are practical within the existing structure of housing finance. Building societies are limited in what they can do to encourage a flow of investment into house maintenance, though administrative reforms could help on the margins. For example, there is scope to simplify building society home loans where current legal costs make banks more competitive. Specifically, it has been suggested that people should be encouraged to maintain their mortgage account so that future improvement loans could be offered without incurring the legal costs associated with proof of title (BSA, 1982b, para. 15). Societies could also play a useful role in ensuring that homes are well maintained at the point of purchase. In this respect, retention practices could act against the desired effect of achieving repairs. The first-time buyer, in particular, might be financially over-extended, and in these cases holding back part of the mortgage simply makes it more difficult to carry out the necessary repairs.

However, it is not easy to see an alternative to retentions. If building societies placed conditions on maintenance standards at the point of sale, effectively transferring responsibility to the vendor, the long-term effect might be a greater incentive for owners to maintain their homes. But, in the short term, the impact would be chaotic. In effect, properties would become unmortgageable, penalizing existing owners of poor property and increasing the difficulty of completing a chain of sales. Schemes could be introduced gradually, but the incentives do not look particularly impressive.

While it can be argued that building societies should take a more positive line when dealing with the maintenance of mortgaged properties, perhaps acting in the role of an enlightened freeholder, it is difficult to envisage circumstances in which building societies would make widespread use of provisions in existing mortgage agreements that mortgagors should maintain their homes in good condition. A possible alternative would be to devise schemes which encourage saving for future maintenance expenditure. For example, it has been recommended that building societies introduce a system where a proportion of mortgage repayments are invested over a period of from five to ten years as a form of maintenance reserve (IEHO, 1983). This idea of a maintenance bond, or a charge added to mortgage interest repayments and subject to tax relief (Thomas, 1979, p. 248), has an interesting precedent in the 1956 Labour Party policy statement 'Homes for the Future'. This proposed that as a condition of a local authority home loan the purchaser should contribute to a repair fund. Nothing came of this, but Section 44 of the Housing (Financial Provisions) Act 1958 allowed a mortgagor to make interest-bearing payments to the local authority to cover the cost of maintenance. This was a rarely used provision which might, nevertheless, suggest a way to develop maintenance packages as part of a wider building society service to home owners.

When improving property, the complexity of the administrative, financial and technical processes remain a major constraint. Agency services can provide the kind of comprehensive support necessary to achieve rehabilitation, but this type of service is resource-intensive. What is being sought are mechanisms which can fund these support costs, and building societies might offer an opportunity to absorb the overheads. In this context, the agency role of building societies has received a degree of government recognition. Given the need for grant applicants to receive integrated advice, particularly on internal improvements following envelope schemes, it has been suggested that building societies might advise on grants, loans and interest-only loans (Stanley, 1983). Reflecting this thinking, building societies like the Abbey National and Nationwide have become more actively involved in the implementation of HAAs from around 1980. Initially, the Abbey National's involvement was simply one of providing mortgage services. But it was soon realized that a relatively passive stance was insufficient, and local staff were then encouraged to become more involved in the community. Referring to the American programme of Neighborhood Housing Services, Abbey National's chief general manager suggested that building societies could act in their non-profit capacity towards similar concerted action, helping to ensure that local government, builders, the professionals and the occupants of the houses themselves were all working as effectively as possible towards overall objectives (Thornton, 1981b).

In extending the agency role of building societies two points are immediately obvious. First, existing building society staff do not have the technical skill to run a comprehensive agency service, though they could fairly readily offer financial advice, and would quickly develop administrative skills. Second, taking on additional staff with the necessary skill to run agency services would, if pursued on a significant scale, have a detrimental impact on competitiveness, due to increased revenue costs. This would not rule out small experiments or, indeed, a longer-term shift in staff expertise within current manpower levels – an argument consistent with trends to reduce time-consuming administrative tasks through computerization, in favour of enhanced services to society customers.

What could occur, as administrative tasks were de-emphasized, would be the emergence of new functions and services. Financial advice along the lines of the Californian savings and loan societies would be an obvious direction in which to move. The stimulus for American home loan counselling centres was the 1978 Community Reinvestment Act, which required all financial institutions in the United States to demonstrate that they were helping to meet the credit needs of their communities, consistent with safe and sound commercial criteria. Assessment of savings and loan performance took into account the emphasis which was placed on effective communication and community development activities. The idea was that community needs were more likely to be met when the community was aware of the types of credit available and the lender was well informed about the credit needs of the community. It was in response to this that the home loan counselling centres were established. Run jointly by a number of savings and loan organizations, they offer free advice and counselling to prospective home buyers, as well as advice on the refinancing of purchase loans and house improvement loans (Bundy, 1980). While there is much to be said in favour of extending this type of advice service to Britain, there are legal problems which make it difficult for building societies to subsidize a comprehensive agency service. As an alternative, societies might be able to develop mechanisms which cover the real costs without these operating as a disincentive to potential clients. Whether inflating improvement loans to cover agency fees acts as a disincentive to take-up will depend in part on the nature of repayment conditions. For some elderly people, use of interest-only or maturity loans will make the issue of marginal importance.

New forms of help for existing home owners would seem to represent a potential area of growth for building societies. The development of housing related services is consistent with the origins of the building society movement and with the need to distinguish themselves from other financial institutions. They must adapt to new factors in the housing market. Doing so need not be in conflict with investment requirements. What is called for is the development of new skills, not the abandonment of financial prudence. There are pressures for building societies to become more like banks, but it would be wrong for societies to develop in any way which compromises their housing objectives. Their early development was closely tied to the growth of owner-occupation. Any further increase in the proportion of owner-occupiers will be less dramatic. But there are mortgaged assets which need to be maintained. In the future, helping owners to repair and improve their homes could be one of the main growth areas in building society activity.

The Role of Housing Associations

The Housing Act 1974 led to a major growth in housing association activity through a new system of subsidy and formal involvement in the implementation of area-based improvement policy. In ten years, housing associations nearly doubled their stock, and in 1981 their activity accounted for 10 per cent of all publicly funded rehabilitation in England, and one in five of all renovations in the public sector. Much of this activity was concentrated within HAAs, where they were an important means of achieving improvement (Niner and Forrest, 1982), while in places like Liverpool (Thompson, 1977) and Glasgow (Maclennan, Brailey and Lawrie, 1983) they were central to local authority rehabilitation policies.

More recently, however, housing associations have found that less money has been available to tackle urban renewal problems. Within the government's expenditure programme, there was a real reduction of 10 per cent in the Housing Corporation's budget between 1977/8 and 1981/2. This was not as severe as the cuts affecting local authorities. But, within the reduced total, housing association development priorities were redefined by the government to favour special needs and new initiatives, at the expense of rehabilitation programmes for general family requirements. At the same time, while local authority loans to housing associations remained relatively steady as a proportion of their total resources, the substantial reduction in authorities' overall capital programmes was translated into a real reduction in funds to housing associations. Local authority lending to housing associations fell from £240 million in 1979/80 to £160 million in 1981/2. The combined result was that the 1982 programme of rented houses provided by housing associations was little better than half that of the late 1970s. And further reductions were to follow. Because housing associations operated on annual cash limits, a relatively modest reduction in the 1984/5 Housing Corporation allocation threatened the entire programme of new approvals because of work already committed. To defend the development pipeline, new commitments in 1983/4 were cut by a quarter, from 22,500 to 16,500, with a similar figure for the new financial year. As such, it represented a programme well below the 20,000 figure which the National Federation of Housing Associations had always argued to be the absolute minimum for a stable and sustainable annual pipeline. The basis for such a figure might be debatable, but as a contribution to a national housing programme it represented an extremely modest target in view of the scale of demand for housing association accommodation.

Private-Sector Finance
Following its rapid growth during the 1970s, a section of the housing association movement became increasingly aware that development in the 1980s would be constrained by the availability of public-sector funds. There was a consequent search for development finance independent of government, so that associations would be free to move in new directions in response to developing problems. The central dilemma was easy to identify. Any innovation which seeks to encourage private-sector investment in older urban areas needs to be attractive to potential investors: it has to carry with it a reasonable expectation of a return on the investment. But how is this return to be achieved, and how can it be done in a way which remains consistent with the aims of housing associations? In looking at investment returns, there are three factors to consider: that in certain circumstances a profit can be made on traditional build-for-sale schemes in the inner areas; that surplus rent income can accrue when advantage is taken of low historic costs and subsequent wage inflation; and that private-sector finance might be used to generate profits to subsidize uneconomic rental provision.

First, the idea of profit is not inconsistent with redevelopment in older urban areas. In certain circumstances there remains scope for conventional private-sector housing investment. Commercial developers are not against inner-city housing projects as such. It is the scheme's profitability rather than its location which is the prime consideration, with the availability of land and its price being the major obstacles to development (Nicholls *et al.*, 1981, p. iii). On these criteria, partnership ventures in places like Liverpool and Birmingham would seem to confirm the view that private-sector housing development is feasible, though a more careful examination shows that such partnerships contain an element of subsidy on land costs. Local authorities can dispose of the land to the developer at market value, even when this represents a loss compared with acquisition costs.

Second, on the idea of offering a return on rented housing investment, there are elements of the housing association sector which have found themselves moving into surplus. This is due to rent inflation after the original capital debt was written off by housing association grant. Economic rents without subsidy have generally been prohibitively high, but only because of the need to meet immediate capital interest repayments. If the mortgage could be tapered to take advantage of historic costs, future rent inflation would be able to service the rescheduled debt. There are, consequently, initiatives in the structuring of mortgages and development finance which might open up new opportunities for cost sale, for private-sector equity participation in shared ownership and for fair rent development through the use of 'index-linked' mortgages.

The third idea concerns subsidy through surplus. Looking at the continuum of outright sale, shared ownership and fair rent, the financing of rental provision is clearly the most challenging. A long history of government subsidy testifies to the failure of the private market to build houses at a rent people can afford. If fair rents continue to rise above the rate of inflation, this will tend to shift the burden from capital subsidies to housing benefits, which will ease the difficulties of privately funded schemes. Even then, however, there may be a gap between rental income and the return needed to service long-term institutional finance. Where this is the case, there is the opportunity to use development cross-subsidy. This would imply housing association involvement in a variety of entrepreneurial activity, with surpluses reinvested in fair rent schemes. The initial steps in this direction have already been taken. In Tower Hamlets, the Abbey Housing Association was able to cross-subsidize assured tenancies within a build-for-sale scheme, with a ratio of six for sale against one for rent. An element of cross-subsidy was also present in a shared ownership scheme by Sutton Hastoe, using deferred-interest mortgages from the Nationwide Building Society. In this type of arrangement, rent income is insufficient to meet loan repayments in the early years, so the building society defers the outstanding interest until a later date. The outstanding sum is added each year to the mortgage, with the year-end balance gradually rising. It was estimated that annual rent rises would meet an increasing proportion of loan repayments, breaking even in year fifteen. After that, further rent increases would produce surplus income, allowing larger repayments than required, and permitting final repayment of the loan in year twenty-seven.

Perhaps the first ambitious example of a mixed-tenure development involving a housing association was Elm Village in Camden. This was developed by the United Kingdom Housing Trust, using building society finance for the build-for-sale element, with Housing Corporation shared ownership and fair rent. In this case the opportunity for cross-subsidy was not exploited. UKHT built and sold fifty houses on a cost-sale basis. It carried out the work through a subsidiary company in the same way as a private developer, but without taking a profit. Instead, UKHT retained a 10 per cent interest in the value of the house so that, at resale, future first-time buyers would benefit from a purchase price below full market value. It is, however, possible to see how similar mixed-tenure developments might use the surplus from value-sale to supplement or replace the Housing Corporation's contribution to shared ownership and fair rent. Having arrived at such a position it would then be logical to maximize the surplus from value-sale schemes by developing in areas which are easily marketable. As a result, new-build schemes for sale in the suburbs might generate surpluses for reinvestment in mixed tenure new build and rehabilitation within older urban areas.

If housing associations become involved in housing reinvestment strategies of this nature, there is the prospect of making continued housing provision during a period where reliance on central government funding would lead to decline. But it is important that, in their attempt to survive and expand, housing associations should continue to meet the requirements of people in special housing need. The objectives of the housing association movement defy succinct definition. The enormous variation might be considered a strength. However, if the role of housing associations is to be justified as a 'third force' in relation to owner-occupation and council housing, a particular function or set of functions has to be identified. A role has sometimes been justified in terms of wider choice. But for many housing associations their priority tenants have no effective choice. People have not necessarily preferred a housing association. It is more likely that their tenancy reflects the high costs of owner-occupation, ineligibility for local authority accommodation and the inadequacy of the private rented sector.

It is significant that the role of housing associations is often described as supplementing that of local authorities – giving priority to the provision of accommodation for special groups and needs not otherwise being met. The available evidence suggests that associations are achieving these goals. A survey in 1978 revealed that nearly half of all new housing associations tenants were over 60, nearly 10 per cent were single-parent families, and nearly 90 per cent earned less than the national average wage (Housing Corporation, 1979). Despite this evidence, the problem remains that, through the Housing Corporation, broad priorities are defined by government policy which need not reflect the interests or developing concerns of the housing associations themselves. It is of some concern that the straitjacket of government policy and finance might inhibit the features of versatility, flexibility and enthusiasm which have been said to characterize the housing association movement. The question is whether housing associations can pursue their special role of 'care and concern' while turning to the private sector for development capital. 'Care and concern' is not a development skill, and there is a danger that, in assembling the necessary expertise, social objectives will be endangered. Existing subsidy systems have been criticized for encouraging growth at the expense of sensitive management. It could be that a more entrepreneurial involvement would exaggerate this dilemma. But this cannot be held to be inescapable. Any development which utilizes private-sector finance means that the housing association can use its non-profit status to reinvest in fair rent housing, which the private sector would not find it economic to provide. In doing so, the housing association is extending the range of available choice and might become involved in a variety of projects within a small area, providing different tenure options to the general benefit of the local community.

The criticism of Housing Corporation initiatives like improvement for sale and shared ownership was that they were not financed by extra allocations but were a response to political priorities and paid for at the expense of fair-rent, general-needs housing. The real challenge is to develop initiatives outside the Housing Corporation framework, allowing housing associations to expand their development programme by supplementing or replacing government subsidies in certain categories of scheme. For example, some housing associations may not be content to provide management services for private developers making profits from the provision of housing for the elderly. If there are profits to be made, it is not inconsistent for a housing association to form a development company, carry out the building work, and use the surplus to reduce the service charge on the scheme. It is the opportunity to substitute cross-subsidy for developer's profit which is the motive behind moves into private-sector finance. It is not an attempt to demonstrate that public-sector intervention is redundant. Given that the non-profit motives of reinvestment have parallels in the philanthropic movement of the nineteenth century, it needs to be borne in mind that 5 per cent philanthropy did not provide housing for the poor on any scale and, indeed, pointed to the need for state intervention to fill the gap left by the failure of the private-sector (Merrett, 1979, p. 19).

While the potential for non-profit reinvestment has considerable attractions, it is an area of legal difficulty. Registered housing associations are not able to carry out building for sale. Following the Housing Act 1980, charitable housing associations had to set up non-charitable registered associations to carry out improvement for sale and shared ownership because it was held that these activities were not charitable. Because of their wish to retain the advantages of charitable status while embarking on a range of non-charitable activities, housing associations have found themselves involved in increasingly complex formal arrangements. The most common is for registered charitable housing associations to have a second, registered non-charitable association for improvement for sale and shared ownership. Less frequent are wholly owned limited companies to carry out architectural services, environmental projects and commercial ventures. As these various satellites generally employ a common core of staff, they are essentially paper organizations which add nothing but legal, accounting and managerial complexity. That they are necessary under present circumstances is partly a result of the need for housing associations to respond to problems with greater flexibility than the Housing Corporation will permit. However, the main reason for the complex organizational arrangements is that the benefits of charitable status are too restrictive to meet the variety of tasks which some housing associations are attempting to perform.

Charitable status is important because it confers a number of tax privileges. There is exemption from income and corporation tax, from capital transfer tax and capital gains tax; and 50 per cent reduction in local rates, no stamp duty, and no employer's national insurance surcharge. At the same time, on gifts and bequests, donors to charities can avoid income tax, corporation tax, capital gains tax and capital transfer tax on the sums donated. These are attractive provisions. But at the root of a number of difficulties facing housing associations is the legal premise that 'trading' is not, as such, a charitable purpose. A charity may freely trade if there is some intrinsic connection with its primary purpose but trading which does not in itself advance the charity's primary purpose is subject to the restriction that it must not dominate the charity's activities (Gladstone, 1982, p. 85). The general principle appears to be that charities should not be allowed to trade without paying tax because this would be unfair competition for the ordinary trader. Arising out of this restriction, the Charity Law Reform Committee (1974) proposed a new category of non-profit-distributing organization. These would be entitled to all the advantages of charities but without the attendant restrictions on their activities. The only prohibition would be on any kind of private benefit. Though attractive in their comparative simplicity, the proposals were criticized because of their scope for tax avoidance and because they would confer tax-exempt status on a wide range of bodies (Gladstone, 1982, p. 140). However, the principles put forward by the Charity Law Reform Committee might yet offer the basis for a more satisfactory tax treatment of housing associations.

Housing Associations and Urban Management
The full substitution of private-sector finance for public-sector funds was still on the horizon in the mid-1980s, and there was no immediate prospect of tax reforms to simplify the organizational structure of housing associations. But, despite their continuing dependence on Housing Corporation funding and the somewhat bizarre spawning of satellite organizations, a number of housing associations had become involved in urban management. Associations like North British and East Midlands acted for local authorities in the implementation of enveloping schemes. Family First Trust in Nottingham had a large youth-training scheme for short-life conversion and community arts, funded by the Manpower Services Commission. Bournville Village Trust, Circle 33 and Merseyside Improved Houses were three of a number of associations experimenting

with agency services for owner-occupiers. Arising out of these initiatives, and from the House of Commons Select Committee on the Management of Urban Renewal, the DOE began to look more closely at extending the role of housing associations in urban regeneration – notably in the area of flats above shops, agency services for the elderly and environmental improvements. The public face of this debate argued that housing associations might be a relatively more important agent of urban renewal, without attempting to displace the function of local authorities in defining local housing policies. However, it was difficult not to speculate on the logical extension of this agency trend.

Historically, in Britain, the lead role in the management of urban renewal has rested with local authorities. This is questioned in a model like Neighbourhood Housing Services, which originated from the United States, where local authorities play a minor role in the housing system. British interest in this type of model, taken with the framework of inner city partnerships and urban development corporations, can be seen as a growing central government preference for intervention through directly funded agencies. A future extension of this thinking might take the form of a body similar to the Scottish Development Agency as a mechanism thought capable of co-ordinating government programmes within core areas. An alternative would be the development of housing associations as agents for integrated urban renewal, using housing funds from central government channelled through the Housing Corporation. The arguments in favour of this are that housing associations have established status and a non-profit orientation. They might be well placed to co-ordinate a partnership with residents, financial institutions and local businesses without this being seen as an attempt to displace the local authority, whose co-operation and resources would be a vital element in any long-term strategy. The role of the housing association would be a detailed involvement at a local level over a long period of time: providing a range of housing tenures, acting as enabler for residents and community groups, encouraging local economic growth and keeping under review opportunities for environmental improvement through a form of gradual renewal implying consultation and a local presence over a long period of time.

The close partnership with local people in a programme of gradual renewal cannot be divorced from a concern with wider economic issues. Because area-based renewal strategies need to be concerned with employment, income and housing as interrelated issues, the enabling role of the housing association as urban manager would be both to link job and training opportunities to the housing programme and to encourage initiatives which would widen the area's employment base. This might be achieved through help with premises and services and by advice and support on product development, marketing and finance. In turn, this advice and support could draw on the resources of the local authority and the business advice services of local banks. In inner city areas, particularly, it might bring together financial institutions and ethnic minority business-men, seeking a better understanding of their needs and helping with an improved presentation of their ideas. These economic initiatives could be formulated within the broad context of community enterprise, and might involve establishing a local enterprise trust as a consortium of business, local authority and housing association, to co-ordinate resources and assistance.

In this type of local programme there has to be a trade-off between participation and intervention. Representation and consultation are necessary if programmes are to benefit local people, but if progress is to be achieved a balance needs to be found between community involvement and efficient project administration. It is here that the role of 'enabler' becomes crucial. The successful management of urban change depends on the co-ordination of resources, appreciating the needs of the area, generating imaginative but feasible options, securing the commitment of all interested parties and then managing efficiently the development work (Falk, 1979, p. 185). Such an approach would have to adopt a planning role which was catalytic and entrepreneurial, looking for ways to remove obstacles standing in the way of investment:

> Rather than concentrating on the problems, it should identify under-utilised resources, whether these are physical, social or economic. Having identified opportunities, it must ensure that good ideas are turned into practical programmes, and that the people and finance needed to implement them are found. Instead of solely searching for investment from outside, it should seek to make full use of local resources, as those with a stake in an area are both sensitive to their community's needs and more inclined to invest. (Falk, 1981)

Because the renewal process is partly political in nature, the enabler has to respond rapidly and flexibly. Local authorities may find this difficult to achieve given the inevitably cumbersome processes of accountability, and it suggests that the enabling role may be better suited to an independent agency like a housing association. It is this lack of accountability, however, which represents a problem. Critics of housing associations in general, and specifically of their expanded role in the management of urban renewal, have commented on their essentially undemocratic structure. Continued interest is therefore expressed in the idea of community-based housing associations along the lines of those operating in Glasgow. These are locally based associations with management committees largely composed of people living in the area. But it should not be assumed that a successful, small and locally based approach necessarily means that housing associations will be either community-based or responsive to local needs. In Glasgow, it has been suggested that 'community-based' may be too strong a description of the thirty-one housing associations working on the rehabilitation programme. The boundaries within which an individual association work were defined by consolidating project areas, themselves formed by grouping declared and potential HAAs. The territory of any housing association, therefore, might subdivide or include more than one locally perceived community (Maclennan, Brailey and Lawrie, 1983). Whether the organizational boundaries of an HAA can or should be related to some notion of geographical community is debatable, and in practical terms may indeed vary from place to place. More important perhaps is the level of control exerted over the housing association at the local level, however defined. Here an assessment of the Glasgow experience suggests only a limited degree of effective control by the management committee. Rehabilitation priorities were pragmatic, control over internal improvements limited to elements like decoration, and much of the technical and financial management left in the hands of professional staff. This led to the conclusion that the association might be more accurately labelled as locally oriented rather than community based (Maclennan, Brailey and Lawrie, 1983). It may be that a more effective level of local representation is required within any body concerned with the implementation of urban renewal. But, taking the model of Neighbourhood Housing Services, this representation could be at a co-ordinating level, leaving a more clearly defined technical role for housing associations in the implementation of agreed partnership proposals.

Intervention and Reform

Urban renewal has had a massive physical and social impact on twentieth-century Britain. Since the 1930s, nearly two million homes have been demolished, while in the postwar period over three million have been improved with grant aid (Gibson and Langstaff, 1982, p. 11). Large-scale comprehensive redevelopment has been displaced by a growing emphasis on policies of rehabilitation linked increasingly with attempts to stimulate economic regeneration. In part this has been a response to changes in the nature of the problem, with substandard housing conditions increasingly associated with disrepair in the owner-occupied and public rented stock. At the same time, growing dissatisfaction with the process of redevelopment coincided with pressures to reduce public-sector capital expenditure. The combined effect has been to redefine the public-sector role towards that of underwriting or subsidising the activities of the private sector rather than intervening through direct public action. But, though the role has changed, urban renewal has been a vehicle of social reform for many years, and it seems reasonable to assume that a concern for housing conditions will continue to be a feature of public policy.

Resources

During the 1970s the main emphasis of urban renewal was on rehabilitation grants and the use of area-based policies. The introduction of enveloping was a radical innovation which changed the scale on which improvement works could be undertaken. But, while enveloping began as a rapid and large-scale external repair programme with a minimum of pre-contract organization, the instinct of government was, in turn, to envelop the approach with all the procedural delays it was designed to avoid. In this sense, the enthusiasm of central government for the political impact of policy initiatives is matched by local authorities' search for new approaches as a way of staying ahead of the weight of interference surrounding mainstream programmes.

By 1984, the early momentum of enveloping programmes had been lost, while the cuts in government housing expenditure had severely affected overall levels of improvement grant activity. The emphasis continued to be on private-sector initiatives in the context of reduced public-sector resources. Lower public expenditure implied a redefinition of the public sector's role and raised questions about its regulatory functions. But there was no automatic need to concede the case for lower levels of public funding. The immediate problems of substandard housing only seem capable of being tackled through a public-sector programme. This can be justified as a reflationary strategy, but it is important that it is seen in the context of a flow of public-sector resources. In the past, frequent reversals of policy have been inconsistent with the need for a sustained and predictable workload in the construction industry. Continuity is important given the concerns which have been expressed about the ability of the building industry to respond to an expanded programme of rehabilitation (RTPI, 1981, p. 23).

Government policy has tended to use urban renewal as an economic regulator without reference to the need for continuity, assuming that if investment capital is made available the building industry will respond by doing the work. However, when improvement grant activity peaked in the early 1970s, the limited evidence which is available suggests that building resources were comparatively inelastic. Because the industry correctly anticipated that the flow of grant work would not be sustained, established builders did not expand, while inexperienced builders were attracted by the work. The result was inflated contract prices, delays in completion, and dissatisfaction with standards of work. One of the attractions of enveloping is its potential to involve larger builders in rehabilitation work and thereby provide a means to expand improvement activity. But it quickly became clear that subcontracting practices draw on a supply of labour similar to that used by the smaller builder. Changing the scale and value of rehabilitation contracts through the enveloping approach does not influence the underlying structure of a building industry which relies on subcontracting as a response to fluctuating demand.

The future emergence of a sustained urban renewal programme seems improbable, and alone would find it difficult to restructure an industry where job security and skill training appear to be rare outside public-sector direct labour organizations. Without this sustained programme, however, it is unlikely that any urban renewal programme can be linked to a planned expansion of small building firms through help with working capital, management assistance and skill training.

There has always been a dramatic relationship within older urban areas between poor housing conditions and unemployment. There is work to be done, and the labour force is available. Consequently, building work promises an important opportunity to generate local employment. The economic impact of renovation activity on the local community is highly speculative, but the multiplier effect of urban renewal is potentially significant. However, there are formidable practical difficulties. A substantial organizational input would be required to enable a wide range of self-help, co-operative and contract developments to proceed. There would be the opportunity to offer work experience and training under government-funded programmes. This would have to be balanced against maintaining union support and ensuring that labour rates were not being undercut in a way which threatened the formal building sector.

Building programmes need not be restricted to housing. In older urban areas, a wide range of projects present themselves. Though requiring varying degrees of financial support, schemes might include the rehabilitation of commercial premises, infrastructure renewal, and environmental projects. In this context, a study in Birmingham showed the unsuitability of much of the city's industrial premises, suggesting the need to improve physical conditions and to provide room for expansion (Williams *et al.*, 1980, p. 62). The report called for selective redevelopment on a small-area basis to rationalize access and provide room for expansion. While the resolution of physical constraints was recognized to be difficult, the necessary rehabilitation work would be a potential source of local employment. Indeed, a combination of funding arrangements and reinvestment strategies would offer the potential for sustained work opportunities, while the use of local labout for projects aimed at stimulating employment growth suggests the possibility of fairly dramatic multiplier effects.

Donnison is perhaps the most influential British proponent of the analysis that housing problems are really problems of unemployment, poverty and inequality, and that a concern for housing is inseparable from the need to provide work opportunities (Donnison, 1980). Similar arguments have been put forward in the United States:

neighbourhood revitalisation must give pre-eminence to economic factors. The causes of urban neighbourhood decay have historically and demonstrably been economic, and it follows therefore that the suggested remedies must be mainly economic if they are to have a chance of succeeding in restoring the viability of neighbourhoods. (Goldstein and Davis, 1977, p. 5).

To bring back jobs and regenerate the economic base of older urban areas is therefore central to any attempt to tackle the root problems of poverty and inadequate housing. Achieving this through structural economic solutions looks uncomfortably like a form of urban employment strategy along the lines of earlier regional policies, and assumes that features of uneven development can be restructured through the control of national economic planning. It seems likely that the creation of new wealth in older urban areas requires the redirection of capital on a massive scale. But considerable doubt surrounds whether this can happen and whether, if it does occur, local residents will benefit. At best, such an approach represents a long-term strategy, and argues for a more ameliorative approach at the community level through the promotion and development of local initiatives.

Increased Clearance

By the early 1980s it has been seen that considerable pressure had been generated for a broad review of approaches to urban renewal. It was commonly argued that improvement policy was too dependent on the voluntary take-up of grants which, when concentrated on the worst housing conditions, imposed too high a cost on low income groups. The result was increased problems in implementing policy and high resource and administrative costs in return for low capital investment. A view also emerged that the pendulum had swung too far in favour of renovation, resulting in levels of clearance which were inadequate. Though many individual authorities continued with a significant clearance programme, rehabilitation had become the dominant activity. The direction of opinion was therefore towards higher levels of demolition. To achieve this, however, was also to encounter the problems of previous redevelopment programmes, notably those of social dislocation, the balance of public and private costs and the allocation of limited public resources.

During the 1960s it seemed that clearance activity met opposition from increasing numbers of owner-occupiers. Any new programme of clearance would be likely to affect a much larger proportion of owner-occupiers, some of whom may have improved their homes with the assistance of rehabilitation grants. The attitudes of these owners towards clearance proposals would be dependent in part on the generosity of compensation arrangements. In this very fundamental sense, increased clearance would be carried out in a radically different tenure context. In the past, redevelopment was implemented through a flow of local authority capital investment and the assumption that people would move into council houses. Indeed, slum clearance legislation was based on the historical pattern of landlord-owned slums. However, with substantial levels of owner-occupation, rehousing in the public rented sector would not be a universally popular option. At the same time, if low levels of new public-sector housebuilding were to continue, it would be unlikely that local authorities could provide housing to match an increased redevelopment programme.

In the context of low levels of public expenditure and the assumed wish of owner-occupiers to remain within the private sector, what might emerge is some form of mixed economy of clearance. This would involve mixed-tenure redevelopment, with the local authority performing an enabling function. People would be rehoused in accordance with their tenure and price preference, but with capital subsidies on the new housing to ensure that local people would not face an increase in their housing costs. The nature of these subsidies require careful thought, as do the implications of involving the private sector in this form of redevelopment. Government are likely to find it initially attractive because it implies a reduced level of public spending. The larger builders, until recently remarkably passive in the lobby for increased clearance, might see the benefits of capital subsidies for new housing construction, linked to an existing local demand for rehousing. But problems can be anticipated, notably in the co-ordination of clearance and rehousing. The involvement of private-sector agencies seems likely to further complicate a process which was always difficult. Questions would also be raised about the obligations which could or should be placed on the private sector to rehouse people affected by redevelopment. Because of these detailed problems, it remains clear that owner-occupation represents a major constraint on future levels of demolition, with implications for the organization and implementation of clearance programmes. The challenge is to make clearance socially and politically more acceptable, perhaps by increasing the element of consumer sovereignty.

Help and Advice

The growth of owner-occupation has been the single most important tenure trend in Britain during the twentieth-century. The general effect of changes in tenure has been to extend owner-occupation down market to include groups of people unable to afford the full costs of ownership. This was apparent in the 1970s, when an overall rise of 5 per cent in home ownership was achieved while the proportion of owners who were unskilled manual workers increased from 21 per cent in 1971 to 26 per cent in 1981 (OPCS, 1973, 1982). Many of these low-income purchasers bought pre-1919 houses, and inherited the problem of a poorly maintained and ageing property. For owners like these, incomes are often inadequate to meet mortgage repayments while carrying out fundamental repairs and undertaking routine maintenance. As a result, the danger is that this property will continue to deteriorate, unless the government intervenes on a much greater scale with grants and other forms of subsidy. The dilemma is that extending support to maintain homes adds further to the costs of financing owner-occupation. Partly for this reason, reform of the grant system began to ask questions about the role of government, of value for money and the benefit of a means-tested grant.

The continued existence of some form of direct assistance was supported by the 1981 House Condition Survey. This made it clear that the majority of those living in the worst housing conditions could not pay for the costs of improvement and repair out of savings or income. Without grants, roughly three-quarters of those in dwellings judged to be unfit or in serious disrepair would have to find a sum greater than their annual income (DOE, 1983a, p. 3). Thus, while it was conceded that some people could afford to improve their homes, the implicit argument was that without grants the worst stock was unlikely to be tackled.

At least for low-income groups, therefore, the House Condition Survey provided a justification for the continuation of grants for house improvements. But this did not answer criticisms levelled at the grant structure. The system has grown incrementally from small beginnings in 1949 to one that in 1983 dispensed about £600 million to about 200,000 owners. Over the years, procedures have been revised but, in aggregate, never simplified. The resulting administration is confusing to applicants, leads to delay and imposes a burden of processing and checking on local authorities. Much of this is applied with the intention of preventing abuse and targeting limited resources at the most needy applicants.

An internal review of improvement policy by the DOE in 1983–4 looked for simplication of the grant system. This involved proposals to remove property criteria such as the rateable value limit, and the introduction of a unitary grant, applying some form of applicant criteria through income limits. But, whatever proposals emerge, it seems likely that a level of detailed control will be maintained. Even though resources are already subject to cash limits, central government continues to perpetuate the myth that local government cannot be entirely trusted to look after people's money.

Even with a simplified grant structure and a substantial level of local authority discretion to establish priorities in the light of local conditions, there would remain two main problems: first, that of grant applications exceeding the available cash; and, second, that of people in need of grants who fail to apply. Consequently, not only is there a danger of demand outstripping supply, but that those in greatest need will not always be competing for the available resources. The problem of a purely passive grant system is that those who need a grant, but do not apply, can be overlooked, while those who do apply are simply prioritized on a date order system. Total demand could be damped down by more restrictive grant conditions, but taking limited resources and attempting to target them at those in greatest need requires a more direct approach to grants as a product or benefit. As part of this, some form of agency service seems to be a prerequisite of improving owner-occupied homes in the poorest condition. Both the 1976 and 1981 House Condition Surveys suggest that a substantial proportion of those living in the most unsatisfactory accommodation require active help and support to improve their homes. The elderly, for example, might be reluctant to undertake work because of an unwillingness to incur debt, or to face the administrative complexities of the grant process or the disruption of building works. The 1981 House Condition Survey concluded that achieving improvement of the poorest housing stock required not only financial help tailored to owners' needs but 'more effective counselling and advice services in order to increase awareness of the importance of maintenance and repair work, and to ease the process of actually obtaining grant and carrying out works' (DOE, 1983a, p. 5).

The existence of an agency service does not, in itself, help to target grant aid. Unless the service is marketed, take-up will not necessarily find the most needy cases. The problem is to target clients rather than simply respond to demand. One solution is to let it be known that the service exists, and then to adopt criteria which select those in most need. Going beyond this, Anchor's 'Staying Put' project showed how client groups might be targeted by making contact with agencies dealing with the elderly, and by visiting day centres and old peoples' clubs. A logical extension of this would be to link an agency service into a carefully devised referral strategy. In this way, information on poor housing conditions could be fed back to the agency service from environmental health officers, social workers, voluntary organizations, health and welfare visitors. The grant system would then begin to operate as part of an integrated welfare service. This would be consistent with a trend towards the treatment of grants as a form of welfare benefit. It might help to get scarce resources to those in need, but only if the familiar problems of benefit take-up are overcome. In the past, grants have been disproportionately enjoyed by those best able to take advantage of the system. Other areas of take-up displayed similar distributions. For example, managerial and professional people got 40 per cent more out of the National Health Service 'in relation to need' than semi-skilled and unskilled manual workers (Le Grand, 1982). For a benefit like improvement grant to be taken up by those who need it most means that the client has to be found, and then given a considerable amount of help and support throughout the improvement process. To do this, thought has to be given to the type of service which might be offered and to the ways in which the service and the client might be brought together.

Progressive Investment
In numerical terms, the 1981 English House Condition Survey confirmed

that the bulk of unfit houses and those in serious disrepair were in the owner-occupied sector. These substandard houses tended to be owned by the elderly, the unemployed and first-time buyers – those least likely to be able to afford the expense of improvement and repair.

The logic of owner-occupation is that government concern for standards need not extend beyond a basic requirement for health and safety. Generous financial assistance on improvement and repair is seemingly inconsistent with policies which disregard the provision of other forms of tenure in favour of a political philosophy of home ownership implying self-reliance and freedom from state intervention. However, such direct help is entirely consistent with a longer tradition of government concern for social inequality in housing, linked with the view that the public benefits accruing from improved housing conditions cannot be rigidly defined to include only the narrow externalities of public health and nuisance. Concerns for individual health, welfare and potential have less easily defined but demonstrable public benefits. At the same time, there is a case for intervention at the level of national self-interest. It is an accepted function of government to ensure that the population is adequately housed, and in this sense the existing housing stock is a national asset which the government has an interest in maintaining. It can do this through subsidy, regulation and direct intervention. Through grant policy, governments have assumed that good housing is a worthwhile goal to be achieved through a subsidy related to a specific end result. A historical distinction has been drawn between works to improve the quality of the original house, which was eligible for public assistance, and works of repair and maintenance, which were the everyday concern of the owners. This distinction has become blurred by the introduction of repair grants and the use of enveloping, but the line of argument can still be followed.

If repair and maintenance problems are a consequence of owners choosing to under-invest, subsidy is a questionable approach. If, on the other hand, under-investment is a consequence of low income, then the effectiveness of direct subsidy through grant aid needs to be compared with a benefit or income supplement approach. In the past, the implementation of urban renewal has been concerned with physical improvement of the stock. If this is the goal, income subsidy would be inappropriate, as higher allowances would not necessarily result in spending on improved housing conditions. In particular, this would be true if a high proportion of income was already devoted to housing, or if higher spending was accompanied by a move away from the older urban areas, so that while there was a general benefit to housing it did not accrue to urban renewal. Alternatively, if the goal of urban renewal was to be defined more widely than the provision of better housing, with a more explicit concern for the overall quality of life, then an income benefits approach becomes a more satisfactory vehicle. Some economists have argued that 'in-kind' transfers like rehabilitation grants are less efficient than money transfers. If this is the case, recipients would be better off, in the sense of a wider range of choice, if they could decide whether or not to buy better-quality housing with enhanced income. However, others might express doubts about an approach which appears to be based on simplistic assumptions about market choice, suspecting that attempts to maximize individual utility would simply drive up the price of poor quality housing because of an inelasticity of supply within local submarkets. Consequently, reliance on income redistribution would remove from government any direct influence over housing conditions, with the possibility that increased housing allowances would be absorbed within the higher costs of consumption.

There remains a case, therefore, for direct intervention. And it is an argument which emphasizes the need for a continued public-sector involvement. It seems likely that government will need to maintain an element of control over older housing policy. If urban renewal is to have a social dimension, reflecting interrelated concerns for employment, income and housing, it is in potential conflict with an emphasis on the role of private-sector institutions. If urban renewal is to be privatized while maintaining a concern for social provision, local government will have to expand its regulatory functions. It seems likely, however, that an emphasis on achieving private market confidence to attract investment will, to some extent, conflict with the control of standards and the welfare of local people. This can already be seen within the assumed externalities of area-based rehabilitation policy. Concentrated grant intervention is effectively designed to stimulate private-sector investment through improved market confidence. This confidence is argued to lead to investment on the expectation of favourable movements in relative property values. But increased confidence is not of any immediate help to people housed in the poorest properties within the area, who may find it difficult to pay their share of improvement works. In a similar way, equally problematic conflicts may develop around increased clearance programmes. There is an uneasy relationship between redevelopment and private-sector involvement, and it will be difficult to establish a clearance programme while trying to reassure building societies of the certain future of older urban areas.

In these circumstances, it seems likely that the public sector will need to reassert itself as an active agent of urban renewal. The role and function of local authorities is changing as they respond to pressure for efficiency and effectiveness. There is a trend towards accountable management which could redefine the distinction between public and private. Local authorities could respond in quite radical ways which combine a social policy dimension with approaches which secure value for money and exploit the opportunities created by public betterment. By its nature, this action will be area-specific, and must be aimed at providing effective help for those within the target areas. There is no reason why these policies should not be unashamedly ameliorative, giving explicit recognition to the uneven development of capital and using public-sector intervention quite deliberately to achieve a more equitable distribution of economic and social opportunities.

While this continues, it is the task of central government to redefine housing subsidies in order to fundamentally alter the pattern of housing obsolescence. Though there remains a need for major capital spending through clearance and area-based rehabilitation policies, the objective should be to move away from intermittent injections of public capital towards the goal of progressive investment in housing maintenance. To do this requires a radical restructuring of housing subsidies to redirect spending away from consumption and towards capital investment in maintenance and new housing production. In this way the use of housing as an investment good would be devalued, and less emphasis placed on profit from exchange. If housing is not to be favourably treated as a form of investment, housing wealth has to be taxed. The political problems are formidable, but the merits of simplicity, equity and impact argue in favour of some form of lifetime expenditure tax. The revenues raised through this mechanism would provide the opportunity to expand capital subsidies to the benefit of new production and the maintenance of the existing stock, creating work in the construction industry with a substantial multiplier effect. Combined with an increase in direct public programmes of clearance and grant-aided rehabilitation, the transfer of subsidies from consumption to production would provide the most favourable method of achieving housing investment on the scale required, and of reversing a trend which, if unchecked, seems likely to continue a spiral of inadequate replacement and increased disrepair.

Appendix 1: *New Building Starts, England and Wales,* 1951–82

('ooos)

Year	Housing associations	Total public sector	Private sector	Total
1951		163·6	24·5	188·1
1952		212·7	50·0	262·7
1953		227·1	80·6	307·7
1954		190·4	104·0	294·4
1955		153·9	123·5	277·4
1956		133.1	115·9	249·0
1957		123·6	122·0	245·6
1958		99·4	133·0	232·4
1959		125·2	164·0	289·2
1960		104·6	175·7	280·3
1961	1·6	103·6	181·1	284·7
1962	1·8	114·6	178·5	293·0
1963	5·5	138·0	192·3	330·3
1964	4·8	151·0	239·2	390·2
1965	2·8	147·8	202·5	350·3
1966	4·4	158·3	185·0	343·3
1967	5·9	178·2	225·4	403·6
1968	8·1	159·8	190·2	349·9
1969	9·6	145·4	158·2	303·6
1970	8·2	125·4	156·9	282·4
1971	10·6	114·5	195·5	310·1
1972	9·4	103·2	214·3	317·4
1973	10·2	95·5	200·2	295·7
1974	11·1	123·8	95·6	219·5
1975	19·0	154·0	137·2	291·2
1976	27·8	156·2	138·3	294·5
1977	27·6	122·3	122·1	244·4
1978	19·1	98·3	140·8	239·1
1979	14·9	73·2	128·7	201·9
1980	13·3	49·3	88·3	137·6
1981	9·7	33·0	105·8	138·8
1982	14·8	46·3	128·1	174·4

Sources: DOE, *Housing Statistics* and *Housing and Construction Statistics* (London: HMSO), various years.

Appendix 2: Slum Clearance, England and Wales, 1960–1980/1

('ooos)

Year	In or adjoining clearance areas	Demolished Not in clearance areas	Total
1960	33·6	16·4	50·0
1961	38·0	17·6	55·6
1962	38·7	18·5	57·2
1963	40·5	16·1	56·6
1964	41·2	15·5	56·7
1965	42·6	14·0	56·6
1966	48·1	13·9	62·0
1967	51·5	14·6	66·1
1968	53·9	13·2	67·1
1969	53·4	11·5	64·9
1970	54·7	11·7	66·4
1971	59·4	10·9	70·3
1972	55·9	9·8	65·7
1973	54·7	8·2	62·9
1974	37·9	3·4	41·3
1975	41·8	4·9	46·7
1976	38·6	5·3	43·9
1977	34·1	4·4	38·5
1978	26·7	4·6	31·3
<u>1979</u>	3·7	4·2	27·9
1979/80	23·1	4·2	27·3
1980/81	21·7	3·4	25·1

Source: DOE, *Housing and Construction Statistics* (London: HMSO), various years.

Appendix 3: Grant Activity in England and Wales, 1960–1982

Year	Local authorities[1]	Housing associations[2] approved	Housing associations[2] completed	Private owners and tenants[3] approved	Private owners and tenants[3] paid	Total
1960	42,510			88,322		130,832
1961	41,988			85,788		127,766
1962	31,877			78,629		110,506
1963	31,311			88,668		119,979
1964	32,368			89,317		121,685
1965	37,750			85,243		122,993
1966	30,239			77,481		107,720
1967	28,808			82,622	70,370	99,178
1968	31,031			81,126	75,305	106,336
1969	29,369	1,457		76,384	73,762	104,588
1970	41,960	2,701		110,533	77,170	121,831
1971	61,138	5,029		130,175	97,656	163,823
1972	103,998	4,200		208,415	137,092	245,290
1973	117,927	3,219		237,976	184,206	305,352
1974	77,314	3,973		149,290	217,076	298,363
1975	37,106	4,617		84,504	92,729	134,452
1976	39,001	13,388		72,762	75,286	127,675
1977	37,551	19,300		68,500	63,972	120,823
1978	60,871	14,632			63,509	139,012
1979	75,967	18,955			71,478	166,400
1980	77,275	17,563	15,084		81,807	176,645
1981						
1982	52,931	14,438	11,960		76,041	143,410
	62,829ᵖ		18,328ᵖ		124,271	205,428

Source: DOE, *Housing and Construction Statistics* (London: HMSO), various years.
Notes:
1 Including new towns. Excluding Wales from 1976. Work completed from 1978.
2 Work under Section 29 Housing Act 1974 and corresponding earlier legislation.
3 Including grants paid to housing associations under private owner legislation.
ᵖ Denotes a provisional figure.

Appendix 4: Grants Approved to Private Owners in England and Wales, by Type, 1960–77

	Conversion and improvement	Intermediate and special	All
1960	38,641	49,681	88,322
1961	37,288	48,500	85,788
1962	30,389	48,240	78,629
1963	32,210	56,458	88,668
1964	33,453	55,864	89,317
1965	27,957	57,268	85,243
1966	25,481	52,000	77,481
1967	25,025	57,597	82,622
1968	23,703	57,423	81,126
1969	24,350	52,034	76,834
1970	50,189	60,344	110,533
1971	74,378	55,797	130,175
1972	153,858	54,557	208,415
1973	198,484	39,492	237,976
1974	127,697	21,593	149,290
1975	73,379	11,125	84,504
1976	61,379	11,383	72,762
1977	58,041	10,459	68,500

Source: DOE, Housing and Construction Statistics (London: HMSO), various years.
Note: Includes housing associations prior to 1967.

Appendix 5: Grants Paid to Private Owners and Tenants, by Type (England), 1969–82

	Conversion and improvement		Intermediate and special[1]		Repairs		All	
	No.	£('ooos)	No.	£('ooos)	No.	£('ooos)	No.	£('ooos)
1969	20,305	6,055	48,274	6,739	—	—	68,579	12,794
1970	26,097	11,125	45,196	6,843	—	—	71,293	17,968
1971	44,428	22,316	46,439	7,367	—	—	90,867	29,683
1972	78,542	48,254	45,634	8,297	—	—	124,176	56,551
1973	128,381	94,060	37,577	7,906	—	—	165,958	101,966
1974	164,525	142,042	27,823	6,518	—	—	192,348	148,560
1975	72,966	60.567	12,368	3,257	59	34	85,393	63,858
1976	57,784	60,073	10,849	4,025	85	27	68,718	64,125
1977	47,788	56,334	9,037	3,734	130	49	56,955	60,117
1978	49,424	71,645	7,935	4,595	219	135	57,578	76,375
1979	57,222	94,902	7,792	5,086	345	210	65,359	100,198
1980[2]	65,809	120,831	8,143	6,096	513	375	74,465	127,302
1981	49,145	119,262	14,743	22,151	5,053	6,739	68,941	148,152
1982[p]	56,560	192,982	23,529	51,306	33,715	62,730	113,804	307,018

Source: DOE, *Housing and Construction Statistics* (London: HMSO), various years.
Notes:
1   Includes standard grants under the Housing Act 1969.
2   Figures from 4th quarter include grants to private and public tenants.
p   Denotes a provisional figure.

Appendix 6: Renovation Grants Paid to Private Owners, 1980 Constant Prices[1]

	Conversion and improvement		Intermediate and special[2]		Repair		All grants	
	total (£'00s)	Av. grant	total (£'000s)	Av. grant	total (£'000s)	Av. grant	total (£'000s)	Av. grant
England and Wales (including housing associations)								
1967	27,265		26,852				54,117	769
1968	27,084		28,155				55,239	733
1969	26,680		26,933				53,613	727
1970	43,168		26,209				69,377	899
England								
1969	23,191	1,142	25,810	535			49,001	715
1970	40,272	1,543	24,772	548			65,044	912
1971	73,643	1,658	24,311	524			97,954	1,078
1972	148,140	1,886	25,472	558			173,612	1,398
1973	265,249	2,066	22,295	593			287,544	1,733
1974	345,162	2,098	15,839	569			361,001	1,877
1975	118,711	1,627	6,384	516	67	1,136	125,162	1,466
1976	100,923	1,747	6,762	623	45	529	107,730	1,568
1977	81,684	1,709	5,414	599	71	546	87,169	1,530
1978	96,004	1,942	6,157	776	181	826	102,342	1,777
1979	111,984	1,957	6,001	770	248	719	118,233	1,809
1980	120,831	1,836	6,096	749	375	731	127,302	1,709
1981	106,143	2,160	1,714	1,337	5,998	1,187	131,855	1,913
1982p	158,245	2,798	42,071	1,788	51,439	1,526	251,755	2,212

Source: DOE, *Housing and Construction Statistics* (London: HMSO), various years.

Notes:
1   Based on RPI.
2   Including standard grants.
p   denotes a provisional figure.

References

Ahlbrandt, R. S., and Brophy, P. C. (1975), *Neighborhood Revitalization: Theory and Practice* (Lexington, Mass.: Lexington Books).

Alexander, J., and Toland, S. (1980), 'Measuring the public sector borrowing requirement' *Economic Trends*, no. 322 (August), pp. 82–98.

AMA (1978), *Policies for Improvement: A Report on Housing Repair and Renovation* (London: Association of Metropolitan Authorities).

AMA (1981a), *Ruin or Renewal: Choices for Our Ageing Housing* (London: Association of Metropolitan Authorities).

AMA (1981b), *Investing in Recovery: An Alternative View of the Economic Future* (London: Association of Metropolitan Authorities).

AMA (1982), *Building for Tomorrow: Housing Investment, Construction and Employment* (London: Association of Metropolitan Authorities).

Anchor Housing Trust (1980), *Staying Put: A Report on the Elderly at Home* (London: Anchor Housing Trust).

Bains, M. A. (1972), *The New Local Authorities: Management and Structure* (London: HMSO).

Ball, M. (1983), *Housing Policy and Economic Power: The Political Economy of Owner-Occupation* (London: Methuen).

Bank of England (1979), *'Real' national saving and its sectoral composition*, Discussion Paper No. 6, C. T. Taylor and A. R. Threadgold (London: Bank of England).

Bank of England (1983), 'Economic commentary', *Bank of England Quarterly Bulletin*, vol. 23, no. 3 (September), pp. 326–36.

Barnes, J. (1974), 'A solution to whose problem?', in *Positive Discrimination and Inequality*, ed. H. Glennerster and S. Hatch, Research Series No. 314 (London: Fabian Society), pp. 9–13.

Barnes, M. (1931), *The Slum: Its Story and Solution* (London: P. J. King).

Barr, A., and Urwin, J. C. (1977), *Phased Residential Redevelopment* (Oldham: Oldham Community Development Programme).

Bassett, K., and Short, J. (1980a), 'Patterns of building society and local authority lending in the 1970s', *Environment and Planning A*, vol. 12, no. 3 (March), pp. 279–300.

Bassett, K., and Short, J. (1980b), *Housing and Residential Structure: Alternative Approaches* (London: Routledge & Kegan Paul).

Benson, D. (1978), 'Rate bills: how they vary for similar houses', *CES Review*, no. 3 (May), pp. 77–84.

Birmingham City Council (1981), 'Housing Investment Programme Submission, 1981/82' (unpublished).

Boddy, M. (1976), 'The structure of mortgage finance: building societies and the British social formation', *Transactions of the Institute of British Geographers*, n.s., vol. 1, no. 1, pp. 58–71.

Boddy, M. (1980), *The Building Societies* (London: Macmillan).

Boleat, M. (1978), *The Building Society Support Scheme for Local Authorities* (London: Building Societies Association).

Boleat, M. (1982), *The Building Society Industry* (London: Allen & Unwin).

Boyer, C. (1973), *Cities Destroyed for Cash* (New York: Follet).

Brading, K. (1981), speech by the Chief Registrar at the Building Societies Association Annual Conference, *Building Societies Gazette*, conference issue, May, pp. 782–90.

Bradley, J. E. (1980), *The Housing Action Area Approach: Monitoring and Evaluation of the Charles Street HAA, South Tyneside*, Research Memorandum No. 77 (Birmingham: Centre for Urban and Regional Studies, University of Birmingham).

Bramley, G. (1979), 'The inner city labour market', in *Urban Deprivation and the Inner City*, ed. C. Jones (London: Croom Helm), pp. 63–91.

Britten, J. R. (1977), *What is a Satisfactory House? A Report of Some Householders' Views*, CP 26/77 (Garston, Herts.: Building Research Establishment).

Britton, R. (1974), *Housing and Related Benefits* (London: Age Concern).

Brown, W. J., Clements, V. R., and Watson, C. J. (1984), *Housing Associations and Older Housing: The Rehabilitation Process*, Research Memorandum No. 96 (Birmingham: Centre for Urban and Regional Studies, University of Birmingham).

Brunt, T., Abbot, C., Eatwell, C., and Downie, J. (1982), 'The Birmingham envelope scheme', *Housing Review*, vol. 31, no. 4 (July–August), pp. 130–3.

BSA (1978), *Evidence Submitted by the BSA to the Committee to Review the Functioning of Financial Institutions* (London: Building Societies Association).

BSA (1979a) *Mortgage Finance in the 1980s*, report of a working party under the chairmanship of Mr Ralph Stow (London: Building Societies Association).

BSA (1979b), *Building Societies and the Savings Market*, report prepared by the British Market Research Bureau (London: Building Societies Association).

BSA (1980), 'The housing market and the allocation of real resources in the economy', *BSA Bulletin*, no. 21 (January) (London: Building Societies Association), pp. 14–16.

BSA (1981a), 'House prices and earnings', *BSA Bulletin*, no. 27 (July) (London: Building Societies Association), pp. 18–23.

BSA (1981b), 'Building societies and the saving ratio', *BSA Bulletin*, no. 27 (July) (London: Building Societies Association), pp. 14–17.

BSA (1981c) 'Bank lending for house purchase', *BSA Bulletin*, no. 28 (October) (London: Building Societies Association), pp. 24–6.

BSA (1982a), *BSA Bulletin*, no. 29 (January) (London: Building Societies Association).

BSA (1982b), *Rehabilitation of Owner-Occupied Homes* (London: Building Societies Association).

BSA (1983a), *Building Societies in 1982* (London: Building Societies Association).

BSA (1983b), *The Future Constitution and Powers of Building Societies* (London: Building Societies Association).

BSA (1984), *New Legislation for Building Societies* (London: Building Societies Association).

Bundy, L. S. (1980), 'Lenders discover advantages and new market with Community Reinvestment Act', *Journal of Housing*, vol. 37, no. 3 (March), pp. 136–8.

Cadman, D. (1981), 'Land, the commercial property market and the impact of urban planning', paper presented at the Urban Future Seminar Series, University of Birmingham, unpublished.

Cambridge Econometrics Ltd (1982), *Policies for Recovery: An Evaluation of Alternatives* (Cambridge: Cambridge Econometrics).

Cantle, E. (1981), 'Is there a future for the revitalisation or urban areas?', *Housing*, vol. 17, no. 7 (July), pp. 22-4.

Carrington, J. C., and Edwards, G. T. (1979), *Financing Industrial Investment* (London: Macmillan).

Carvel, J. (1983), 'Where pensioners can find the money to repair their houses', *Guardian*, 12 March, p. 22.

CDP (1977), *Gilding the Ghetto: The State and the Poverty Experiments* (London: Community Development Project).

CHAC (1966), *Our Older Homes: A Call for Action* (the Denington Report), Central Housing Advisory Committee (London: HMSO).

Clarke, S., and Ginsburg, N. (1975), 'The political economy of housing', in *Political Economy and the Housing Question*, ed. M. Edwards, *et al.* (n.p.: Conference of Socialist Economists), pp. 3-33.

CLRC (1974), *Charity Law: Only a New Start Will Do* (London: Charity Law Reform Committee).

Coates, K., and Silburn, R. (1970), *Poverty: The Forgotten Englishmen* (Harmondsworth: Penguin).

Community Forum (1983), *Are You Being Enveloped? A Residents' Guide to Enveloping* (Birmingham: Community Forum).

Craig, J., and Driver, A. (1972), 'The identification and comparison of small areas of adverse social conditions', *Journal of the Royal Statistical Society*, ser. C, vol. 21, no. 1, pp. 25-35.

Croham, Lord (1979), 'Home ownership could have raised industry's borrowing costs', *Building Societies Gazette*, vol. 111, no. 139 (December), pp. 1490-2.

CSD (1981), *Cash Limits and External Financing Limits*, Civil Service Department (London: HMSO).

CSO (1980), *Financial Statistics*, February 1980 (Supplementary Table C), Central Statistical Office (London: HMSO).

CSO (1981), *National Income and Expenditure*, Central Statistical Office (London: HMSO).

CSO (1983), *Financial Statistics* (September), Central Statistical Office (London: HMSO).

Cullingworth, J. B. (1960), *Housing Needs and Planning Policy* (London: Routledge & Kegan Paul).

Cullingworth, J. B. (1966), *Housing and Local Government in England and Wales* (London: Allen & Unwin).

Davis, E. P., and Saville, I. D. (1982), 'Mortgage lending and the housing market', *Bank of England Quarterly Bulletin*, vol. 22, no. 3 (September), pp. 390-8.

Deakin, N. (1983), 'Peter Shore and inner city policy: the last, best hope?', in *Government and Urban Poverty: Inside the Policy Making Process*, ed. J. Higgins, N. Deakin, J. Edwards and M. Wicks (Oxford: Blackwell), pp. 117-69.

Demuth, C. (1977), *Government Initiatives on Urban Deprivation* (London: Runnymede Trust).

Dennis, R. (1978), 'The decline of manufacturing employment in Greater London: 1966-1974', *Urban Studies*, vol. 15, pp. 63-73.

Department of Employment (1976), *Employment Gazette*, vol. 84 (August), pp. 839-50.

Devereux, M. P., and Morris, C. N. (1983), 'Budgetary arithmetic and the 1983 budget', *Fiscal Studies*, vol. 4, no. 2 (May), pp. 29–42.

Dicken, P., and Lloyd, P. E. (1978), 'Inner metropolitan industrial change, enterprise structures and policy issues: case studies in Manchester and Merseyside', *Regional Studies*, vol. 12, pp. 181–97.

DOE (1973a), *House Condition Survey 1971: England and Wales* (London: DOE).

DOE (1973b), *Better Homes: The Next Priorities*, Cmnd 5339 (London: HMSO).

DOE (1974a), 'Studies of distribution of improvement grants: 1972–73 and 1973–74', unpublished.

DOE (1974b), *Rate Fund Expenditure and Rate Calls in 1975/76*, Circular 171/74 (London: HMSO).

DOE (1975a), *Renewal Strategies*, Circular 13/75 (London: HMSO).

DOE (1975b), *Housing Action Areas, Priority Neighbourhoods and General Improvement Areas*, Circular 14/75 (London: HMSO).

DOE (1975c), *Gradual Renewal*, Area Improvement Occasional Paper 2/75 (London: DOE, repr. from *Architects' Journal*).

DOE (1976a), *Housing Action Areas: A Detailed Examination of Declaration Reports*, Improvement Research Note 2/76 (London: DOE).

DOE (1976b), *Local Government Finance: Report of the Committee of Enquiry* (the Layfield Report), Cmnd 6453 (London: HMSO).

DOE (1977a), *Housing Policy: A Consultative Document*, report (Cmnd 6851) and three technical volumes (London: HMSO).

DOE (1977b), *Housing Act 1974*, Circular 86/77 (London: HMSO).

DOE (1977c), *Inner Area Studies: Liverpool, Birmingham and Lambeth: Summaries of Consultants' Final Reports* (London: HMSO).

DOE (1977d), *Policy for the Inner Cities*, Cmnd 6845 (London: HMSO).

DOE (1977e), *Local Government and the Industrial Strategy*, Circular 71/77 (London: HMSO).

DOE (1978a), *English House Condition Survey 1976. Part 1: Report of the Physical Condition Survey* (London: HMSO).

DOE (1978b), *National Dwelling and Housing Survey* (London: HMSO).

DOE (1978c), *Rate Support Grant Settlement 1978–79*, Circular 8/78 (London: HMSO).

DOE (1979a), *English House Condition Survey 1976. Part 2: Report of the Social Survey* (London: HMSO).

DOE (1979b), *Housing Action Areas: An Analysis of Annual Progress Reports for 1977*, Improvement Research Note 5/78 (London: DOE).

DOE (1980), *Housing Acts 1974 and 1980: Improvement of Older Housing*, Circular 21/80 (London: HMSO).

DOE (1981a), *Compulsory Purchase Orders Made Under Housing Powers*, Circular 13/81 (London: HMSO).

DOE (1981b), *Housing and Construction Statistics 1970–1980* (London: HMSO).

DOE (1982a) *English House Condition Survey 1981. Part 1: Report of the Physical Condition Survey* (London: HMSO).

DOE (1982b), *Housing and Construction Statistics 1971–81* (London: HMSO).

DOE (1982c), *Improvement of Older Housing: Enveloping*, Circular 29/82 (London: HMSO).

DOE (1983a), *English House Condition Survey 1981. Part 2: Report of the Interview and Local Authority Survey* (London: HMSO).

DOE (1983b), *Housing and Construction Statistics 1972–82* (London: HMSO).

Doling, J. (1982), 'Housing finance and the British city', *Area*, vol. 14, no. 1, pp. 33–8.

Doling, J. (1983), *Does Home Ownership Mean Home Disrepair?*, Working Paper No. 91 (Birmingham: Centre for Urban and Regional Studies, University of Birmingham).

Doling, J. (1985), 'Owner-occupation, house condition and government subsidies', in *Low Cost Home Ownership*, ed. A. D. H. Crook (Aldershot: Gower), forthcoming.

Doling, J., and Thomas, A. D. (1982), 'Disrepair in the national housing stock', *Town Planning Review*, vol. 53, no. 3 (July), pp. 241–56.

Donnison, D. V. (1974), 'Policies for priority areas', *Journal of Social Policy*, vol. 3, no. 2, pp. 127–35.

Donnison, D. V. (1979), 'Housing the poorest people: how can we help poor owner-occupiers keep their houses in decent repair?', *Housing Review*, vol. 28, no. 2 (March/April), pp. 48–9.

Donnison, D. V. (1980), 'A policy for housing', *New Society*, 6 November, pp. 283–4.

Duncan, S. S. (1976), 'Self-help: the allocation of mortgages and the formation of housing sub-markets', *Area*, vol. 8, no. 4, pp. 307–16.

Duncan, T. L. C. (1974), *Housing Improvement Policies in England and Wales*, Research Memorandum No. 28 (Birmingham: Centre for Urban and Regional Studies, University of Birmingham).

Edwards, J., and Batley, R. (1978), *The Politics of Positive Discrimination: An Evaluation of the Urban Programme 1967–77* (London: Tavistock).

English, J., Madigan, R., and Norman, P. (1976), *Slum Clearance: The Social and Administrative Context in England and Wales* (London: Croom Helm).

Ermisch, J. (1981), 'Housing in the eighties: demographic impetus and policy response', *Policy Studies*, vol. 2, pt 1 (July), pp. 34–48.

Evans, A. (1980), 'An economist's perspective', in *The Inner City: Employment and Industry*, ed. A. Evans and D. Eversley (London: Heinemann), pp. 445–59.

Falk, N. (1979), 'Enabling change', *Built Environment*, vol. 5, no. 3, pp. 184–8.

Falk, N. (1981), 'Counteracting commercial decline', paper to the Urban Renaissance Conference, Norrkoping, Sweden, unpublished.

Farmer, M. K., and Barrell, R. (1981), 'Entrepreneurship and government policy: the case of the housing market', *Journal of Public Policy*, vol. 1, no. 3, pp. 307–32.

Fleetwood, M. (1975), 'What gradual renewal means', *Architects' Journal*, vol. 161, no. 5 (February), pp. 283–4.

Fleming, M., and Nellis, J. (1982), 'A new housing crisis?', *Lloyds Bank Review*, no. 144 (April), pp. 38–53.

Forrest, R., and Williams, P. (1980), *The Commodification of Housing: Emerging Issues and Contradictions*, Working Paper No. 73 (Birmingham: Centre for Urban and Regional Studies, University of Birmingham).

Fothergill, S., and Gudgin, G. (1979), 'Regional employment change: a subregional explanation', *Progress in Planning*, vol. 12, no. 3, pp. 155–219.

Fothergill, S., and Gudgin, G. (1982), *Unequal Growth: Urban and Regional Employment Change in the UK* (London: Heinemann).

Frieden, B. J. (1964), *The Future of Old Neighbourhoods* (Cambridge, Mass.: MIT).

Frost, D., and Sharman, N. (1975), 'Housing and community based renewal',

Housing Review, vol. 24, no. 6 (November/December), pp. 157-9.

Gibson, M. (1979), 'From redevelopment to envelopment? Housing Action Areas in Birmingham', *Housing Review*, vol. 28, no. 2 (March/April), pp. 35-9.

Gibson, M., and Langstaff, M. (1977), 'Policies and strategies in gradual renewal', *The Planner*, vol. 63 (March), pp. 35-8.

Gibson, M., and Langstaff, M. (1982), *An Introduction to Urban Renewal* (London: Hutchinson).

Gladstone, F. (1982), *Charity Law and Social Justice* (London: Bedford Square Press/National Council for Voluntary Organizations).

GLC (1980), *Grant Take-Up for House Renovation in Housing Action Areas*, Reviews and Studies Series No. 6 (London: Greater London Council).

GLC (1981), *The Greater London House Condition Survey*, Reviews and Studies Series No. 7 (London: Greater London Council).

GLC (1982), *People and Dwellings*, Statistical Series No. 13 (London: Greater London Council).

Goldstein, B., and Davis, R. (eds) (1977), *Neighbourhoods in the Urban Economy: The Dynamics of Decline and Revitalization* (Lexington, Mass.: Lexington Books).

Goss, S., and Lansley, S. (1981), *What Price Housing? A Review of Housing Subsidies and Proposals for Reform* (London: Shelter Housing Advice Centre).

Gough, T. J., and Taylor, T. W. (1980), 'Home ownership has been the best hedge against inflation', *Building Societies Gazette*, vol. 140 (June), pp. 692-6.

Great Britain (1977), *Royal Commission on the Distribution of Income and Wealth* (the Diamond Commission), Third Report on the Standing Reference, Cmnd 6999 (London: HMSO).

Great Britain (1979), *Royal Commission on the Distribution of Income and Wealth* (the Diamond Commission), Fourth Report on the Standing Reference, Cmnd 7595 (London: HMSO).

Great Britain (1980), *The Government's Expenditure Plans 1980-81 to 1983-84*, Cmnd 7841 (London: HMSO).

Great Britain (1981), *The Government's Expenditure Plans 1981-82 to 1983-84*, Cmnd 8175 (London: HMSO).

Great Britain (1982), *The Government's Expenditure Plans 1982-83 to 1984-85*, Cmnd 8494, 2 vols (London: HMSO).

Great Britain (1983), *The Government's Expenditure Plans 1983-84 to 1985-86*, Cmnd 8789, 2 vols (London: HMSO).

Greer, S. (1965), *Urban Renewal and American Cities* (Indianapolis, Ind.: Bobbs-Merrill).

Grey, A., Hepworth, N. P., and Odling-Smee, J. (1981), *Housing Rents, Costs and Subsidies: A Discussion Document* (London: Chartered Institute of Public Finance and Accountancy).

Grigsby, W. G., White, S. B., Levine, D. U., Kelly, M. R. P., and Claflen, G. L. (1977), *Re-thinking Housing and Community Development Policy* (Philadelphia, Pa: University of Pennsylvania Press).

Gripaios, P. (1977), 'Industrial decline in London: an examination of the causes', *Urban Studies*, vol. 14, pp. 181-9.

Guterbock, T. M. (1980), 'The political economy of urban revitalization: competing theories', *Urban Affairs Quarterly*, vol. 15, no. 4 (June), pp. 429-38.

Habraken, N. J. (1972), *Supports: An Alternative to Mass Housing* (London: Architectural Press).

Hall, P. (ed.) (1981), *The Inner City in Context: The Final Report of the SSRC Inner Cities Working Party* (London: Heinemann).

Hammersmith and Fulham (1981), 'Designation of the North Fulham Housing Improvement Zone', report of the Director of Housing, unpublished.

Hamnett, C. (1973), 'Improvement grants as an indicator of gentrification in inner London', *Area*, vol. 5, no. 4, pp. 252–61.

Hancock & Hawkes (1967), *Greater Peterborough Draft Basic Plan* (London: Hancock & Hawkes, Architects and Planners).

Haringey (1975), *First Steps Towards a Housing Action Area* (London: Borough of Haringey).

Harloe, M., Issacharoff, R., and Minns, R. (1974), *The Organization of Housing: Public and Private Enterprise in London* (London: Heinemann).

Harrison, A. (1977), 'The valuation gap: a danger signal?', *CES Review*, no. 2 (December), pp. 101–3.

Harrison, M. L., and Stevens, L. (1983), *Down-Market Lending: Mortgages and the Support Scheme in Leeds*, Occasional Paper No. 7 (Birmingham: Centre for Urban and Regional Studies, University of Birmingham).

Harrop, K. J., Mason, T., Vielba, C. A., and Webster, B. A. (1978), *The Implementation and Development of Area Management*, Area Management Monitoring Project (Birmingham: Institute of Local Government Studies, University of Birmingham).

Harvey, D. (1977), 'Government policies, financial institutions and neighbourhood change in United States cities', in *Captive Cities*, ed. M. Harloe (London: Wiley), pp. 123–39.

Hatch, S., and Sherrott, R. (1973), 'Positive discrimination and the distribution of deprivations', *Policy and Politics*, vol. 1, no. 3, pp. 223–40.

Higgins, J., Deakin, N., Edwards, J., and Wicks, M. (1983), *Government and Urban Poverty: Inside the Policy Making Process* (Oxford: Blackwell).

Hirsch, F. (1977), *Social Limits to Growth* (London: Routledge & Kegan Paul).

Holman, R. (1977), 'Poverty: consensus and alternatives', in *Welfare in Action*, ed. M. Fitzgerald (Milton Keynes: Open University), pp. 184–91.

Holmes, C. (1973), *Tomorrow in Upper Holloway: A Plan for Area Improvement* (London: North Islington Housing Rights Project).

Holtermann, S. (1975), 'Areas of urban deprivation in Great Britain: an analysis of 1971 census data', *Social Trends* (HMSO), no. 6, pp. 33–47.

Holtermann, S. (1978), 'The welfare economics of priority area policies', *Journal of Social Policy*, vol. 7, no. 1, pp. 23–40.

Home Office (1968), *Urban Programme Circular No. 1*, 4 October (London: HMSO).

Home, R. K. (1982), *Inner City Regeneration* (London: Methuen).

House of Commons (1949), *Parliamentary Debates (Hansard)*, 5th ser., vol. 462, 16 March, col. 2130.

House of Commons (1972), *Parliamentary Debates (Hansard)*, 5th ser., vol. 833, 23 March, cols 1698–1700.

House of Commons (1973), *House Improvement Grants. Volume 1: Report*, Tenth Report from the Expenditure Committee, Session 1972-3, HC 349-1 (London: HMSO).

House of Commons (1975), *Parliamentary Debates (Hansard)*, 5th ser., vol. 899, 10 November, cols 425–54.

House of Commons (1980), *Enquiry into Implications of Government's Expenditure Plans 1980–81 to 1983–84 for the Housing Policies of the Department of the Environment*, House of Commons Environment Committee, First Report, Session 1979–80, HC 714 (London: HMSO).

House of Commons (1981a), *DOE's Housing Policies: Enquiry into Government's Expenditure Plans 1981/82 to 1983/84 and the Updating of the Committee's First Report for Session 1979/80*, House of Commons Environment Committee, Third Report, Session 1980–1, HC 383 (London: HMSO).

House of Commons (1981b), *Monetary Policy*, Third Report from the Treasury and Civil Service Committee, 3 vols, HC 163 (London: HMSO).

House of Commons (1981c), *Parliamentary Debates (Hansard)*, 6th ser., vol. 12, 11 November, col. 563.

House of Commons (1981d), *Parliamentary Debates (Hansard)*, 5th ser., vol. 998, 11 February, col. 899.

House of Commons (1983), *The Government's Expenditure Plans 1983–84 to 1985–86*, Treasury and Civil Service Committee, Third Report, Session 1982–3, HC 204 (London: HMSO).

Housing Centre Trust (1975), *Housing Finance Review*, evidence to the Secretary of State for the Environment (London: Housing Centre Trust).

Housing Centre Trust (1981), *Rescuing Our Housing*, report of the Housing Centre Working Party (London: Housing Centre Trust).

Housing Corporation (1979), *Housing Association Tenants* (London: Housing Corporation).

Housing Corporation (1981), *Schemework Procedure Guide* (London: Housing Corporation).

Housing Monitoring Team (1978), *The Structure and Functioning of Building Societies: A Head Office View*, Research Memorandum No. 64 (Birmingham: Centre for Urban and Regional Studies, University of Birmingham).

Hughes, G. A. (1979), 'Housing income and subsidies', *Fiscal Studies*, vol. 1, no. 1 (November), pp. 20–38.

Hughes, G. A. (1980), 'Housing and the tax system', in *Public Policy and the Tax System*, ed. G. A. Hughes and G. M. Heal (London: Allen & Unwin), pp. 67–105.

Huntly, J. (1980), *Neighbourhood Revitalisation: American and German Experience of Commmunity Involvement in the Revitalisation of Older Housing Areas*, Occasional Paper No. 4 (Reading: School of Planning Studies, University of Reading).

IEHO (1981), *Area Improvement: The Report of the Area Improvement Working Party* (London: Institution of Environmental Health Officers).

IEHO (1983), *The Future of the Housing Stock* (London: Institution of Environmental Health Officers).

Inner City Working Group (1977), *Inner Area Studies: A Contribution to the Debate* (Birmingham: Centre for Urban and Regional Studies/Institute of Local Government Studies, University of Birmingham).

Jackson, P. M. (1980), 'The socio-economic impact of urban renewal', in *The Future of the British Conurbations*, ed. G. C. Cameron (London: Longman), pp. 224–9.

Jennings, H. (1962), *Societies in the Making* (London: Routledge & Kegan Paul).

Jones, P. (1980), 'Housing Action Areas: the facts', *Housing and Planning Review* (Spring), pp. 5–8.

Karn, V. (1979), 'Low income owner-occupation in the inner city', in *Urban Deprivation and the Inner City*, ed. C. Jones (London: Croom Helm), pp. 160–90.

Karn, V., Kemeny, J., and Williams, P. (1982), 'Final report of the Inner City Home-Ownership Project', unpublished.

Kay, J. A., and King, M. A. (1980), *The British Tax System*, 2nd edn (Oxford: Clarendon).

Keeble, D. E. (1978), 'Industrial decline in the inner city and conurbation', *Transactions, Institute of British Geographers*, n.s., vol. 3, no. 1, pp. 101–14.

Kemeny, J. (1981), *The Myth of Home Ownership: Private Versus Public Choices in Housing Tenure* (London: Routledge & Kegan Paul).

Kemeny, J. (1983), *Privatized City: Critical Studies in Australian Housing and Urban Structure* (University of Birmingham: Centre for Urban and Regional Studies).

Kemeny, J., with Karn, V. A., and Williams, P. (1981), *Polarisation in the Inner Birmingham Housing Market, 1972–80: First Interim Report of the Inner City Home-Ownership Project*, Working Paper No. 81 (Birmingham: Centre for Urban and Regional Studies, University of Birmingham).

Kemeny, J., and Thomas, A. D. (1984), 'Capital leakage from owner-occupied housing', *Policy and Politics*, vol. 12, no. 1, pp. 13–30.

Kilroy, B. (1979), 'Housing finance: why so privileged?', *Lloyds Bank Review*, no. 133 (July), pp. 37–52.

Kilroy, B. (1981a), 'The real competition for resources in housing', *Housing Review*, vol. 30, no. 4 (July/August), pp. 113–16.

Kilroy, B. (1981b), 'Why is housing investment being cut so much?', *Housing Review*, vol. 30, no. 2 (March/April), pp. 46–8.

King, M. A., and Atkinson, A. B. (1980), 'Housing policy, taxation and reform', *Midland Bank Review*, Spring, pp. 7–15.

Kirby, A. (1977), *Housing Action Areas in Great Britain, 1975–77* (Reading: Department of Geography, University of Reading).

Lansley, S. (1982), 'The road to Toxteth', *New Society*, 22 April, pp. 133–4.

Lawless, P. (1981), *Britain's Inner City Problems and Policies* (London: Harper & Row).

Lawson, N. (1980), 'Speech by the Financial Secretary to the Treasury at the BSA Annual Conference', *Building Societies Gazette*, conference issue, May, pp. 752–6.

Leather, P. (1982), 'Cardiff's poor home owners', *Roof*, vol. 7, no. 6 (November/December), p. 5.

Leather, P., and Murie, A. (1983), *Community Based Urban Renewal: An Evaluation of the South Riverside Urban Renewal Project*, Working Paper No. 35 (School for Advanced Urban Studies, University of Bristol).

Le Grand, J. (1982), *The Strategy of Equality* (London: Allen & Unwin).

Leigh-Pemberton, R. (1979), 'Banks, building societies and personal savings', *National Westminster Bank Quarterly Review*, May, pp. 2–10.

Lever, H., and Edwards, G. T. (1980), 'Why Germany beats Britain', *Sunday Times*, 2 November, pp. 16–18.

Lewis, O. (1965), *The Children of Sanchez* (Harmondsworth: Penguin).

Lipsey, D. (1983a), 'Lawson taxes our patience', *Sunday Times*, 16 October, p. 16.

Lipsey, D. (1983b) 'Home owners – and the others', *Sunday Times*, 3 July, p. 62.

Llewellyn, D. T. (1979), 'Do building societies take deposits away from banks?', *Lloyds Bank Review*, no. 131, pp. 21–34.

Lloyd, P. E. (1979), 'The components of industrial change for Merseyside inner area: 1966–1975', *Urban Studies*, vol. 16, pp. 45–60.

Lomas, G. (1978), *Clough Street Housing Action Area, Burnley, Lancashire*, Policy Series No. 3 (London: Centre for Environmental Studies).

Lomas, G., and Howes, E. (1979), 'Private improvement in Leicester', *CES Review*, no. 6 (May), pp. 50–5.

London, B. (1976), 'Functionalism, Marxism and the city: ideology versus science or competing ideocentrisms?', *Comparative Urban Research*, no. 4 (Spring), pp. 26–9.

Maclennan, D. (1982), *Housing Economics: An Applied Approach* (London: Longman).

Maclennan, D., Brailey, M., and Lawrie, N. (1983), *The Rehabilitation Activities and Effectiveness of Housing Associations in Scotland* (Edinburgh: Central Research Unit, Scottish Office).

MacMurray, T. (1973), 'Community renewal at Swinbrook', *Built Environment*, vol. 2, no. 4 (April), pp. 229–32.

Malpass, P., and Murie, A. (1982), *Housing Policy and Practice* (London: Macmillan).

Massey, D. (1983), 'The shape of things to come', *Marxism Today*, April, pp. 18–27.

Massey, D., and Meegan, R. (1982), *The Anatomy of Job Loss* (London: Methuen).

Matthews, R. (1983), 'Conditions suspicions', *Roof*, vol. 8, no. 2 (March/April), pp. 22–4.

McCarthy, J. (1975), *Some Social Implications of Improvement Policy in London*, Social Research Division (London: DOE).

McCarthy, J., and Buckley, M. (1982), *Birmingham Enveloping Schemes Survey* (London: Research Bureau Ltd for DOE).

McIntosh, N. (1982), 'Owning-up: housing finance – reform at last?', *Roof*, vol. 7, no. 2 (March/April), pp. 10–12.

McKay, D., and Cox, A. W. (1979), *The Politics of Urban Change* (London: Croom Helm).

McKie, R. (1971), *Housing and the Whitehall Bulldozer*, Hobart Paper No. 52 (London: Institute of Economic Affairs).

McKie, R. (1974), 'Cellular renewal', *Town Planning Review*, vol. 45, no. 3 (July), pp. 274–90.

Merrett, S. (1979), *State Housing in Britain* (London: Routledge & Kegan Paul).

Metcalf, D., and Richardson, R. (1980), 'Unemployment in London', in *The Inner City: Employment and Industry*, (eds) A. Evans and D. Eversley (London: Heinemann), pp. 193–203.

MHLG (1953), *Housing: The Next Step*, Cmd 8996 (London: HMSO).

MHLG (1954), *New Homes for Old* (London: HMSO).

MHLG (1965a), *Report of the Committee on Housing in Greater London* (the Milner Holland Report), Cmnd 2605 (London: HMSO).

MHLG (1965b), *Report of the Committee on the Management of Local Government* (the Maud Report) (London: HMSO).

MHLG (1966), *The Deeplish Study: Improvement Possibilities in an Area of Rochdale* (London: HMSO).

MHLG (1968), *Old Houses into New Homes*, Cmnd 3602 (London: HMSO).

MHLG (1969) *Housing Act, 1969: Area Improvement*, Circular 65/69 (London: HMSO).

Monck, E., with Lomas, G. (1980), *Housing Action Areas: Success and Failure*,

Policy Series No. 10 (London: Centre for Environmental Studies).

Moore, R. (1971), 'Progressive redevelopment', *Official Architecture and Planning*, vol. 304, no. 10 (October), pp. 775-7.

Moore, R. (1980), *Reconditioning the Slums: The Development and Role of Housing Rehabilitation*, Planning Studies No. 7 (London: School of Environment Planning Unit, Polytechnic of Central London).

Morton, J. (1982), *Ferndale: A Caring Repair Service for Elderly Home Owners* (London: Shelter).

Murie, A. (1981), *Housing Policy and the Inner City*, Working Paper No. 12 (School for Advanced Urban Studies, University of Bristol).

Murie, A. (1983), *Housing Inequality and Deprivation* (London: Heinemann).

Murie, A., and Forrest, R. (1980a), 'Wealth, inheritance and housing policy', *Policy and Politics*, vol. 8, no. 1 (January), pp. 1-19.

Murie, A., and Forrest, R. (1980b), *Housing Market Processes and the Inner City*, The Inner City in Context, 10 (London: SSRC).

NBA (1979), *The Colville/Tavistock Housing Action Area* (London: National Building Agency).

NCC (1981), *Building Societies and the Consumer* (London: National Consumer Council).

NEDO (1975), *Finance for Investment* (London: National Economic Development Office).

Needleman, L. (1965), *The Economics of Housing* (London: Staples Press).

Needleman, L. (1969), 'The comparative economics of improvement and new building', *Urban Studies*, vol. 6, no. 2 (June), pp. 196-209.

Nicholls, D. C., Turner, D. M., Kirby-Smith, R., and Cullen, J. D. (1981), *Private Housing Development Process: A Case Study*, Inner Cities Research Programme No. 4 (London: DOE).

Niner, P., and Forrest, R. (1982), *Housing Action Area Policy and Progress: The Residents' Perspective*, Research Memorandum No. 91 (Birmingham: Centre for Urban and Regional Studies, University of Birmingham).

Niner, P., Karn, V. A., Murie, A., and Watson, C. J. (1975), *The Beeches Road Area Study: A Potential Housing Action Area*, Research Memorandum No. 49 (Birmingham: Centre for Urban and Regional Studies, University of Birmingham).

Norman, P. (1975), *Managerialism: Review of Recent Work*, Conference Paper No. 14 (London: Centre for Environmental Studies).

Northern Region Strategy Team (1977), *Strategic Plan for the Northern Region: Main Report* (Newcastle upon Tyne: Northern Region Strategy Team).

OECD (various years), *Main Economic Indicators* (Paris: OECD).

Office of Fair Trading (1983), *Home Improvements*, report by the Director General of Fair Trading (London: Office of Fair Trading).

OPCS (1973), *General Household Survey: Introductory Report* (London: HMSO).

OPCS (1982), *General Household Survey 1980* (London: HMSO).

Paris, C. (1977), 'Housing Action Areas', *Roof*, vol. 2, no. 1 (January), pp. 9-14.

Paris, C., and Blackaby, B. (1979), *Not Much Improvement: Urban Renewal Policy in Birmingham* (London: Heinemann).

Pepper, S. (1971), *Housing Improvement: Goals and Strategy*, Architectural Association Paper No. 8 (London: Lund Humphries).

Perry, J. (1983), 'What boom?', *Roof*, vol. 8, no. 6 (November/December), pp. 25-7.

Pickup, D. (1975), 'The provisions of the Housing Act, 1974', *Housing Review*, vol. 24, no. 2 (March/April), pp. 53–7.

Plowden Report (1967), *Children and their Primary Schools*, Central Advisory Committee for Education (London: HMSO).

Poor Law Commissioners (1842), *Report on the Sanitary Conditions of the Labouring Population of Great Britain* (London: HMSO).

Price, R. W. R., and Chouraqui, J. C. (1983), 'Public sector deficits: problems and policy implications', *Economic Outlook* (OECD), June, pp. 13–44.

Property Advisory Group (1980), *Structure and Activity of the Development Industry* (London: HMSO).

Redpath, R. U., and Chivers, D. J. (1974), 'Swinbrook: a community study applied', *Greater London Intelligence Quarterly*, no. 26, pp. 5–17.

Richardson, H. W. (1971), *Urban Economics* (Harmondsworth: Penguin).

Richardson, H. W. (1978), *Regional and Urban Economics* (Harmondsworth: Penguin).

Richardson, I. (1983), 'Speech by the Governor of the Bank of England to the BSA Annual Conference', *Building Societies Gazette*, conference issue, vol. 115, no. 1396 (May), pp. 768–71.

Roberts, J. T. (1976), *General Improvement Areas* (Farnborough: Saxon House).

Rocheford Tenants' Association (1976), *Pre-allocation at Pepper Lane* (Leeds: Rocheford Tenants' Association).

Rodwell, D. F. G. (1981), 'Occupants and home maintenance', *Housing Review*, vol. 30, no. 1 (January/February), pp. 15–20.

RTPI (1981), *Renewal of Older Housing Areas: In the 1980s: A Policy Paper Prepared by the Housing Working Party* (London: Royal Town Planning Institute).

Rutter, M., and Madge, N. (1976), *Cycles of Disadvantage* (London: Heinemann).

Ryan, W. (1971), *Blaming the Victim* (London: Orbach & Chambers).

Saunders, P. (1980), *Urban Politics: A Sociological Interpretation* (Harmondsworth: Penguin; 1st edn London: Hutchinson, 1979).

Schoor, A. L. (1964), *Slums and Social Insecurity* (London: Nelson).

Seebohm Report (1969), *Committee on Local Authority and Allied Personal Social Services*, Cmnd 3703 (London: HMSO).

Shelter (1981), *Build Homes, Build Hope: A Report on Britain's Mounting Housing Crisis* (London: Shelter).

Shelter (1982), *Housing and the Economy: A Priority for Reform* (London: Shelter).

SNAP (1972), *Another Chance for Cities: SNAP 69/72* (London: Shelter Neighbourhood Action Project).

Shore, P. (1976a), 'Inner city policy', speech at Manchester Town Hall, *Press Notice 835* (DOE), 17 September.

Shore, P. (1976b), 'Dealing with the problems of inner cities and housing', Annual Conference of the National Housing and Town Planning Council, *Press Notice 926* (DOE).

Shore, P. (1977), address by the Secretary of State for the Environment to the Save Our Cities Conference, Bristol, *Press Notice 63* (DOE), 9 February.

Sigsworth, E. M., and Wilkinson, R. K. (1967), 'Rebuilding or renovation', *Urban Studies*, vol. 4, no. 2 (June), pp. 109–21.

Sigsworth, E. M., and Wilkinson, R. K. (1970), 'Rebuilding or renovation? A rejoinder', *Urban Studies*, vol. 7, no. 1 (February), pp. 92–4.

Sigsworth, E. M., and Wilkinson, R. K. (1971), 'The finance of improvements: A study of low quality housing in three Yorkshire towns', *Bulletin of Economic Research*, vol. 23, no. 2 (November), pp. 113–28.

Sizer, J. (1974), 'Four years GIAs', paper given at the Planning and Transport Research and Computation Summer Annual Meeting, University of Warwick, 8–12 July.

Skinner, N. P. (1981), 'House condition, standards and maintenance', *Housing Review*, vol. 30, no. 4 (July/August), pp. 106–9.

Spencer, K. M. (1970), 'Older urban areas and housing improvement policies', *Town Planning Review*, vol. 41, no. 3 (July), pp. 256–62.

Spencer, K. M. (1980), 'The genesis of Comprehensive Community Programmes', *Local Government Studies*, vol. 6, no. 5 (September/October), pp. 17–28.

Stanley, J. (1983), 'The building societies and home improvement', in BSA, *Rehabilitation of Owner-Occupied Homes* (London: Building Societies Association), pp. 21–7.

Stone, P. A. (1970), *Urban Development in Britain: Standards, Costs and Resources 1964–2004* (Cambridge: Cambridge University Press).

Struyk, J. R., and Soldo, B. J. (1980), *Improving the Elderly's Housing: A Key to Preserving the National Housing Stock and Neighborhoods* (Cambridge, Mass.: Ballinger).

Taylor, N. (1973), *The Village in the City* (London: Temple Smith).

Thomas, A. D. (1979), *Area Based Renewal: Three Years in the Life of an HAA*, Research Memorandum No. 72 (Birmingham: Centre for Urban and Regional Studies, University of Birmingham).

Thomas, A. D. (1981), *Local Authority Agency Services: Their Role in House Improvement*, Research Memorandum No. 88 (Birmingham: Centre for Urban and Regional Studies, University of Birmingham).

Thomas, A. D., Karn, V. A., and Gibson, M. (1984), *Research on Urban Renewal* (London: Economic and Social Research Council).

Thompson, A. (1977), *The Role of Housing Associations in Major Urban Areas: A Case Study of Merseyside Improved Houses*, Research Memorandum No. 60 (Birmingham: Centre for Urban and Regional Studies, University of Birmingham).

Thornton, C. (1981a), 'Summary of speech to Regional Conference', *Building Societies Gazette*, vol. 113, no. 1364 (January), pp. 34–5.

Thornton, C. (1981b), 'Building societies' role in urban renaissance', *Housing Review*, vol. 30, no. 2 (March/April), pp. 44–5.

Tinker, A., and White, J. (1979), 'How can elderly owner-occupiers be helped to improve and repair their homes?', *Housing Review*, vol. 28, no. 3 (May/June), pp. 74–5.

Townsend, P. (1979), *Poverty in the United Kingdom: A Survey of Household Resources and Standards of Living* (Harmondsworth: Penguin).

Treasury (1983), *Financial Statement and Budget Report 1983–84* (London: HMSO).

Treble, J. H. (1971), 'Liverpool working-class housing 1801–1851', in *The History of Working-Class Housing*, ed. S. D. Chapman (Newton Abbot: David & Charles), pp. 165–220.

TUC (1981a), *Plan for Growth: The Economic Alternative* (London: Trades Union Congress).

TUC (1981b), *The Reconstruction of Britain* (London: Trades Union Congress).

TUC (1981c), *Regenerating Our Inner Cities* (London: Trades Union Congress).

TUC (1983), *The Battle for Jobs: TUC Economic Review 1983* (London: Trades Union Congress).

US Congress (1977), *Developments in Aging: 1976, Part 1*, report of the Senate Committee on Aging.

Urbed (1980), *Local Economic Development: A Guide to US Experience* (London: Urbed Research Trust).

Weir, S. (1976), 'Red line districts', *Roof*, vol. 1, no. 4 (July), pp. 109–14.

Welsh Office (1975), *Housing Act 1974: Renewal Strategies*, Circular 4/75 (London: HMSO).

Wheeler, R. (1982), 'Staying-put: a new development in policy', *Ageing and Society*, vol. 2, pt 3 (November), pp. 299–329.

Wheeler, R. (1983), 'The housing problems of elderly owner-occupiers', in BSA, *The Rehabilitation of Owner-Occupied Homes* (London: Building Societies Association), pp. 8–20.

Wicks, M. (1983), 'The lost years', in *Government and Urban Poverty*, ed. J. Higgins, N. Deakin, J. Edwards and M. Wicks (Oxford: Blackwell), pp. 86–116.

Williams, H., Bozeat, N., Cook, A., and Hardy, B. (1980), *Industrial Renewal in the Inner City: An Assessment of Potential and Problems*, Inner Cities Research Programme No. 2 (London: DOE).

Williams, P. (1976), 'The role of institutions in the inner London housing market: the case of Islington', *Transactions of the Institute of British Geographers*, n.s., vol. 1, no. 1, pp. 72–82.

Williams, P. (1978), 'Urban managerialism: a concept of relevance', *Area*, vol. 10, pp. 236–40.

Williams, P. (1982), 'Restructuring urban managerialism: towards a political economy of urban allocation', *Environment and Planning A*, vol. 14, pp. 95–105.

Williamson, A., and Wrigley, E. (1978), *General Improvement Areas 1969–1976*, Improvement Research Note 3–77 (London: DOE).

Wilson, H. (1971), *The Labour Government 1964–1970: A Personal Record* (London: Weidenfeld & Nicolson).

Wilson Committee (1979a), *Committee to Review the Functioning of Financial Institutions*, Second Stage Evidence, Vol. 3 (London: HMSO).

Wilson Committee (1979b), *The Financing of Small Firms*, the Wilson Committee Interim Report, Cmnd 7503 (London: HMSO).

Wilson Committee (1980), *Report of the Committee to Review the Functioning of Financial Institutions*, Cmnd 7937 (London: HMSO).

Wintour, J. (1980), 'Bradford: first year figures', *Roof*, vol. 5, no. 1, pp. 5–6.

Wintour, J., and Van Dyke, S. (1977), 'Housing Action Areas but where's the action?', *Roof*, vol. 2, no. 4, pp. 113–15.

Wohl, A. S. (1971), 'The housing of the working classes in London', in *The History of Working-Class Housing*, ed. S. D. Chapman (Newton Abbot: David & Charles), pp. 13–54.

Yates, D. (1982), 'The English housing experience: an overview', *Urban Law and Policy*, vol. 5, pp. 203–33.

Young, J. (1979), 'Bradford City's promotion prospects', *Roof*, vol. 4, no. 2, pp. 55–6.

Young, M., and Willmott, P. (1957), *Family and Kinship in East London* (London: Routledge & Kegan Paul).

Index

For Product Safety Concerns and Information please contact our EU
representative GPSR@taylorandfrancis.com
Taylor & Francis Verlag GmbH, Kaufingerstraße 24, 80331 München, Germany

www.ingramcontent.com/pod-product-compliance
Lightning Source LLC
Chambersburg PA
CBHW070407270326
41926CB00014B/2733